ARROW IMPOSSIBILITY
THEOREMS

ECONOMIC THEORY AND MATHEMATICAL ECONOMICS

Consulting Editor: Karl Shell

UNIVERSITY OF PENNSYLVANIA
PHILADELPHIA, PENNSYLVANIA

ARROW IMPOSSIBILITY THEOREMS

JERRY S. KELLY

Department of Economics
Syracuse University
Syracuse, New York

ACADEMIC PRESS   New York   San Francisco   London   1978

A Subsidiary of Harcourt Brace Jovanovich, Publishers

ACADEMIC PRESS, INC.
111 Fifth Avenue, New York, New York 10003

United Kingdom Edition published by
ACADEMIC PRESS, INC. (LONDON) LTD.
24/28 Oval Road, London NW1 7DX

Library of Congress Cataloging in Publication Data

Kelly, Jerry S.

Arrow impossibility theorems.

(Economic theory and mathematical economics series)
Bibliography: p.
Includes index.
1. Social choice—Mathematical models—   2.   Welfare
economics.   I.   Title.
HB99.3.K45   330.15'5   77-82417
ISBN 0-12-403350-4

To Meredith

CONTENTS

PREFACE

Economists and political scientists have recently directed a great deal of research to a very old problem: the design of good procedures for making social choices. Political scientists often approach the problem from the viewpoint of democratic theory and suggest that an alternative ought not to be chosen if there is available another alternative that a plain majority or perhaps a larger fraction (say, two-thirds) find superior. Such an approach flounders on the classic voting paradox: Suppose there are three individuals of whom the first prefers outcome A to outcome B and outcome B to outcome C (and so A to C), while the second prefers B to C and C to A (and so B to A), and the third prefers C to A and A to B (and so C to A). Then A is rejected, losing on a two-to-one vote to C, B is rejected, losing to A, and C is rejected, losing to B. Majority voting can narrow the choice down to nothing.

Economists, on the other hand, approach the problem from the viewpoint of Pareto efficiency, which says that an alternative ought not to be chosen if there is available another alternative that everyone believes superior. But this approach fails to narrow the choice enough and leads each individual to have what may sometimes seem excessive power. Even if everyone but the first individual prefers A to B, the first prefers B to A; he keeps B from being rejected, and neither A nor B is chosen over the other.

These difficulties lead to two important questions: What criteria should we expect to be satisfied by a "good" procedure for making social choices on the basis of individual preferences? Given a list of such criteria, do there exist *any* procedures satisfying all of them? In 1950, Kenneth J. Arrow exhibited a set of apparently reasonable criteria and a proof that they could not be jointly satisfied. This was the start of a vigorous industry of constructing impossibility theorems about social choice. This book is an effort to systematically organize these results, especially the large number of very recent theorems that have appeared since the publication of Amartya K. Sen's *Collective Choice and Social Welfare*.

Despite its sources in political and economic theory, this material does not require any previous background in these fields. Nor is the formal mathematical background required very extensive. Bits and pieces of logic, set theory, and the theory of binary relations are used; the main results needed are presented here in a Mathematical Appendix. The most important prerequisite is a willingness to approach the very practical problem of collective decisionmaking from an extremely abstract and formal point of view.

ACKNOWLEDGMENTS

I wish to offer my profound thanks

to Syracuse University, the University of Virginia, and the University of Minnesota for providing research facilities and support;

to JoAnn O'Keefe at the University of Minnesota for expert secretarial support;

to Karl Shell, editor of this series, and the staff at Academic Press for facilitating the publication of this book;

to the *Journal of Economic Theory*, *Econometrica*, and *Economica* for permission to use material I originally published in those places;

to David Schmeidler, Hugo Sonnenschein, and Charles Plott for permission to include some of their as-yet-unpublished research;

to Marcel Richter for mathematical help;

to Douglas Blair, Georges Bordes, and Kotaro Suzumura for the contributions they made to our joint work [45], as reported in Chapter 4;

to the students in my social choice seminar at the University of Minnesota who brought countless corrections to my attention and who helped to greatly improve one of the theorems (see Chapter 8);

to Peter Fishburn and Amartya Sen for their generous remarks on an earlier version of this manuscript and for their constant stimulation.

INTRODUCTION

The historians and sociologists of thought have always been struck by the special drama of the extraordinarily seminal paper. Examples become very carefully studied and we see analysts poring over such milestones as Einstein's 1905 paper on the electrodynamics of moving bodies, Gödel's 1931 paper on the undecidability of Whitehead and Russell's *Principia Mathematica*, Crick and Watson's 1953 *Nature* paper on DNA structure, or, less widely known, but enormously influential, Eilenberg and Mac Lane's 1945 paper on category theory. These papers have initiated or completely transformed entire fields (relativity physics, logic, molecular biology, and much of pure mathematics, respectively). A similar dramatic case is Kenneth Arrow's 1950 *Journal of Political Economy* paper, "A Difficulty in the Concept of Social Welfare." This paper (or the book, *Social Choice and Individual Values*, which extended the paper) has been a principle source for almost all contemporary collective choice theory and has deeply influenced theoretical welfare economics, moral and political philosophy, and mathematical approaches to microeconomic theory.

In part, the interest stimulated by Arrow's work was its introduction of a whole new theme, that of provable impossibility, into economics. This theme had already played an important role in mathematics. For more than twenty centuries, mathematicians labored to build an apparatus, culminating in Galois theory, for proving the impossibility of the three classical problems for solving, with straightedge and compass, the duplication of the cube, trisection of an arbitrary angle, and quadrature of the circle.

In logic, the seminal paper of Gödel served to prove an impossibility result for obtaining proofs in formal systems. The tools developed for that

1

purpose have been extended and applied to other mathematical domains, so that we have proofs by Novikov and Boone of the unsolvability of the word problem for finitely presented groups, a proof by Markov for the unsolvability of the homeomorphy problem for simplicial complexes, and, recently, a proof by Matijasevic of the impossibility of deriving an algorithm for determining the solvability, in integers, of polynomial equations with integer coefficients, thus completely solving Hilbert's tenth problem.

In statistics and econometrics, a similar idea is reflected in studies establishing conditions for underidentification of parameters.

Measure theory provides an example closer to the results of this book. First some desirable criteria to be imposed on the concept of a "measure" μ are developed:

1. μ maps bounded subsets of R^n into the nonnegative reals;
2. If A and B are congruent subsets of R^n, then $\mu(A) = \mu(B)$;
3. $\mu([0,1]^n) > 0$;
4. if $A = A_1 \cup \cdots \cup A_m$ & $A_i \cap A_j \neq 0$ for $i \neq j$, then

$$\mu(A) = \mu(A_1) + \cdots + \mu(A_m).$$

For $n \geq 3$, these criteria are shown to be inconsistent by the Banach–Tarski paradox [22]: assuming the axiom of choice, "a sphere of fixed radius may be decomposed into a finite number of parts and put together again in such a way as to form two spheres with the given radius" (Suppes [328, p. 250]).

This same theme pervades Arrow's paper and the subsequent literature on "social welfare functions"; some combination of properties that appear to be desirable for social choice procedures are shown to be impossible to be jointly satisfied. Now nothing is new in showing that desirable social choices are very hard to define and difficult to arrange. "Best" social choices require working out all the catches in the definition of "best," and this problem has been with us since antiquity. Norbert Wiener has related the problem to the ageless fairy tales showing how hard it is to state three wishes in a sufficiently foolproof way to ensure a happy ending (cf. [3, p. 52]). But "difficult" and "logically impossible" require markedly different modes of analysis for their establishment, and Arrow's contribution is in sharp contrast to anything preceding it in the literature of social theory.

When we are presented with a set of formalizations of intuitive ethical constraints on social choice procedures and shown that these formalizations are logically incompatible, we seem to be left with three general kinds of response. At one extreme, working with the formalizations, we could deny that the proof of inconsistency is valid. We could look for a mathematical error. And, indeed, Julian Blau [46] found an error in Arrow's logical analysis, one deep enough to render Arrow's original theorem false. But apparently mild alterations in the constraints and the subsequent analysis by Blau [46] and Arrow [12] have left us with proofs that have survived scrutiny by two decades of mathematically sophisticated scholars. This extreme response no longer seems fruitful.

At the other extreme, one could treat the impossibility proofs as *revelations* in the field of ethics and set about rejecting one's intuitive moral ideas. This has been a very rarely developed response.

The "moderate" and most common response has been to accept the mathematics and still retain one's ethical ideas by impunging the formalizations as inadequate reflections of the intuitive ethics. For economists and social thinkers not intimately aware of very recent collective choice theory, the standard reaction has been to point to *one* of Arrow's conditions (usually, but not always, the one called "independence of irrelevant alternatives") and, by denying its reasonableness as a formalization of an ethical precept, dispose of Arrow's theorem as a barrier to welfare theory. The difficulty this reaction now faces is very simple: *for each of Arrow's conditions, there is now an impossibility theorem not employing that condition.* The number and variety of impossibility theorems has increased so much recently that we need a reassessment of the moderate reaction. One central purpose of this book is to aid this by presenting a complete description of existing impossibility theorems.

As a field guide to impossibility theorems, this book must be concerned with a great number of formalizations of ethical constraints appearing in such variety that they seem to have, like the contents of the bottle that Alice found down the rabbit-hole, "a sort of mixed flavor of cherry-tart, custard, pineapple, roast turkey, toffey and hot buttered toast." The book has been arranged according to a scheme that classifies these varied constraints. As such, we will be going beyond an assessment of already existing theorems. Field guides tell us how we are to describe species not yet cataloged: look at their habitat, markings, food sources, wing-span, and so on. After having read this book, I hope you will not only know the theorems already cataloged but also what to look for in new theorems; principally, simplicity conditions, rights assignments, and rights-exercising rules.

After a chapter introducing the framework and notation for this study, the main impossibility results appear in Chapters 2 and 4–6. Chapter 3 presents some concepts and an apparatus of relations among those concepts which are important for the theorems of Chapter 4. Chapters 7–9 present some impossibility results that serve to point out serious difficulties in some plausible escape routes from the theorems of earlier chapters. The final chapter describes important areas of research that have arisen in the collective choice field in the transition away from studying the conditions of Arrow's theorem alone to the totality of all impossibility theorems.

Lemmas, theorems, corollaries, and examples are numbered in a common consecutive sequence, starting afresh in each chapter, and prefixed, in all instances, with the chapter number, e.g. Theorem 2-3. A mathematical appendix has been included, but it is more a method of gaining agreement with the reader on notation and terminology than a presentation of new concepts. For the reader unfamiliar with this material, all that we will use, and much more besides, is available in Fishburn's *Mathematics of Decision Theory* [117].

I FRAMEWORK

We will let E be the set of all possible *social states*. Except in Chapter 8, the word *alternative* will be used interchangeably with "social state." (In Chapter 8, alternatives have a more complicated structure, consisting of both a social state and a specification of an individual.) For each of our theorems, E is assumed fixed. Depending on the purposes of the investigator, E may be interpreted as a set of political candidates; a set of legislative or committee proposals; a set of income distributions; a set of complete descriptions of consumption, production, exchange, and inventory situations for all agents in an economy or a set of probability distributions over such descriptions. The only universal constraint on E is that its elements must be incompatible with one another. Only *one* social state can prevail at the end of the choice procedure.

Some theorems that we will present depend on additional assumptions about E. Inequality restrictions on the cardinality of E will occasionally be required. Analyses for theorems that involve continuous "utility" function representations of preferences will require that E have topological structure. We will be careful to take pains to point out any assumptions on E that might limit the reasonableness of interpretations of that set.

2^E is the power set of E, the set of all subsets of E. Thus $2^E - \{\varnothing\}$ is the set of all nonempty subsets of E. An element v of $2^E - \{\varnothing\}$ is called an *agenda*. A choice function will serve the role of picking out an element from an agenda, the pick corresponding to the element to be "chosen" from the agenda.

Of the possible kinds of information that could be used as a basis for making choices, we will concentrate almost entirely on the preferences individuals have with respect to the alternatives. The set of individuals, labeled as integers, is $N = \{1, \ldots, n\}$. We let R_E be the set of all complete, reflexive, transitive binary relations on E. (For definitions, see the Mathematical Appendix.) R_E^n is the n-fold Cartesian product of R^E. If

$$u = (R_{1u}, R_{2u}, \ldots, R_{nu})$$

is an element of R_E^n, we call u a *profile* of n individuals and R_{iu} is the *individual preference ordering* at u for the ith individual. If $(x, y) \in R_{iu}$, we write $xR_{iu}y$ and read this as "x is at least as good as y in the eyes of i at u" or "i at u prefers x to y or is indifferent between them" or some similar phrase. From R_{iu} we define P_{iu}, "strict" preference, and I_{iu}, indifference, as

$$
\begin{aligned}
xP_{iu}y \quad & \text{if and only if} \quad xR_{iu}y \quad \text{and } not \quad yR_{iu}x, \\
xI_{iu}y \quad & \text{if and only if} \quad xR_{iu}y \quad \text{and} \quad yR_{iu}x.
\end{aligned}
$$

I_{iu} and P_{iu} are the symmetric and asymmetric parts of R_{iu} respectively. $xP_{iu}y$ is read "i at u strictly prefers x to y" and $xI_{iu}y$ is read "i at u is indifferent between x and y."

I_{iu} is an equivalence relation, i.e., it is reflexive, symmetric, and transitive. Completeness of R_{iu} implies the *Trichotomy law*: exactly one of $xP_{iu}y$, $xI_{iu}y$, $yP_{iu}x$ holds. The set of all possible profiles is

$$R_E^* = \bigcup_{n=1}^{\infty} R_E^n.$$

Whatever additional information is used in making choices we will assume is captured by the value of a (possibly multidimensional) variable x, which assumes values in a set X. We wish to explicitly allow for the possibility that the value of x is determined in part by the result of a random drawing. If we must choose from $\{a, b\}$ and everyone is indifferent between these two alternatives, we might choose according to the result of a coin toss.

Let V be a nonempty set of agendas from E. Elements of V will be called *admissible agendas*. A *partial choice function* Ch on V is any mapping from V to 2^E satisfying

$$\text{Ch}(v) \subseteq v.$$

The set of all such mappings is $\mathscr{C}(V)$. Because of our initial requirement that elements of E be mutually incompatible, it is natural to require that final choices, given *all* relevant information, not be multiple valued. Thus we would require that $\text{Ch}(v)$ not contain two distinct elements. We will allow for the possibility that $\text{Ch}(v) = \varnothing$, in which case we say Ch *fails* at v. If $\text{Ch}(v) \neq \varnothing$ for all v in V, we say Ch is a *total* choice function on V.

Now let U be a set of profiles from R_E^*. Elements of U will be called *admissible profiles*. With each element u of U and each value of x, we wish to associate a corresponding partial choice function $\text{Ch}_{u,x}$. Thus, we define a *partial collective choice rule* as a mapping, f^1, from $U \times X$ to $\mathscr{C}(V)$. If each image of f^1 is a total choice function, we call f^1 a *total* collective choice rule.

Since most of the impossibility theorems we deal with do not involve the structure of X, we adopt a notation and language that eliminates reference to X. Let C_u be the element of $\mathscr{C}(V)$ defined by

$$C_u(v) = \bigcup_{x \varepsilon X} \mathrm{Ch}_{u,x}(v).$$

We extend our use of the term *partial collective choice rule* to cover the mapping f from U to $\mathscr{C}(V)$ which assigns C_u to $u \in U$. Clearly now we do *not* maintain the requirement that no two distinct alternatives may be in $C_u(v)$. This remark becomes of great importance in Chapter 6. f will be called a *total collective choice rule* on V, U if each C_u in its image set is a total choice function on V. Most proofs will proceed by discovering a $u \in U$ and $v \in V$ such that C_u fails at v. Note that C_u is confronted with all of V for every u in U. We are excluding the possibility that certain preferences will prevail only when special agenda are being considered or that certain agenda will arise only in the face of special sets of preferences.

If we are to establish violations of totality, this must be done by unraveling the consequences of some other constraints imposed on collective choice rules.

Most of these constraints on f are intended to be formalizations of ethical beliefs about criteria for good social choice processes. Constraints of this type will be discussed throughout the remaining chapters, and we will observe here only that the reader must always be aware that the desirability of a criterion depends importantly on the specific interpretation of E used, on which individuals get their preferences counted, and on what other kinds of information (via X) are to be used in making the "final" choice $\mathrm{Ch}_{u,x}(v)$ from among the elements of $C_u(v)$.

Before turning to such ethical constraints, we first discuss a set of restrictions on V and U that we employ to force f to be flexible with respect to the agenda and profiles on which it will work. The most stringent requirement would be: $V = 2^E - \{\varnothing\}$ and $U = R_E^*$. In effect, this would be a way of asserting complete lack of information about the settings in which choices will be made. None of our theorems will require this much. As for $V = 2^E - \{\varnothing\}$, Plott [267, p. 5] points out:

> In the case of infinite E the set of all subsets may be "too large" to be of interest. For example choice over "open" sets or nonconvex sets may be too much to demand.

Most of our results will be obtained by weakening this condition to the requirement that V contain all nonempty subsets of E of sufficiently small cardinality.

Turning to $U = R_E^*$, we will find that impossibility results arise without requiring f to work on societies of all possible sizes. What we will require is that f work on all societies of some one size, not too small. This discussion is summarized in what we will call the *standard domain constraint*:

   (i) V contains all finite numbers of $2^E - \{\varnothing\}$,
   (ii) $|E| \geq 3$,
   (iii) there is an n, $3 \leq n < \infty$, with $U = R_E^n$,
   (iv) f is total on V, U.

When (i) is modified to say only

   (i)′ V contains all members v of $2^E - \{\varnothing\}$ with $|v| \leq m$,

we will call the combination of (i)′, (ii), (iii), and (iv) the *standard domain constraint (m)*.

We must mention one important dissent from part (iii) of this restriction. Part (iii) is a statement of ignorance about the settings in which f is to be applied—either because we do not know current preferences for *the* choice to be made now or because f is designed to be used repeatedly in the future and we do not know with certainty what future preferences are to be. But if we are concerned with a single choice *now* and *know* current preferences to be $(R_1, R_2, \ldots, R_n)$, then we need only $(R_1, R_2, \ldots, R_n) \in U$, and for a long time there did not exist any impossibility theorems with such a weak domain restriction. This has been the essence of Samuelson's quarrel [261] with impossibility research and his support of the Bergson social welfare function [33]. Recent impossibility theorems of Parks [244] and Kemp and Ng [198], which we will deal with in Chapter 7, use only a single profile and seriously affect Samuelson's dissent.

2 DECISIVENESS

Clearly we want a choice function to do more than give us a nonempty choice set at each point of a carefully specified domain. We have some informal ideas, loosely tied to moral and political philosophy, about "good" social choice procedures. These ideas are to be reflected in restrictions on the choice function.

The restrictions that most directly reflect ethical ideas are those specifying which groups of individuals have a deciding voice on which issues. These descriptions of power relations are the *decisiveness* conditions and are organized around a fourfold classification system. A set S of individuals and a pair x, y of alternatives being given such that we want to say S decides for x against y, we take as the first part of our classification the list of agenda on which decisiveness plays a role. If S is only known to rule on the agenda $\{x, y\}$, we will speak of *pairwise* decisiveness; if S has an impact on all agenda containing x and y, we are dealing with *general* decisiveness (although we will not usually use this term explicitly, understanding its presence whenever we do not say "pairwise").

The second part of our classification deals with the nature of the outcome. S can exclude y from the choice set when x is available or merely ensure that x is chosen if y is. In the pairwise case, these two possibilities correspond to $\{x\} = C(\{x, y\})$ and $x \in C(\{x, y\})$. In the general case, the first version is

$$x \in v \to y \notin C(v),$$

and the second is

$$x \in v \ \& \ y \in C(v) \to x \in C(v).$$

For total choice functions which reflect a "social preference relation" (to be discussed in Chapter 4), the first version here corresponds to strict social preference, while the second corresponds to weak social preference-or-indifference. The language we adopt in our classification refers to the first as *decisive* and the second as *semidecisive*.

The third part of our classification describes what preferences of individuals in S must be like in order for them to be the deciding factor. If *all* members of S must strictly prefer x to y, we will talk about *weak* decisiveness. *Strong* decisiveness then refers to the case where it is sufficient that at least one individual in S strictly prefers x to y and no one in S strictly prefers y to x (but some in S are allowed to be indifferent).

The fourth and last part of our classification describes what preferences of individuals outside of S must be like in order for S to be the deciding factor. If S is decisive for all possible preferences of individuals outside of S we will talk about *global* decisiveness. *Local* decisiveness of S for x against y then refers to the case where S is only known to decide when everyone outside S strictly prefers y to x.

Formalizing all this, we have the following definitions, where

$$u = (R_{1u}, R_{2u}, \ldots, R_{nu}), S = \{1, 2, \ldots, n\} - \tilde{S},$$

and

$$C_u = f(u):$$

The set S is *weakly, globally decisive* for x against y if

$$(\forall i)(i \in S \to xP_{iu}y) \to (x \in v \to y \notin C_u(v)).$$

The set S is *weakly, globally semidecisive* for x against y if

$$(\forall i)(i \in S \to xP_{iu}y) \to (x \in v \,\&\, y \in C_u(v) \to x \in C_u(v)).$$

The set S is *strongly, globally decisive* for x against y if

$$((\forall i)(i \in S \to xR_{iu}y) \,\&\, (\exists i)(i \in S \,\&\, xP_{iu}y)) \to (x \in v \to y \notin C_u(v)).$$

The set S is *strongly, globally semidecisive* for x against y if

$$((\forall i)(i \in S \to xR_{iu}y) \,\&\, (\exists i)(i \in S \,\&\, xP_{iu}y)) \to (x \in v \,\&\, y \in C_u(v) \to x \in C_u(v)).$$

The set S is *weakly, locally decisive* for x against y if

$$(\forall i)((i \in S \to xP_{iu}y) \,\&\, (i \in \tilde{S} \to yP_{iu}x)) \to (x \in v \to y \notin C_u(v)).$$

The set S is *weakly, locally semidecisive* for x against y if

$$(\forall i)((i \in S \to xP_{iu}y) \,\&\, (i \in \tilde{S} \to yP_{iu}x)) \to (x \in v \,\&\, y \in C_u(v) \to x \in C_u(v)).$$

The set S is *strongly, locally decisive* for x against y if

$$((\forall i)(i \in S \to x R_{iu} y) \& (x \in \tilde{S} \to y P_{iu} x)) \& (\exists i)(i \in S \& x P_{iu} y)) \to (x \in v \to y \notin C_u(v)).$$

The set S is *strongly, locally semidecisive* for x against y if

$$((\forall i)(i \in S \to x R_{iu} y) \& (x \in \tilde{S} \to y P_{iu} x)) \& (\exists i)(i \in S \& x P_{iu} y))$$
$$\to (x \in v \& y \in C_u(v) \to x \in C_u(v)).$$

In each of the preceding cases we were dealing with general decisiveness. The modifications for pairwise decisiveness are fairly straightforward. As an example, a set S is *weakly, globally pairwise semidecisive* for x against y if

$$(\forall i)(i \in S \to x P_{iu} y) \to (x \in C_u(\{x, y\})).$$

Some additional jargon has been built up from these definitions. If S is weakly, globally decisive both for x against y and for y against x, we say S is weakly, globally decisive *between* x and y. Similar language is used for the other expressions.

We now use our decisiveness language to introduce some of the restrictions on choice functions that have been used in impossibility proofs:

1. *The weak Pareto condition* The set, $N = \{1, 2, \ldots, n\}$, of all individuals is weakly, globally decisive between every pair of alternatives.

2. *The strong Pareto condition* The set N is strongly, globally decisive between every pair of alternatives.

3. *General nondictatorship* No set of just a single individual is weakly, globally decisive between every pair of alternatives.

4. *Nonimposition* For no pair of alternatives x, y is the null set weakly, globally semidecisive for x against y.

5. *Majoritarianism* Any set S of at least $[n/2] + 1$ (see Mathematical Appendix) individuals is weakly, globally decisive between every pair of alternatives.

6. *Minimal Liberalism* There are at least two individuals for each of whom there is a pair of alternatives between which that individual is weakly, globally decisive.

The version of decisiveness that will show up most frequently is weak decisiveness, general or pairwise, and so we introduce a new notation to abbreviate this expression in proofs. "S is weakly, globally decisive for x against y" will become $x \bar{D}_S y$, and "S is weakly, globally pairwise decisive for x against y" will become $x \overline{PD}_S y$. Correspondingly, "S is weakly, locally decisive for x against y" is abbreviated $x D_S y$, and "S is weakly, locally pairwise decisive for x against y" becomes $x P D_S y$. Clearly, $x \bar{D}_S y$ implies $x D_S y$ and also $x \overline{PD}_S y$ implies $x P D_S y$.

To illustrate how it is sometimes possible to reverse the results just mentioned and derive a global result from a local one, we introduce a new condition of a sort that will play a major role in subsequent chapters. A collective choice rule f on V, U is said to satisfy *nonnegative responsiveness* if, whenever u, $u' \in U$, $v \in V$ and the profiles $u = (R_1, R_2, \ldots, R_n)$ and $u' = (R_1', R_2', \ldots, R_n')$ are related by

(i) for all i, $x'R_i y'$ implies $x'R_i' y'$ for all x', y' distinct from x,
(ii) for all i, $xR_i y'$ implies $xR_i' y'$ for all $y' \neq x$,
(iii) for all i, $xP_i y'$ implies $xP_i' y'$ for all $y' \neq x$,

then, if $x \in v \to y \notin C_u(v)$, we have $x \in v \to y \notin C_{u'}(v)$, where $C_u = f(u')$ and $C_{u'} = f(u')$.

Nonnegative pairwise responsiveness is defined similarly with the conclusion being altered to: if $C_u(\{x, y\}) = \{x\}$, we have $C_{u'}(\{x, y\}) = \{x\}$.

Theorem 2-1 If f satisfies nonnegative responsiveness, then $xD_S y$ implies $x\bar{D}_S y$; if f satisfies nonnegative pairwise responsiveness, then $xPD_S y$ implies $x\overline{PD}_S y$.

Proof We will confirm only the first half since the second is dealt with in the same manner. Suppose $xD_S y$ and that $u' = (R_1', R_2', \ldots, R_n')$ is *any* society in which $xP_i' y$ for all $i \in S$. Construct a society $u = (R_1, R_2, \ldots, R_n)$ by taking x to the bottom of each R_i' for $i \notin S$, i.e.,

$$qR_i r \quad \text{if and only if} \quad \begin{cases} i \in S \quad \text{and} \quad qR_i'r, \\ \text{or} \\ i \notin S \quad \text{and} \quad (q \neq x \text{ and } qR_i'r) \quad \text{or} \quad r = x. \end{cases}$$

Then, at u, $xP_i y$ for all $i \in S$ and $yP_i x$ for all $i \notin S$. By $xD_S y$, $x \in v \to y \notin C_u(v)$. By nonnegative responsiveness, $x \in v \to y \notin C_{u'}(v)$. Thus $x\bar{D}_S y$. $\quad\square$

For suitably strong domain restrictions, these decisiveness conditions will yield no difficulties. For example, we could require that V and U satisfy

(A) $v \in V \to |v| < \infty$,

and, for all x and y,

(B) $u \in U \to ((\exists i)(xP_{iu} y) \;\&\; (\forall i)(xR_{iu} y))$

   $\qquad$ or $((\exists i)(yP_{iu} x) \;\&\; (\forall i)(yR_{iu} x))$.

With this restriction, if C is required to satisfy the strong Pareto condition, each v will have a unique Pareto optimal alternative and it will be the unique element of the chosen set. But it simply does not make sense to design choice procedures which work only when the kind of consensus expressed in (B) prevails. The heart of welfare theory must be a concern with choices in the context of conflict. It is the collective choice theorist who is professionally concerned with the hollowness of "power to the people" or "in the public interest" or "promote the general welfare" as guidelines for public choice. All this is the rationale for combining our decisiveness conditions with a flexibility restriction like the standard domain restriction of the previous chapter.

We now have the background material required for presenting some impossibility theorems. A widely used technique for resolving a social choice problem is "counting heads," weighing the number of individuals who favor one alternative over another against the number in opposition. In our current language, this involves assigning decisiveness properties to a set of individuals based on the size of the set. Our first impossibility theorem reveals the difficulties in this technique for the case of many alternatives. [The only trick in this theorem is determining an expression, in part (iii), for how many alternatives it does take to generate difficulties.]

Theorem 2-2 There is no collective choice rule f on V, U satisfying

(i)   decisiveness constraint: there is an integer m, $0 < m < n$ (so that $n \geq 2$) such that for all sets $S \subset N$ and all pairs x, y of alternatives, $|S| \geq m$ implies S is weakly, globally decisive between x and y,

(ii)   the standard domain constraint,

(iii)   parameter constraint: $|E| \geq -[n/(m-n)]$.

Proof   CASE 1: $n - m$ *evenly divides* n Then $-[n/(m-n)] = n/(n-m)$. Let r be this integer, $n/(n-m)$. By (iii), $|E| \geq r$, so we can pick out from E a set of r alternatives, $X = \{x_1, x_2, \ldots, x_r\}$. Using (ii), we examine a profile u such that the preference orderings (restricted to X) of individuals are (see Section F, Notation Note, in the Mathematical Appendix)

$$
\begin{array}{ll}
1: & x_1 x_2 x_3 \cdots x_{r-1} x_r \\
2: & x_2 x_3 x_4 \cdots x_r x_1 \\
3: & x_3 x_4 x_5 \cdots x_1 x_2 \\
\vdots & \\
r: & x_r x_1 x_2 \cdots x_{r-2} x_{r-1}
\end{array} \left.\rule{0pt}{6em}\right\} \text{Block 1,}
$$

$$
\begin{array}{ll}
r+1: & x_1 x_2 x_3 \cdots x_{r-1} x_r \\
\vdots & \\
2r: & x_r x_1 x_2 \cdots x_{r-2} x_{r-1}
\end{array} \left.\rule{0pt}{4em}\right\} \text{Block 2.}
$$
$$\vdots$$

The block of r serial permutations of X are assigned to successively higher numbered blocks of individuals. Within any block, $r - 1$ individuals prefer x_1 to x_2, $r - 1$ prefer x_2 to $x_3, \ldots, r - 1$ prefer x_{r-1} to x_r, and $r - 1$ prefer x_r

to x_1. Since, for this case, $r = n/(n - m)$, we have $n/r = n - m$; there are $n - m$ complete blocks and no incomplete blocks. Thus, overall, the number of individuals who prefer x_1 to x_2 in u is

$$(r - 1)(n - m) = (n/(n - m) - 1)(n - m) = n - (n - m) = m.$$

By (i), $x_2 \notin C_u(X)$. Similar calculations allow us to eliminate $x_3, x_4, \ldots, x_r, x_1$. Thus $C_u(X) = \varnothing$, contrary to the totality requirement in (ii).

CASE 2: $n - m$ *does not evenly divide* n Then $-[n/(m - n)] = [n/(n - m)] + 1$. For this case we will let $r = [n/(n - m)] + 1$, an integer. By (iii), we can again pick out from E a set of r alternatives, $X = \{x_1, x_2, \ldots, x_r\}$. Using (ii), we again examine a profile u, in which individual preference orderings (restricted to X) are assigned as in Case 1. Now how many prefer x_1 to x_2? Within each *complete* block, $r - 1$ do. With $[n/r]$ complete blocks, this gives $(r - 1)[n/r]$ preferring x_1 to x_2. But now, since $n - m$ does not evenly divide n, there will be an incomplete block of (less than r) highest-numbered individuals, $n - r[n/r]$ in number, of whom at most one can prefer x_2 to x_1. Thus we can add at least $n - r[n/r] - 1$ to get a total of at least

$$(r - 1)[n/r] + n - r[n/r] - 1 = n - [n/r] - 1$$

who prefer x_1 to x_2.

By $r = [n/(n - m)] + 1$, we have $r > n/(n - m)$, so $n - m > n/r$ or $n - m - 1 > (n/r) - 1$. Since $n - m - 1$ is an integer,

$$n - m - 1 \geq [n/r] \qquad \text{or} \qquad n - [n/r] - 1 \geq m.$$

Therefore at least m individuals prefer x_1 to x_2. By (i), $x_2 \notin C_u(X)$. Similar calculations allow us to eliminate $x_3, x_4, \ldots, x_r, x_1$. Thus $C_u(X) = \varnothing$, again contrary to (ii). $\square$

It should be noted that this result could be expressed as a "possibility" result if we required $|E|$ to be small rather than large. This, basically, is the approach of Ferejohn and Grether [100], essentially the result of Theorem 2-2, although the equivalence is somewhat masked by their addition of a condition of acyclic rationality (this condition will be discussed in detail in the next chapter).

We can use the inequality $|E| \geq -[n/(m - n)]$ from Theorem 2-2 to illustrate three special cases that have been treated in the literature.

(1)   *Minorities* $m \leq [n/2]$; less than a strict majority is decisive.   Then we would expect a contradiction by examining two disjoint decisive sets in opposition on *a single pair* of alternatives. This is confirmed in our theorem, where (iii) would require $|E| \geq -[n/(m - n)]$. By $m \leq [n/2]$,

$$m - n \leq [n/2] - n \leq -n/2$$

so $n/(m - n) \geq -2$. Since $m > 0$, we have $n - m < n$, so $n/(m - n) < -1$. Combining, we have $-2 \leq n/(m - n) < -1$, so $[n/(m - n)] = -2$. Thus (iii) requires $|E| \geq 2$, i.e., that we can find a single pair.

(2) *Majorities* $m = [n/2] + 1$. (Note: $m < n$ then implies $n \geq 3$.) This is the case of the often rediscovered "paradox of voting," a history of which can be found in Black [40]. For this case our theorem is a sort of distilled essence of an impossibility theorem of MacKay [208], although MacKay's analysis is cluttered by an unnecessary use of rationality and independence assumptions together with insufficient attention to the sizes of m and n.

CASE 1: *n is even (and so $n \geq 4$).*

$$m = (n/2) + 1,$$
$$m - n = -(n/2) + 1,$$
$$\frac{n}{m - n} = \frac{n}{-(n/2) + 1} = \frac{2n}{-n + 2}.$$

What is $[2n/(-n + 2)]$? First note that $2n/(-n + 2) < -2$, since this is equivalent to $2n > -2(-n + 2) = 2n - 4$. Also we have $2n/(-n + 2) \geq -3$ if $2n \leq -3(-n + 2) = 3n - 6$ or $n \geq 6$. For $n = 4$, $m = 3$ and $n/(m - n) = -4$. Combining, we obtain

$$-\left[\frac{n}{m - n}\right] = \begin{cases} 4 & \text{if } n = 4 \\ 3 & \text{if } n \geq 6 \text{ and } n \text{ is even.} \end{cases}$$

CASE 2: *n is odd (and $n \geq 3$).*

$$m = (n/2) + (1/2),$$
$$m - n = -(n/2) + (1/2),$$
$$\frac{n}{m - n} = \frac{2n}{-n + 1}.$$

What is $[2n/(-n + 1)]$? First note that $2n/(-n + 1) < -2$, since this is equivalent to $2n > -2(-n + 1) = 2n - 2$. Also we have $2n/(-n + 1) \geq -3$, since that is equivalent to $2n \leq -3(-n + 1) = 3n - 3$ or $n \geq 3$, which holds here. Thus $[2n/(-n + 1)] = -3$. Summarizing the two cases, we have

$$-\left[\frac{n}{m - n}\right] = \begin{cases} 4 & \text{if } n = 4 \\ 3 & \text{if } n = 3 \text{ or } n \geq 5. \end{cases}$$

Arrow [8, pp. 46–48] already noted that majority voting avoided the problems of his impossibility result if $|E| = 2$.

It takes three alternatives to illustrate the paradox of voting unless there are just four individuals, in which case four alternatives are required. The anomalous case with $n = 4$ allows an interesting application of Dirichlet's pigeonhole principle: if j objects are distributed in k pigeonholes, and if $j > k$, then at least one pigeonhole must contain at least two objects. Let three alternatives be called the three pigeonholes. The pigeons will be individuals and are assigned as follows: put individual i in pigeonhole x if and only if x is maximal in i's ordering. With four individuals, at least four pigeons will be distributed and so by Dirichlet at least one alternative must be maximal for two individuals. Such an alternative cannot lose a majority (3–to–1) vote to any of the other two alternatives and so will be chosen from the agenda of three alternatives; the choice set will be nonempty. For four alternatives, we have enough pigeonholes to avoid this. With five or more individuals, the pigeonhole principle still tells us that some alternative is maximal for two individuals but now there are enough individuals to beat that alternative on majority vote.

(3) *All but one $m = n - 1$.* Then

$$\left[\frac{n}{m-n}\right] = \left[\frac{n}{n-1-n}\right] = -[-n] = n.$$

This gives us an impossibility result of Fishburn [109] Further light is here shed on the $n = 4$ anomalous case for majority voting, for then $[n/2] + 1 = n - 1$, where we have just seen that n alternatives are required.

Theorem 2-2 rules out the possibility that, because of size alone, groups of less than all individuals might be decisive between *all* pairs of alternatives. A somewhat more surprising result is that we must deny most small groups decisiveness between *any* pairs of alternatives, at least if we are to impose the weak Pareto condition on our choice procedure. This will be obtained as a derivative result (Theorem 2-5) of the following theorem, due to Sen [309, 310].

Theorem 2-3 (*Impossibility of a Paretian liberal*) There is no collective choice rule on V, U satisfying

(i)   the standard domain constraint,
(ii) decisiveness constraints,
    (a) the weak Pareto condition,
    (b) minimal liberalism.

Proof Let x and y be the alternatives such that $\{i\}$ is decisive between them and w and z be alternatives such that $\{j\} \neq \{i\}$ is decisive between them.

CASE 1: $\{x, y\} = \{w, z\}$; *say, $w = x$ and $z = y$.* Consider a profile u, with preference orderings for i and j restricted to $\{x, y\}$ such that

$$i: \quad xy,$$
$$j: \quad yx \qquad \text{(i.e., } zw\text{).}$$

By minimal liberalism, $y \notin C_u(\{x, y\})$ and $x = w \notin C_u(\{x, y\})$. Then $C_u(\{x, y\}) = \varnothing$, contrary to (i).

CASE 2: $\{x, y\}$ and $\{w, z\}$ have exactly one element in common, say $w = x$. Consider a profile u with preference orderings restricted to $\{x, y, z\}$ such that

$$i: \quad xyz,$$
$$j: \quad yzx(= w),$$
$$k: \quad yzx \qquad \text{for all} \quad k \in N - \{i, j\}.$$

Then by minimal liberalism, $y \notin C_u(\{x, y, z\})$ and $x \notin C_u(\{x, y, z\})$. By the weak Pareto condition (comparing with y), $z \notin C_u(\{x, y, z\})$. Thus $C_u(\{x, y, z\}) = \varnothing$ contrary to (i).

CASE 3: $\{x, y\} \cap \{z, w\} = \varnothing$. Consider a profile u with preference orderings restricted to $\{x, y, z, w\}$ such that

$$i: \quad wxyz,$$
$$j: \quad yzwx,$$
$$k: \quad yzwx \qquad \text{for all} \quad k \in N - \{i, j\}.$$

Then by minimal liberalism, $y \notin C_u(\{x, y, z, w\})$ and $w \notin C_u(\{x, y, z, w\})$. Using the weak Pareto condition, comparison with y gives $z \notin C_u(\{x, y, z, w\})$ and comparison with w gives $x \notin C_u(\{x, y, z, w\})$. Thus $C_u(\{x, y, z, w\}) = \varnothing$ contrary to (i). $\square$

Fairly minor revisions of the proof can yield two further theorems:

Theorem 2-4 (Sen [310, p. 154]) There is no collective choice rule on V, U satisfying

(i) the standard domain constraint,
(ii) decisiveness constraints,
    (a) the weak Pareto condition,
    (b) there is an individual i and two alternatives x, y such that $\{i\}$ is weakly, globally decisive for x against y, and there is an individual $j \neq i$ and two alternatives w, z with $\{x, y\} \cap \{w, z\} = \varnothing$ such that $\{j\}$ is weakly globally decisive for z against w.

Sen refers to Theorem 2-4 as a strengthening of Theorem 2-3, noting that (iib) in Theorem 2-4 only requires i be decisive for x against y and not necessarily for y against x and similarly for j. Technically, however, this is not a strengthening as we must add the requirement that $\{x, y\}$ be disjoint from $\{z, w\}$. A clear strengthening is provided by:

Theorem 2-5 (*Impossibility of Paretian federalism*)   There is no collective choice rule f on V, U satisfying

   (i)   standard domain constraint,
  (ii)   decisiveness constraints,
      (a)   the weak Pareto condition,
      (b)   minimal federalism: there is a nonempty subset S_1 of N and two alternatives x, y such that S_1 is weakly, globally decisive between x and y, and there is a nonempty subset S_2 of N, disjoint from S_1, and two alternatives w, z such that S_2 is weakly, globally decisive between w and z.

The minimal federalism requirement first appeared in an impossibility theorem by Batra and Pattanaik [31]. As noted in [191], this change from Theorem 2-3 may be important:

> It is interesting that the examples Sen uses to illustrate the liberalism requirement (like sleeping on your stomach or your back, or reading *Lady Chatterly's Lover* or not) are not appropriate to the standard interpretations of E and N in welfare economics. There, E is a set of vectors describing commodity holdings by members of N, which, in turn, is the set of consumers and firms. Members of E differ because of trades between consumers (exchanges), trades between consumers and firms (purchase of consumables, sale of factors), trades between firms (intra- and interindustry sales), production by firms or disposal by consumers. We may well imagine an ethic in which no consumer is to be able to throw away a scarce commodity if everyone else is opposed and no firm is to use up a scarce resource in production if that activity generates externalities that make everyone else opposed. No single member of E is to be decisive between the kinds of alternatives considered in the standard interpretation. If disjoint S_1 and S_2 contain two individuals each, engaged in costless trades internal to an S_i, liberalism in Sen's sense may be desirable. You may object to my using up scarce resources to manufacture copies of *Lady Chatterly's Lover* (which you may or may not find offensive) and we might want to take into account the external effects of resource use (even if not the external effects involving literary judgement). But liberalism may still defend a right of pairs of individuals engaging in non-resource-using exchange (e.g., where I give a friend my copy of *Lady Chatterly's Lover* for her copy of *Lolita*).

There is a drama in the simplicity and appeal of these last theorems that has encouraged a great deal of the most recent research in collective choice theory. We shall be encountering this work repeatedly in the rest of this book, especially in Chapters 8 and 9. For a review of the Paretian liberal literature, the reader is advised to consult Sen [317].

elements are collected, and then a choice is made from them. Path independence, in this case, would mean that the final result would be independent of the way the alternatives were initially divided up for consideration.

Clearly, this could be a description of either individual choice or social choice. The case of social choice might be of special interest, however, where the outcomes that *should* result when the process is functioning "correctly" have been prespecified and the welfare economist is charged with the responsibility of creating or repairing the process in a manner which assures that the prespecified outcomes will, in fact, occur. A problem of path independence can arise in this case from what appears to be fundamental limitations on institutions. For example, the concept of "majority rule," inherently, refers to a choice over a two-element set. The idea of a proposal either "passing" or "failing" is, at base, binary. Without pursuing this much further, one can easily imagine a group restricting deliberations to four or five issues at a time because of overriding considerations relating to communication costs and other logistical problems. If the institutions a welfare economist has at his disposal for the creation of social choice processes can only operate on "small" sets, how then can he create a choosing process which will handle a "non-small' set? The answer is simple. If the institutions will operate on *any* "small" set, he can apply them repeatedly. He would thereby "extend" choice from smaller sets to a choice over the non-small set. For example, if his institutions operated on any set with five elements or less, he would split a larger set into smaller sets of five elements or less and then proceed as above to choose, collect choices, and choose again.

Now, if he can design the process so that the outcomes are independent of the initial groupings, that parameter, "path," is one less that he has to worry about. Suppose individuals 1, 2, and 3 have, respectively, preference relations $x \succ y \succ z$, $y \succ z \succ x$, and $z \succ x \succ y$. Suppose further that the process he is to create, in this case, must yield x as the outcome. If he can only use the binary process of majority rule and if he has no control over the parameter, "path," then it would appear that he has an unsolvable problem. [260, pp. 1079–1080]

However, as we shall see as soon as we have formalized the property of path independence, that property is weaker than rationality. There exist non-rational path-independent social choice functions. Arrow has defended path-independence not rationality.

The remaining argument for rationality is that, since it directs our attention to best elements, it provides a reason for stuffing our tool box with mathematical optimization techniques (on the value of which, see Samuelson's Nobel address [293]). Two remarks are appropriate here. One is that this argument will be telling only if the rationalization satisfies additional properties that permit use of existing optimization methods—we might want the social preference relation to have a representation that is continuous, or differentiable, or maybe even linear. Secondly, this argument is clearly one of computational simplicity and *not related to ethical ideas*.

The following examples (from Plott [267]) show that rational choice functions may differ in their degree of rationality.

Example 3-4a A choice function may be total, reflexive, and rational but *not* acyclic:

$$C(\{a,b\}) = \{a\}, \qquad C(\{b,c\}) = \{b\}, \qquad C(\{a,c\}) = \{c\}.$$

Example 3-4b A choice function may be total, reflexive, and acyclic but *not* quasitransitive:

$$C(\{a,b\}) = \{a\}, \qquad C(\{b,c\}) = \{b\}, \qquad C(\{a,c\}) = \{a,c\}.$$

Example 3-4c A choice function may be total, reflexive, and quasitransitive rational but not transitive rational:

$$C(\{a,b\}) = \{a,b\}, \qquad C(\{b,c\}) = \{b,c\}, \qquad C(\{a,c\}) = \{a\}.$$

However, trivially, transitive rationality is stronger than quasitransitive rationality, which is stronger than acyclic rationality.

Theorem 3-5 If V contains all finite subsets of E, any rationalization of a total choice function is acyclic.

Proof If not, $x_1 P x_2, \ldots, x_{n-1} P x_n, x_n P x_1$. Then

$$C(\{x_1, \ldots, x_{n-1}, x_n\}) = \varnothing,$$

contrary to our totality assumption. $\square$

The *path independence* (PI) formalization that we promised earlier is

$$C(v_1 \cup v_2) = C(C(v_1) \cup C(v_2)).$$

We will follow Ferejohn and Grether [101] in factoring the PI condition into two parts:

$$\text{PI*:} \quad C(v_1 \cup v_2) \subseteq C(C(v_1) \cup C(v_2)),$$
$$\text{*PI:} \quad C(v_1 \cup v_2) \supseteq C(C(v_1) \cup C(v_2)).$$

Ferejohn and Grether argue that Arrow's defense of path independence is really a defense of *PI. We also mentioned earlier the next result.

Theorem 3-6 For total choice functions, transitive rationality implies path independence.

Proof Let R be a transitive rationalization of C. If $x \in C(v_1 \cup v_2)$, then xRy for all y in $v_1 \cup v_2$ and thus for all y in $C(v_1) \cup C(v_2) \subseteq v_1 \cup v_2$. Also $x \in v_1 \cup v_2$, so $x \in C(v_1)$ or $x \in C(v_2)$, so $x \in C(v_1) \cup C(v_2)$. Therefore $x \in C(C(v_1) \cup C(v_2))$ and

$$C(v_1 \cup v_2) \subseteq C(C(v_1) \cup C(v_2)). \tag{PI*}$$

(Note that rationality but neither totality nor transitivity were required to establish PI*.)

Now suppose $x \in C(C(v_1) \cup C(v_2))$ and let $y \in v_1 \cup v_2$, say $y \in v_1$. Using totality, look at any $z \in C(v_1)$. xRz by $x \in C(C(v_1) \cup C(v_2))$ and zRy by $z \in C(v_1)$. By transitivity, xRy. Therefore $x \in C(v_1 \cup v_2)$ and

$$C(C(v_1) \cup C(v_2)) \subseteq C(v_1 \cup v_2). \qquad (\text{*PI})$$

PI and PI combine to give path independence. □

Important for the position we have shown Plott to have taken is that a total choice function may satisfy path independence but not rationality. The following example is from Plott [266]:

$$C(\{x, y\}) = \{x, y\}, \qquad C(\{y, z\}) = \{y, z\}, \qquad C(\{x, z\}) = \{x, z\},$$
$$C(\{x, y, z\}) = \{x, y\}.$$

By Theorem 3-3, the only possible rationalization is relexive with xIy, xIz, yIz, so that z is R-best in $\{x, y, z\}$. But $z \notin C(\{x, y, z\})$; thus C is not rational. To show path independence, note $C(v) = v$ if $v \subsetneqq \{x, y, z\}$. Then we divide our analysis into two cases.

CASE 1: $v_1 \cup v_2 \subsetneqq \{x, y, z\}$. $C(v_1) \cup C(v_2) = v_1 \cup v_2$ since each of v_1 and v_2 must be a proper subset of $\{x, y, z\}$. Thus $C(C(v_1)) = C(v_1 \cup v_2)$.

CASE 2: $v_1 \cup v_2 = \{x, y, z\}$. Then $C(v_1 \cup v_2) = \{x, y\}$. We must calculate $C(C(v_1) \cup C(v_2))$. Note x and y are chosen from any agenda containing them. $x \in v_1 \cup v_2$; suppose $x \in v_1$. Then $x \in C(v_1)$, so $x \in C(v_1) \cup C(v_2)$ and thus $x \in C(C(v_1) \cup C(v_2))$. Similarly, $y \in C(C(v_1) \cup C(v_2))$. It remains to show $z \notin C(C(v_1) \cup C(v_2))$. But suppose z is in this choice set so that $z \in C(v_1) \cup C(v_2)$. Then $C(v_1) \cup C(v_2) = \{x, y, z\}$ and so $C(C(v_1) \cup C(v_2)) = C(\{x, y, z\}) = \{x, y\}$, contrary to the assumption we just made about z. Thus $z \notin C(C(v_1) \cup C(v_2)) = \{x, y\} = C(v_1 \cup v_2)$. □

Example 3-7 A total choice function can satisfy path independence and have a complete, reflexive rationalization without the relation being transitive:

$$C(\{x, y\}) = \{x, y\}, \qquad C(\{y, z\}) = \{y, z\}, \qquad C(\{x, z\}) = \{z\},$$
$$C(\{x, y, z\}) = \{y, z\}.$$

The unique, complete, reflexive rationalization is xIy, yIz, xPz, which is not transitive. Confirming that C satisfies path independence is left as an exercise for the reader.

We define a new regularity condition,[2] called *Property* α as follows, where v and v' are elements of V:

$$v \subseteq v' \quad \text{implies} \quad v \cap C(v') \subseteq C(v).$$

Theorem 3-8   Path independence implies Property α.

Proof   Suppose C satisfies independence of path, that $x \in C(v')$, and $x \in v \subset v'$. Partition v' into v and $v' - v$. $C(v') = C(v \cup (v' - v)) = C(C(v) \cup C(v' - v))$. Since $x \in C(v')$, $x \in C(v) \cup C(v' - v)$. $x \notin C(v' - v)$, for otherwise $x \in v' - v$, contrary to $x \in v$. Therefore $x \in C(v)$. $\square$

Combining Theorems 3-6 and 3-8, we see that for total choice functions transitive rationality implies Property α. We also note that Property α does not imply transitive rationality. Otherwise, with Theorem 3-8, we would have path independence implying transitive rationality contrary to Plott's example. In fact, we can establish a stronger result:

Example 3-9   There exist total social choice functions satisfying Property α but not path independence:

$$C(\{a,b\}) = \{a\}, \qquad C(\{a,c\}) = \{a,c\}, \qquad C(\{b,c\}) = \{c\},$$
$$C(\{a,b,c\}) = \{a\}.$$

Confirming Property α is straightforward and is left to the reader. To see that independence of path is violated, we split $\{a,b,c\}$ as $\{a,b\} \cup \{b,c\}$:

$$C(\{a,b\} \cup \{b,c\}) = C(\{a,b,c\}) = \{a\},$$
$$C(C(\{a,b\}) \cup C(\{b,c\})) = C(\{a\} \cup \{c\}) = C(\{a,c\}) = \{a,c\}.$$

Just as we introduced pairwise versions of decisiveness conditions, we will make use of pairwise versions of regularity conditions. The main pairwise version of α is α_p. A choice function C satisfies α_p if for every x and every $S \in V$,

$$x \in C(S) \rightarrow x \in C(\{x,y\}) \quad \text{for all} \quad y \in S.$$

Sen [318] discusses two weakenings of α_p. A choice function C satisfies $\alpha_p(-)$ if for every $S \in V$ there exists at least one x in $C(S)$ such that

$$x \in C(\{x,y\}) \quad \text{for all} \quad y \in S.$$

A choice function satisfies $\alpha_p(--)$ if for every *triple* $S \in V$, there exists at least one x in $C(S)$ such that

$$x \in C(\{x,y\}) \quad \text{for all} \quad y \in S.$$

---

[2] This property has frequently appeared in the choice and decision theory literature (cf. e.g. [11], [81], [232], [270]) and under a variety of names including, unfortunately, independence of irrelevant alternatives (on this, see [94], [184], [272]).

We now embark on a series of theorems that show the *fundamental* nature of Property α by characterizing many regularity conditions as α plus something else. The first "something else" is *Property β*, defined as follows, where v and v' are elements of V:

$$v \subseteq v' \to [C(v) \cap C(v') \neq \varnothing \to C(v) \subseteq C(v')].$$

Property β is a strengthening of Sen's *Property δ*:

If $x, y \in C(S)$ and $S \subset T$, then neither x nor y can be *uniquely* best in T.

β is weaker than Bordes' *Property $\beta(+)$*:

$$x \in C(S) \ \& \ y \in S \subseteq T \to [y \in C(T) \to x \in C(T)].$$

$\beta(+)$ will play an interesting role in Chapter 5. $\beta(+)$ implies *PI [60].

Theorem 3-10 If a total choice function with V containing all finite subsets of E satisfies both Properties α and β, then it has a complete, reflexive, transitive rationalization (Sen [307]).

Proof The only *possible* rationalization is the base relation: xRy if and only if $x \in C(\{x, y\})$. We will first show that R *is* a rationalization of C and then that R is transitive.

Suppose $y \in v \in V$ is not R-best in v. There is an $x \in v$ with xPy, i.e., $C(\{x, y\}) = \{x\}$. If $y \in C(v)$, then α would dictate $y \in C(\{x, y\})$, contrary to our choice of x. Thus $y \notin C(v)$, which contains only R-best elements of v. We must show it contains *all* such elements. So let $x \in v$ be an R-best element of $v \in V$. Since $C(v)$ is not empty, there is a z in $C(v)$. If $z = x$, we are done. Otherwise consider $v' = \{x, z\} \subseteq v$. By Property α, $z \in C(v')$. Thus $z \in C(v') \cap C(v)$ and Property β tells us $C(v') \subseteq C(v)$. But $x \in C(v')$ since x is R-best in v. Therefore $x \in C(v)$.

Suppose transitivity fails, i.e., there are alternatives x, y, and z, with xRy, yRz but zPx. Equivalently,

$$x \in C(\{x, y\}), \qquad y \in C(\{y, z\}) \qquad \text{but} \qquad C(\{x, z\}) = \{z\}.$$

Since $y \in C(\{y, z\})$, we have either $C(\{y, z\}) = \{y, z\}$ or $C(\{y, z\}) = \{y\}$.

CASE 1: $C(\{y, z\}) = \{y, z\}$. Then z is R-best in $\{x, y, z\}$, $z \in C(\{x, y, z\})$. Applying Property β, $\{y, z\} = C(\{y, z\}) \subseteq C(\{x, y, z\})$. $y \in C(\{x, y, z\})$ implies y is R-best in that set, so yRx, $y \in C(\{x, y\})$. Applying Property β again, $\{x, y\} = C(\{x, y\}) \subseteq C(\{x, y, z\})$. But that means x is R-maximal contrary to zPx.

CASE 2: $C(\{y, z\}) = \{y\}$. Then yPz, so neither z nor x are R-maximal in $\{x, y, z\}$. Since $C(\{x, y, z\}) \neq \varnothing$, we need $y \in C(\{x, y, z\})$. By Property α,

$y \in C(\{x, y\})$. Applying Property β, $\{x, y\} = C(\{x, y\}) \subseteq C(\{x, y, z\})$. But $x \in C(\{x, y, z\})$ would imply x is R-best, contrary to zPx. $\square$

We will express quasitransitive rationality in terms of Property α by first expressing quasitransitive rationality in terms of path independence and then expressing independence of path in terms of Property α. Define *Property γ_p* as[3]

$$[x \in v \in V \& (\forall y)(y \in v \rightarrow x \in C(\{x, y\}))] \rightarrow x \in C(v).$$

Property γ_p is a pairwise version of Sen's Property γ:

$$C(v_1) \cap C(v_2) \subseteq C(v_1 \cup v_2).$$

Theorem 3-11 If a total choice function has a V consisting of exactly the finite subsets of E, then it has a complete, reflexive, quasitransitive rationalization if and only if it satisfies both path independence and Property γ_p (Plott [266]).

Proof First, assume C has the required rationalization which must be the usual one:

$$xRy \qquad \text{if and only if} \quad x \in C(\{x, y\}).$$

Suppose $x \in v \in V$ and $(\forall y)(y \in v \rightarrow x \in C(\{x, y\}))$. Then for all y in v, xRy. Since x is R-best in v, $x \in C(v)$. Thus C satisfies Property γ_p. To establish path independence, let $x \in C(v_1 \cup v_2)$; xRy for all $y \in v_1 \cup v_2$. Also $x \in v_1 \cup v_2$, say $x \in v_1$. Since xRy for all $y \in v_1$, $x \in C(v_1)$. Also xRy for all $y \in C(v_1) \cup C(v_2)$, so $x \in C(C(v_1) \cup C(v_2))$. This establishes

$$C(v_1 \cup v_2) \subseteq C(C(v_1) \cup C(v_2)). \qquad \text{(PI*)}$$

To confirm the reverse inclusion, suppose $x \in C(C(v_1) \cup C(v_2))$ but $x \notin C(v_1 \cup v_2)$. There is a $y_1 \in v_1 \cup v_2$ with $y_1 Px$. Assume without loss of generality that $y_1 \in v_1$. $y_1 \notin C(v_1)$, for otherwise $y_1 \in C(v_1) \cup C(v_2)$ and then $x \in C(C(v_1) \cup C(v_2))$ says xRy_1, contrary to our choice of y_1. Since $y_1 \notin C(v_1)$, there is a y_2 in v_1 with $y_2 Py_1$. By quasitransitivity, $y_2 Px$. Again, $y_2 \notin C(v_1)$, for otherwise $y_2 \in C(v_1) \cup C(v_2)$ and then xRy_2 contrary to $y_2 Px$. Since $y_2 \notin C(v_1)$, there is a y_3 in v_1 with $y_3 Py_2$ and so $y_3 Py_1$ and $y_3 Px$. y_1, y_2, and y_3 are thus all distinct. Continuing in this fashion, for any m, we can get a set of m distinct alternatives, $\{y_1, y_2, \ldots, y_m\} \subseteq v_1$ with no y_i in $C(v_1)$, contrary to the assumption that v_1 is admissible and finite. Thus

$$C(C(v_1) \cup C(v_2)) \subseteq C(v_1 \cup v_2), \qquad \text{(*PI)}$$

which combined with (PI*) combined path independence.

---

[3] This property has also been called the generalized Condorcet property [45].

Now we will assume C satisfies path independence and Property γ_p and show that C is quasitransitive rational. The candidate rationalization is the base relation

$$xRy \qquad \text{if and only if} \quad x \in C(\{x, y\})$$

which is complete and reflexive. First we show that R is a rationalization and then that R is quasitransitive. Suppose $x \in v$ is R-best in v, i.e., $x \in C(\{x, y\})$ for all y in v; by Property γ_p, $x \in C(v)$. If $x \in v$ is not R-best in v, there is a $w \in v$ with wPx, i.e., $C(\{x, w\}) = \{w\}$. Partitioning v into $\{x, w\}$ and $v - \{x, w\}$, we see that x is in neither $C(\{x, w\})$ nor $C(v - \{x, w\})$ and so, by path independence, x is not in $C(v)$. Combining these two results, $C(v)$ is the set of R-best elements of v, i.e., R is a rationalization.

Suppose R is not quasitransitive. There exist x, y, and z with xPy, yPz but not xPz, i.e.,

$$C(\{x, y\}) = \{x\}, \qquad C(\{y, z\}) = \{y\}, \qquad \text{but} \qquad z \in C(\{x, z\}).$$

Since yPz, $z \notin C(\{x, y, z\})$. But

$$C(\{x, y, z\}) = C(C(\{x, y\}) \cup C(\{z\})) = C(\{x\} \cup \{z\}) = C(\{x, z\})$$

which contains z. This contradiction proves that our claim that R is not quasitransitive was wrong. $\square$

Now, as promised, we decompose path independence. C satisfies *Property ε* if $v \subseteq v'$ implies $C(v')$ is not a *proper* subset of $C(v)$.[4]

Theorem 3-12 A choice function satisfies path independence if and only if it satisfies both Properties α and ε [45].

Proof First we show that path independence implies Property α. Let $v \subseteq v'$ and let $x \in v \cap C(v')$. By path independence,

$$C(v') = C(C(v' - v) \cup C(v)) \subseteq C(v' - v) \cup C(v).$$

Since $x \in v$, $x \notin v' - v$, so $x \notin C(v' - v)$. Therefore $x \in C(v)$. Hence $v \cap C(v') \subseteq C(v)$.

Next we show that path independence implies Property ε. Let $v \subseteq v'$ and suppose, contrary to Property ε, that $C(v') \subsetneq C(v)$. By path independence,

$$C(v') = C(C(v) \cup C(v')) = C(C(v)).$$

By the first part of this proof, Property α holds, so that from $C(v) \subseteq v$ we can derive $C(v) \cap C(v) \subseteq C(C(v))$, so $C(v) = C(C(v))$. This yields $C(v') = C(v)$, a contradiction. Therefore Property ε is satisfied.

---

[4] Property ε has been called the *superset property* [45].

Finally, from Properties α and ε we will obtain path independence. Suppose $x \in C(v_1 \cup v_2)$. If $x \in v_1$, then, by Property α, $x \in C(v_1)$; if $x \in v_2$, then $x \in C(v_2)$. Hence $x \in C(v_1) \cup C(v_2) \subseteq v_1 \cup v_2$. By another application of Property α, $x \in C(C(v_1) \cup C(v_2))$. Thus,[5]

$$C(v_1 \cup v_2) \subseteq C(C(v_1) \cup C(v_2)).$$

But this inclusion cannot be strict because of Property ε and the observation that $C(v_1) \cup C(v_2) \subseteq v_1 \cup v_2$. Thus

$$C(v_1 \cup v_2) = C(C(v_1) \cup C(v_2)). \quad \square$$

As we observed earlier, Theorems 3-11 and 3-12 together yield a refined decomposition of quasitransitive rationality. A total choice function with V equal to the set of finite nonempty subsets of E has a complete, reflexive, quasitransitive rationalization if and only if it satisfies Properties α, ε, and γ_p. Continuing our decomposition exercises, we have[6]:

Theorem 3-13 If a total choice function has a V containing all finite nonempty subsets of E, then it has a complete, acyclic, and reflexive rationalization if and only if it satisfies Properties α_p and γ_p [45].

Proof First assume C satisfies the latter two conditions. Again the only possible rationalization is the base relation

$$xRy \qquad \text{if and only if} \quad x \in C(\{x, y\}).$$

If $x \in C(v)$, then by Property α_p, $x \in C(\{x, y\})$ for each $y \in v$, so that $C(v)$ consists of only R-best elements. If $x \in v$ is R-best in v, $x \in C(\{x, y\})$ for all $y \in v$ and then, by Property γ_p, $x \in C(v)$. Thus $C(v)$ is the set of R-best elements of v. Completeness and reflexivity of R are trivial; acyclicity follows from Theorem 5.

Now assume C has a complete, acyclic, reflexive rationalization R. If $x \in C(v)$ and $y \in v$, we observe that xRy, and so $x \in C(\{x, y\})$. Also, if $x \in C(\{x, y\})$ for all y in v, xRy for all such y and so $x \in C(v)$. $\quad \square$

Many of these conditions fit a classification that Sen has shown to be useful in understanding impossibility theorems [318]. A *contraction-consistency* condition gives information on what elements are chosen from subsets from information on what elements are chosen from supersets. Equivalently, they inform us of what is not chosen from supersets according

---

[5] This result together with the proof of Theorem 8 shows that Property α is equivalent to PI* (cf. Parks [245]).

[6] Since V contains all pairs, this is equivalent to Sen's theorem that C is normal if and only if Properties α and γ are satisfied.

to what is not chosen from subsets. An *expansion-consistency* condition gives information on what is chosen from supersets from information on what is chosen from subsets or, equivalently, information on what is not chosen from subsets according to what is not chosen from supersets. Examples of contraction-consistency conditions are Properties α, α_p, $\alpha_p(-)$, and $\alpha_p(--)$. Examples of expansion-consistency conditions are Properties δ, β, $\beta(+)$, γ, and γ_p.

We now turn to the other class of simplicity conditions, with fixed agenda and variable profile. A collective choice rule f on U is said to satisfy *independence of irrelevant alternatives* if, whenever $v \in V$, $C_u = f(u)$, and $C_{u'} = f(u')$, where u and u' are both in U with $u|_v = u'|_v$, then $C_u(v) = C_{u'}(v)$. (For the $u|_v$ notation, see the Mathematical Appendix.)

A variant,[7] due to Murakami [232] and Blau [47], has independence for agenda of a fixed size. A collective choice rule f satisfies *m-ary independence* if, for every set $v \in V$ with cardinality m, $u|_v = u'|_v$ implies $C_u(v) = C_{u'}(v)$, where $C_u = f(u)$ and $C_{u'} = f(u')$. Since f is a function, we can say that if $|E| = m < \infty$, f is m-ary independent. Also every collective choice rule is 1-ary independent. Clearly, independence of irrelevant alternatives is equivalent to saying that C is m-ary independent for every m for which there is an admissible agenda with cardinality m. The next few results strive to establish independence of irrelevant alternatives from *apparently* weaker m-ary independence conditions.

We first observe that if C satisfies rationality and V contains all two-element subsets of E, then 2-ary independence implies independence of irrelevant alternatives. For suppose $u|_v = u'|_v$, $C_u = f(u)$, and $C_{u'} = f(u')$:

$$
\begin{aligned}
C_u(v) &= \{x \mid xR(u)y \text{ for all } y \in v\} \\
&= \{x \mid x \in C_u(\{x, y\}) \text{ for all } y \in v\} \\
&= \{x \mid x \in C_{u'}(\{x, y\}) \text{ for all } y \in v\} \\
&= \{x \mid xR(u')y \text{ for all } y \in v\} \\
&= C_{u'}(v).
\end{aligned}
$$

In fact, given rationality and suitably large V, similar calculations can establish independence of irrelevant alternatives for finite E from k-ary independence, where k can be any integer, $2 \le k < |E|$. We will develop this in two steps.

Lemma 3-14   If f is a collective choice rule that satisfies

    (i)   rationality,

    (ii) V contains all k-element subsets of E, then k-ary independence implies $(k + 1)$-ary independence for $2 < k + 1 \le |E|$.

---

[7] Other interesting variants are presented by Mayston [221].

Proof   Let $|v| = k + 1$ and suppose $u|_v = u'|_v$, $C_u = f(u)$, and $C_{u'} = f(u')$:

$$C_u(v) = \{x \mid xR(u)y \text{ for all } y \in v\}$$
$$= \{x \mid x \in C_u(\{x\} \cup v') \text{ for all } v' \text{ such that } |v'| = k - 1 \text{ and } x \notin v' \subseteq v\}$$
$$= \{x \mid x \in C_{u'}(\{x\} \cup v') \text{ for all } v' \text{ such that } |v'| = k - 1 \text{ and } x \notin v' \subseteq v\}$$
$$= \{x \mid xR(u')y \text{ for all } y \in v\}$$
$$= C_{u'}(v). \quad \square$$

Theorem 3-15   If f satisfies

  (i)   rationality,
  (ii) the standard domain constraint,
  (iii) $|E| < \infty$,

then if f is k-ary independent for $2 \le k < |E|$, f satisfies independence of irrelevant alternatives.

Proof   By repeated applications of the lemma, f is $(k + 1)$-ary independent, $(k + 2)$-ary independent, $\ldots$, $|E|$-ary independent. What remains is a derivation of $(k - 1)$-ary independence which can then be repeated to derive $(k - 2)$-ary independence and so on down to 2-ary independence.

Suppose $|v| = k - 1$ and $u|_v = u'|_v$. Let c and d be distinct alternatives in $E - v$ and define a profile u'' as

$$(x, y) \in R_i'' \quad \text{if and only if} \quad \begin{cases} \text{neither } x \text{ nor } y \text{ is } d \text{ and } (x, y) \in R_i, \\ (x = d \text{ or } y = d) \text{ and } (x, y) \in R_i'. \end{cases}$$

Then $u|_{v \cup \{c\}} = u'|_{v \cup \{c\}}$ and $u'|_{v \cup \{d\}} = u''|_{v \cup \{d\}}$. By k-ary independence, $R(u)|_{v \cup \{c\}} = R(u'')|_{v \cup \{c\}}$ and $R(u')|_{v \cup \{d\}} = R(u'')|_{v \cup \{d\}}$, hence $R(u)|_v = R(u')|_v$, so that $C_u(v) = C_{u'}(v)$ as was to be established. $\square$

We will illustrate independence of irrelevant alternatives and show ties between the simplicity conditions of this chapter and the responsiveness and decisiveness conditions of the previous chapter by the following results, which will play an important role early in the next chapter.

Lemma 3-16   Suppose a collective choice rule f satisfies

  (i)   the standard domain restriction,
  (ii) independence of irrelevant alternatives,
  (iii) Property α,
  (iv) nonnegative responsiveness,

then, for every x, y, if $u = (R_1, \ldots, R_n)$ and $u' = (R_1', \ldots, R_n')$ satisfy $xR_iy \rightarrow xP_i'y$, then with $C_u = f(u)$ and $C_{u'} = f(u')$,

$$(x \in v \rightarrow y \notin C_u(v)) \rightarrow (x \in v \rightarrow y \notin C_{u'}(v)).$$

Proof   Define two new profiles $u^* = (R_1^*, \ldots, R_n^*)$ and $u'^* = (R_1'^*, \ldots, R_n'^*)$ as

aR_i^*b if and only if
aR_ib with either $\{a, b\} \subseteq \{x, y\}$ or $\{a, b\} \cap \{x, y\} = \varnothing$
or
$a \in \{x, y\}$,

$aR_i'^*b$ if and only if
aR_ib and $\{a, b\} \subseteq \{x, y\}$ or
aR_ib and $\{a, b\} \cap \{x, y\} = \varnothing$ or
$a \in \{x, y\}$.

R_i^* is obtained from R_i by taking x and y to the top of R_i but otherwise preserving the R_i relations between x and y and among the members of $E - \{x, y\}$. $R_i'^*$ is obtained from R_i by taking x and y to the top, preserving the R_i relations among the members of $E - \{x, y\}$, but the R_i' relations between x and y. Let $C_{u^*} = f(u^*)$ and $C_{u'^*} = f(u'^*)$.

By independence of irrelevant alternatives, $C_u(\{x, y\}) = C_{u^*}(\{x, y\})$. By hypothesis, $x \in v \to y \notin C(v)$; in particular, $C_u(\{x, y\}) = \{x\}$. Hence $C_{u^*}(\{x, y\}) = \{x\}$. By Property α, $x \in v \to y \notin C_{u^*}(v)$. Then, by nonnegative responsiveness, $x \in v \to y \notin C_{u'^*}(v)$. In particular, $C_{u'^*}(\{x, y\}) = \{x\}$. Another application of independence of irrelevant alternatives yields $C_{u'}(\{x, y\}) = \{x\}$ and a final use of Property α gives $x \in v \to y \notin C_{u'}(v)$. $\square$

Theorem 3-17   Suppose f satisfies

  (i)   the standard domain restriction,
 (ii)   independence of irrelevant alternatives,
(iii)   Property α,
(iv)   nonnegative responsiveness.

Suppose for some $u = (R_1, \ldots, R_n)$ such that xP_iy for all $i \in S$ and yP_ix for $i \notin S$, we have $C_u(\{x, y\}) = \{x\}$, where $C_u = f(u)$. Then S is weakly, globally decisive for x against y.

Proof   Note that by Property α, $x \in v \to y \notin C_u(v)$. Now if $u' = (R_1', \ldots, R_n')$ is any profile with $xP_i'y$ for all $i \in S$, the previous lemma tells us $x \in v \to y \notin C_{u'}(v)$. But this is just the assertion $x\bar{D}_Sy$.

Theorem 3-18   Suppose f satisfies

  (i)   the standard domain restriction,
 (ii)   independence of irrelevant alternatives,
(iii)   Property α,

(iv)   nonnegative responsiveness,
(v)   nonimposition.

Then f also satisfies the weak Pareto condition.

Proof   By nonimposition, there is at least one profile u with $C_u = f(u)$ and $C_u(\{x, y\}) = \{x\}$; by Property α, $x \in v \to y \notin C_u(v)$. Consider u' derived from u by advancing x to the most preferred position on each R_i in u. By the lemma, $x \in v \to y \notin C_{u'}(v)$, where $C_{u'} = f(u')$; in particular, $C_{u'}(\{x, y\}) = \{x\}$. By the previous theorem, the set of all individuals is weakly, globally decisive for x against y, i.e., f satisfies the weak Pareto condition. $\square$

Exercises

1.   Prove Theorem 3-3.
2.   Prove Property $\beta(+)$ implies *PI.
3.   Show the need for Property α in each of Lemma 3-16, Theorem 3-17, and Theorem 3-18 by giving examples in which all assumptions but Property α hold and the conclusion fails.
4.   Prove the following result (similar to a theorem of Weldon [343]) which uses a property almost the opposite of liberalism.
     There does not exist a collective choice rule f on V, U satisfying
     (i)   the standard domain constraint,
     (ii)   for each $S \subseteq N = \{1, 2, \ldots, n\}$ with $|S| = n$ or $n - 1$, S is weakly, globally decisive between every pair of alternatives,
     (iii) each $f(u)$ has a reflexive and complete rationalization,
     (iv)   independence of irrelevant alternatives.
     (*Hint*:   Show first that if $|S| = n - 2$, then S is weakly globally decisive; next deal with $|S| = n - 3$, etc.)

4 SIMPLICITY: IMPOSSIBILITY THEOREMS

As a prelude to a series of impossibility results, we prove an important result on decisiveness.

Lemma 4-1 [45] Suppose a collective choice rule satisfies

(i) the standard domain restriction (2),
(ii) the weak pairwise Pareto condition,
(iii) independence of irrelevant alternatives,
(iv) base quasitransitivity, i.e., quasitransitivity of the base relation for $C_u = f(u)$ for all u:

$$C_u(\{x, y\}) = \{x\} \ \& \ C_u(\{y, z\}) = y \to C_u(\{x, z\}) = \{x\}.$$

Then, if a set S is weakly, *locally* pairwise decisive for *some* alternative against another, it is weakly, *globally* pairwise decisive between *any* two alternatives.

Proof Suppose $xPD_S y$. If $S = N$, the conclusion is immediate by the weak pairwise Pareto condition. So we assume $N - S \neq \emptyset$. Let z be any third alternative (known to exist by the standard domain restriction), suppose u is any profile with $xP_i z$ for $i \in S$ and $zP_i x$ for $i \notin S$. Consider a profile u_0 for which the restrictions of the orderings to $\{x, y, z\}$ are

$$S: \quad xyz,$$
$$N - S: \quad yzx.$$

$C_{u_0}(\{x,y\}) = \{x\}$ by xPD_Sy. $C_{u_0}(\{y,z\}) = \{y\}$ by the weak Pareto condition. Therefore, by base quasitransitivity, $C_{u_0}(\{x,z\}) = \{x\}$. By independence of irrelevant alternatives, $C_u(\{x,z\}) = \{x\}$, so xPD_Sz.

$$xPD_Sy \to xPD_Sz. \tag{1}$$

Start again, letting u satisfy the condition that zP_iy for all $i \in S$ while yP_iz for all $i \in N - S$. Consider a profile u_1 for which the restrictions of the orderings to $\{x,y,z\}$ are

$$S: \quad zxy,$$
$$N - S: \quad yzx.$$

$C_{u_1}(\{x,y\}) = \{x\}$ by xPD_Sy. $C_{u_1}(\{x,z\}) = \{z\}$ by the weak Pareto condition. Therefore, by base quasitransitivity, $C_{u_1}(\{y,z\}) = \{z\}$. IIA then yields $C_u(\{y,z\}) = \{z\}$, so zD_Sy.

$$xPD_Sy \to zPD_Sy. \tag{2}$$

From (2), interchanging y and z gives

$$xPD_Sz \to yPD_Sz. \tag{3}$$

Combining this with (1), we have

$$xPD_Sy \to yPD_Sz. \tag{4}$$

From (1), using the permutation $\begin{pmatrix} x & y & z \\ y & z & x \end{pmatrix}$, we get $yPD_Sz \to yPD_Sx$. Combining this with (4), we obtain

$$xPD_Sy \to yPD_Sx. \tag{5}$$

From (3), using the permutation $\begin{pmatrix} x & y & z \\ y & z & x \end{pmatrix}$ again, we get $yPD_Sx \to zPD_Sx$. Combining this with (5), we get

$$xPD_Sy \to zPD_Sx. \tag{6}$$

Together, (1), (2), and (4)–(6) tell us

$$\text{if} \quad xPD_Sy, \quad \text{then} \quad rPD_St \quad \text{for every} \quad \{r,t\} \subseteq \{x,y,z\}. \tag{7}$$

By an adaptation of an argument of Blau [46, p. 310] to our notation, we use this result to prove that if xPD_Sy, then rPD_St for all r, t in E. If $\{r,t\} = \{x,y\}$, (7) guarantees rPD_St. Suppose $\{r,t\} \cap \{x,y\}$ consists of just one alternative, say, $r = x$. Then letting $z = t$ in (7), we get rPD_St. Finally, suppose $\{r,t\} \cap \{x,y\} = \varnothing$. Using (7) once, with $z = r$ we have $xPD_Sy \to rPD_Sy$.

Then using (7) again with $x = r$ and $z = t$ we obtain $rPD_S y \to rPD_S t$. Therefore $xPD_S y \to rPD_S t$.

All that remains is a demonstration that these local results can all be converted to global results. Still assuming $xPD_S y$, let u be any profile with $xP_i y$ for all $i \in S$:

$$S: \quad xy,$$

$$N - S: \quad [xy].$$

Insert a z to get a u_0 for which the restricted orderings are

$$S: \quad xzy,$$

$$N - S: \quad z[xy].$$

By $xPD_S y$ we see from the first part of our proof that $xPD_S z$. Therefore $C_{u_0}(\{x, z\}) = \{x\}$. By the weak Pareto condition, $C_{u_0}(\{y, z\}) = \{z\}$. Then, by base quasitransitivity, $C_{u_0}(\{x, y\}) = \{x\}$. By independence of irrelevant alternatives, $C_u(\{x, y\}) = \{x\}$ as was to be shown. $\square$

This contagion result is clearly disturbing; to confer apparently little power to a set S is to confer global pairwise decisiveness between all alternatives. (An interesting variant of this lemma, not using independence of irrelevant alternatives, has been employed by Sen [317].) Many of the following theorems are simply ways of dramatizing the disturbing nature of Lemma 4-1.

Theorem 4-2 (*Arrow's first impossibility theorem*)   There is no collective choice rule f satisfying

  (i) $|E| = 3$,
  (ii)   domain; there is a subset $T \subseteq E$, with $|T| = 3$ and
      (a) $V \supseteq 2^T - \{\varnothing\}$,
      (b) $\{u|_T | u \in U\} = R_T{}^n,\ 3 \leqq n \leqq \infty$,
  (iii)   each $C_u = f(u)$ has a complete, reflexive, and transitive rationalization $R(u)$,
  (iv)   independence of irrelevant alternatives,
  (v)   nonimposition,
  (vi)   general nondictatorship,
  (vii)   nonnegative responsiveness.

Proof   With (i), (ii) and (iii), the standard domain constraint holds. (Totality can be obtained for finite agenda when a complete, reflexive, and transitive rationalization exists.)

By transitive rationality, each $C_u = f(u)$ satisfies Property α and base quasitransitivity. By Theorem 3-18, f satisfies the weak Pareto condition.

By Lemma 4-1, any set weakly, locally pairwise decisive for some alternative against another is weakly, globally, pairwise decisive between any two alternatives. Any such set we will call *pairwise decisive*. Let W be the *smallest* pairwise decisive set (this exists by the weak pairwise Pareto condition which tells us N is pairwise decisive). By global nondictatorship and Property α, we see W must contain at least two individuals. (Property α is used to show that pairwise dictators are general dictators.) Partition W into $\{i\}$ and $W - \{i\} \neq \varnothing$. Consider a profile u with *complete* orderings

$$
\begin{aligned}
i: &\quad xyz, \\
W - \{i\}: &\quad zxy, \\
N - W: &\quad yzx.
\end{aligned}
$$

Since W is pairwise decisive, $xP(u)y$. If $zR(u)x$, then, by transitivity, $zP(u)y$. By Theorem 3-17 $z\overline{PD}_{W-\{i\}}y$ and so, by Lemma 4-1, $W - \{i\}$ is pairwise decisive, contrary to our choice of W. Therefore $xP(u)z$. But then, by Theorem 3-17, $x\overline{PD}_{\{i\}}z$ and so, by Lemma 4-1, $\{i\}$ is pairwise decisive. With Property α, this says i is a general dictator. $\square$

This is not quite the theorem that Arrow stated. For he dropped (i), allowing $|E| > 3$.

But with this relaxation, it is not possible to establish the standard domain constraint and so it is not possible to establish Theorem 3-18 and Lemma 4-1 which Arrow had dealt with as if $|E| = 3$.

Arrow's original version was shown to be false by Blau [46] by means of the following example. Let $E = \{a, b, c, d\}$. We take $V = 2^E - \{\varnothing\}$, but U is the *largest* subset of $R_E{}^n$ satisfying the condition:

If $u = (R^1, \ldots, R^n) \in U$, then *either* individual 1 strictly prefers d to the others and everyone else strictly prefers the others to d *or* 1 strictly prefers all the others to d while everyone else strictly prefers d to the others. Given u, $R(u)$ is determined as follows:

(1)   If 1 strictly prefers d to the others, then $R(u) = \{(d, d), (a, d), (b, d), (c, d)\} \cup R_1|_{\{a,b,c\}}$.

(2)   If 1 strictly prefers the others to d, then $R(u) = \{(d, d), (d, a), (d, b), (d, c)\} \cup R_1|_{\{a,b,c\}}$.

It is left as an exercise for the reader to show that this *is* a counterexample to Arrow's original version of Theorem 4-2.

In response to this discovery, Arrow constructed a theorem very similar to Theorem 4-2 that does work for $|E| \geq 3$. In his second theorem, he uses the full standard domain constraint (2) and then assumes the weak Pareto condition rather than starting from nonimposition and nonnegative responsiveness and working through Theorem 3-18.

Theorem 4-3 (*Arrow's second impossibility theorem*)   There is no collective choice rule f satisfying

    (i)   the standard domain constraint (2),
    (ii) each $C_u = f(u)$ has a complete, reflexive, and transitive rationalization $R(u)$,
    (iii) independence of irrelevant alternatives,
    (iv) the weak pairwise Pareto condition,
    (v) general nondictatorship.

Proof   As before, Lemma 4-1 allows us to talk about pairwise decisive sets. If W is the smallest decisive set, nondictatorship and Property α tell us $|W| \geq 2$. Partitioning $W = \{i\} \cup (W - \{i\})$, we examine a profile u with *restricted* orderings:

$$i:\quad xyz,$$
$$W - \{i\}:\quad zxy,$$
$$N - W:\quad yzx.$$

Just as before decisiveness of W gives $xP(u)y$; $zP(u)y$ gets ruled out to keep $W - \{i\}$ from being decisive for z against y; but $yR(u)z$ and transitivity give $xP(u)z$ and then independence and Property α ensure that i is a general dictator. $\square$

These results have been of sufficient importance to attract a variety of alternative proofs. A recent, "direct" proof is due to Blau [48]. Proofs with an algebraic flavor have been developed by Wilson [353] using his theory of "frames" and by Hansson [158] and Kirman and Sondermann [199] using the theory of filters. Because these algebraic approaches are particularly useful when we relax the condition that individuals' tastes are captured by the idea of a complete, reflexive, and transitive relation, we will defer discussion of these techniques to Chapter 8. Here we present an alternative proof by Fishburn [111] that the finiteness of n is violated if Arrow's remaining conditions are satisfied. The heart of Fishburn's analysis is the establishment of an induction step: if $n > k$, then $n > k + 1$. A precursor of the idea of establishing Arrow's theorem by Property α and by induction on n is found in a paper by Weldon [343].

Alternative Proof of Theorem 3   (Fishburn [111])   The set of individuals is $N = \{1, 2, \ldots, n\}$. If $n = 1$, the weak Pareto condition contradicts the nondictatorship requirement. Hence $n > 1$. Let xky be the proposition: Any subset of N consisting of all but k individuals is locally pairwise decisive for

x against y. We will first establish $x1y$ for all distinct x, y. Then we will prove an induction statement:

$$\forall x, y, x \neq y \rightarrow [(n > k \text{ \& } xky) \rightarrow (n > k + 1 \text{ \& } x(k + 1)y)].$$

Together with $(n > 1 \text{ \& } x1y)$, this suffices to show that n must exceed every finite integer, contrary to the standard domain constraint.

To prove $x1y$, consider arbitrary $i \in N$ and define $N' = N - \{i\}$. By nondictatorship, there are distinct alternatives a, b and a profile $u \in U$ with restricted orderings:

$$i: \quad ab,$$
$$N': \quad [ab],$$

such that $bR(u)a$. Let z be a third alternative. And consider u_1 with restrictions:

$$i: \quad azb,$$
$$N': \quad [ab]z.$$

Then by IIA, $bR(u_1)a$. Weak pairwise Pareto yields $aP(u_1)z$. By transitive rationality, $bP(u_1)z$. Hence by IIA, $bPD_{N'}z$. By Lemma 1, $xPD_{N'}y$ for all x, $y \in E$. Thus $x1y$.

For the induction step, suppose $n > k$ and xky for all distinct x, y. Let $\{a, b, c\}$ be three distinct alternatives and S a proper subset of N with $|S| = k$. Take $i \in N - S$ and examine the profile u with restricted orderings as follows (note the voting paradox formation):

$$i: \quad cba,$$
$$S: \quad acb,$$
$$N - (S \cup \{i\}): \quad bac.$$

By $a1c$, $aP(u)c$. By bka, $bP(u)a$. Hence $bP(u)c$ and by Lemma 4-1, $N - (S \cup \{i\})$ is a pairwise decisive set. This contradicts nondictatorship unless $|N - S| > 1$, i.e., $N > k + 1$. Moreover, since i, S, a, b, and c are arbitrary, pairwise decisiveness of the $n - (k + 1)$ element set, $N - (S \cup \{i\})$ yields $x(k + 1)y$ for all distinct x, y. $\square$

Fishburn has also established, using measure-theoretic tools, the result that if $|N|$ is infinite, the other Arrow conditions *are* consistent. Fishburn's example and a new impossibility theorem by Kirman and Sondermann for the infinite $|N|$ case will be taken up in Chapter 8 where we can use the filter theory tools developed there.

Immediately after Arrow presented his first theorem, there arose critiques of the conditions used. In response to those critiques there have developed several series of impossibility theorems, each seeking to remove the use of a condition not found compelling. We shall examine one of those series, dealing with the condition of transitive rationality, in the next few theorems.

Our first result stems from Sen's observation [307] that if the condition of transitive rationality is weakened to only quasitransitive rationality, choice rules do exist satisfying that and all of the remaining Arrow conditions. Sen's example is the function that selects the Pareto optimals from v:

$$C_u^P(v) = \{x/x \in v \text{ and there is no } y \in v \text{ such that}$$
$$yR_{iu}x \text{ for all } i \text{ and } yP_{iu}x \text{ for at least one } i\}.$$

This example draws our attention to the decisiveness conditions. Individual i is said to be a *weak pairwise dictator* for collective choice rule f if, for all x, y, whenever u has xP_iy, then $x \in C_u(\{x, y\})$. For C_u^P, *everyone* is a weak pairwise dictator. This is what causes C_u^P to be "nonselective"; $C_u^P(v) = v$ quite frequently. The close relationship between the regularity constraint of quasitransitive rationality and the presence of weak pairwise dictators is brought out in the next theorem, independently discovered by Gibbard [141], Schwartz, Guha, Mas-Colell and Sonnenschein, Schick, and Murakami and first published by Mas-Colell and Sonnenschein [211]. A *general oligarchy* for f is a set S of individuals such that

    (i) S is weakly globally generally decisive between any two alternatives, and

    (ii)   every member of S is a weak pairwise dictator.

If a collective choice rule has a dictator, say individual i, then $\{i\}$ is a general oligarchy. But a collective choice rule can have a nonempty general oligarchy without having a dictator. On the other side, a collective choice rule with a nonempty general oligarchy must have a weak dictator, but a rule can have a weak dictator without having a general oligarchy. A small but nonempty general oligarchy is undesirable as it concentrates the power of decisiveness between all pairs of alternatives in a small group of individuals. A large general oligarchy is undesirable because the multiplicity of weak pairwise dictators will make the choice functions nonselective.

Theorem 4-4   There does not exist a collective choice rule f satisfying

    (i)   the standard domain constraint (2),

    (ii)   each $C_u = f(u)$ has a complete, reflexive, and quasitransitive rationalization $R(u)$,

    (iii)   independence of irrelevant alternatives,

    (iv)   the weak pairwise Pareto condition,

    (v)   there is no nonempty general oligarchy for f.

Proof   By quasitransitive rationality, f satisfies base quasitransitivity. By Lemma 4-1, any set weakly, locally pairwise decisive for some alternative against another is weakly, globally, pairwise decisive between any two alternatives and by quasitransitive rationality, is weakly, globally, generally decisive between any two alternatives, i.e., is a decisive set.

We next prove that if A and B are decisive sets, so is $A \cap B$. Let x and y be any alternatives and u be a profile with

$$A \cap B: \quad xy,$$
$$N - (A \cap B): \quad yx.$$

Consider profile u_1 with alternative z inserted to give

$$A \cap B: \quad xzy,$$
$$A - B: \quad yxz,$$
$$N - A: \quad zyx.$$

By the decisiveness of A, $xP(u_1)z$; by the decisiveness of B, $zP(u_1)y$. By quasitransitivity, $xP(u_1)y$ and by IIA, $xP(u)y$. Hence $A \cap B$ is locally pairwise decisive for x against y and so, by Lemma 4-1, is decisive.

Now let W be the smallest decisive set (known to exist by the weak pairwise Pareto condition and quasitransitive rationality). To show that W is a general oligarchy, it remains to show that if individual $k \in W$, then k is a weak pairwise dictator. Suppose not. Suppose there is a u such that $xP_{ku}y$ but $C_u(\{x, y\}) = \{y\}$. We partition N according to preferences on $\{x, y\}$ in u:

$$B_1: \quad xy,$$
$$B_2: \quad (xy),$$
$$B_3: \quad yx,$$

with $k \in B_1$. Consider a profile u_1 with preferences on $\{x, y, z\}$ given by

$$B_1: \quad xzy,$$
$$B_2: \quad (xy)z,$$
$$B_3: \quad yxz.$$

By IIA, $C_{u_1}(\{x, y\}) = \{y\}$; by the weak pairwise Pareto condition, $C_{u_1}(\{x, z\}) = \{x\}$. Therefore, by base quasitransitivity, $C_{u_1}(\{y, z\}) = \{y\}$. By Theorem 3-17, $B_2 \cup B_3$ is weakly, globally decisive for y against z and so, by Lemma 1, is a pairwise decisive set. By an earlier part of this proof, $W \cap (B_2 \cup B_3)$ is a pairwise decisive set. But $W \cap (B_2 \cup B_3)$ is a *proper* subset of W since it does not contain k and this violates our choice of W as the smallest pairwise decisive set. $\square$

As we saw in the remark following Theorem 3-12, in the presence of the standard domain condition, quasitransitive rationality is equivalent to the conjunction of Properties α, ε, and γ_p. If we throw away Property γ_p we are left with independence of path (cf. Theorem 3-12); if we throw away Property

ε we are left with acyclic rationalization (Theorem 3-13). We will now develop impossibility results on each of these weaker conditions. First we deal with path independence. In the statement of Theorem 4-5, a *pairwise oligarchy* is a set S of individuals such that

(i) S is weakly, globally pairwise decisive between any two alternatives, and

(ii)   every member of S is a weak pairwise dictator.

Theorem 4-5 [45]   There does not exist a collective choice rule f satisfying

(i)   independence of path,
(ii)   the weak pairwise Pareto condition,
(iii) independence of irrelevant alternatives,
(iv)   the standard domain restriction (2),
(v)   there is no pairwise oligarchy.

Instead of providing a separate proof of Theorem 4-5, we observe that it is a corollary to Theorem 4-6, which uses only base quasitransitivity instead of the stronger path independence.

Theorem 4-6 [45]   There is no collective choice rule f satisfying

(i)   base quasitransitivity,
(ii)   the weak pairwise Pareto condition,
(iii) independence of irrelevant alternatives,
(iv)   the standard domain restriction,
(v)   there is no pairwise oligarchy.

Proof   As before, we can invoke Lemma 4-1, allowing us to conclude that a set is pairwise decisive if it is weakly, locally pairwise decisive for at least one alternative against another. Let W be a smallest pairwise decisive set. The weak pairwise Pareto condition ensures that such a W exists and is nonempty. Pick one individual $k \in W$ and so partition W as $\{k\} \cup W^*$. If $W^* = \varnothing$, k is a pairwise dictator and $\{k\}$ is a pairwise oligarchy; therefore assume $W^* \neq \varnothing$. We want to show that k is a weak pairwise dictator. So pick any pair of alternatives x and y and let u be any profile in which $xP_{ku}y$:

$$k: \quad xy,$$
$$W^* \cup (N - S): \quad [xy].$$

Picking any third alternative z, examine a profile u_0 in which the orderings restricted to $\{x, y, z\}$ are

$$k: \quad xzy,$$
$$W^*: \quad [xy]z,$$
$$N - W: \quad z[xy].$$

By the lemma, xPD_Wz. Therefore $C_{u_0}(\{z,x\}) = \{x\}$. If $x \notin C_{u_0}(\{x,y\})$, then $C_{u_0}(\{x,y\}) = \{y\}$ and then $C_{u_0}(\{y,z\}) = \{y\}$ by base quasitransitivity. But then, by independence of irrelevant alternatives, $yPD_{W*}z$, contrary to our choice of W. Therefore $x \in C_{u_0}(\{x,y\})$ and another application of independence of irrelevant alternatives gives $x \in C_u(\{x,y\})$, i.e., k is a weak pairwise dictator and W is a pairwise oligarchy. $\square$

Comparing this result with Arrow's second impossibility theorem (Theorem 4-3), we have weakened the regularity constraint from transitive rationality to base quasitransitivity at the cost of a strengthening from nondictatorship to absence of pairwise oligarchies. Alternatively, we could keep nondictatorship and (in a pairwise form) use a responsiveness property. A collective choice rule f is said to satisfy *positive pairwise responsiveness* if, whenever $u = (R_1, \ldots, R_n)$ and $u' = (R_1', \ldots, R_n')$ are related by

   (i)   for all i, $xP_iy \to xP_i'y$ and $xI_iy \to xR_i'y$,
   (ii)   there is a k such that either xI_ky and $xP_k'y$ or yP_kx and $xR_k'y$,

then

$$x \in C_u(\{x,y\}) \to \{x\} = C_{u'}(\{x,y\}).$$

Theorem 4-7   There is no collective choice rule f satisfying

   (i)   the standard domain restriction (2),
   (ii)   base quasitransitivity,
   (iii)   the weak pairwise Pareto condition,
   (iv)   independence of irrelevant alternatives,
   (v)   no pairwise dictator, i.e., $\{i\}$ is a pairwise decisive set for no $i \in N$,
   (vi)   positive pairwise responsiveness.

Proof   Lemma 4-1 is still applicable. If we let W be the smallest pairwise decisive set, then, by nondictatorship, W contains at least two individuals, say 1 and 2. As in the proof of Theorem 4-6, we see that both 1 and 2 are weak pairwise dictators. Let u be such that xP_1y and yP_2x. By weak pairwise dictatorship, $C_u(\{x,y\}) = \{x,y\}$. This has been determined without reference to the preferences of the third individual, with respect to whom we have a violation of positive pairwise responsiveness. $\square$

This condition of positive pairwise responsiveness also allows us to get an impossibility result on acyclic rationality. Theorem 4-8 is due to Mas-Colell and Sonnenschein [211]. Note that it requires *both* absence of weak dictators and positive pairwise responsiveness.

Theorem 4-8   There does not exist a collective choice rule f satisfying

   (i)   each $C = f(u)$ has a complete, reflexive, and acyclic rationalization,
   (ii)   independence of irrelevant alternatives,

   (iii)   the weak pairwise Pareto condition,
   (iv)   the standard domain restriction (2) (strengthened to require $n \geq 4$),
   (v)   positive pairwise responsiveness,
   (vi)   there is no weak pairwise dictator.

This theorem will be a corollary to Theorem 4-10 below. We now have impossibility theorems separately on independence of path and acyclic rationality. What those two regularity conditions have in common is Property α. Thus we are led to hope for an impossibility theorem directly on Property α.

Theorem 4-9   [45]   There is no collective choice rule f satisfying

   (i)   Property α,
   (ii)   independence of irrelevant alternatives,
   (iii)   the weak pairwise Pareto condition,
   (iv)   the standard domain restriction (2) (strengthened to require $n \geq 4$),
   (v)   positive pairwise responsiveness,
   (vi)   there is no weak pairwise dictator.

This theorem is also a corollary of Theorem 4-10, which replaces Property α by the requirement of *triple acyclicity of the base relation*:

$$[C_u(\{x, y\}) = \{x\} \ \& \ C_u(\{y, z\}) = \{y\}] \rightarrow x \in C_u(\{x, z\}).$$

Triple acyclicity is strictly weaker than both Property α and base quasi-transitivity.

Theorem 4-10   [45]   There is no collective choice rule f satisfying

   (i)   triple acyclicity of the base relation,
   (ii)   independence of irrelevant alternatives,
   (iii)   the weak pairwise Pareto condition,
   (iv)   the standard domain restriction (2) (strengthened to require $n \geq 4$),
   (v)   positive pairwise responsiveness,
   (vi)   there is no weak pairwise dictator.

We will develop the proof of this theorem out of a preliminary result:

Lemma 4-11   [45]   If a collective choice rule f satisfies

   (i)   triple acyclicity of the base relation,
   (ii)   the standard domain restriction (2),
   (iii)   the weak pairwise Pareto condition,
   (iv)   independence of irrelevant alternatives,
   (v)   positive pairwise responsiveness,

then there is an individual i and alternatives x and y in E such that if in u

$$xP_i y \ \& \ (\forall j)(j \in N - \{i\} \rightarrow yP_j x), \qquad \text{then} \quad x \in C_u(\{x, y\}).$$

Proof of the Lemma Suppose not; then for all x, $y \in E$, and all $i \in N$, if in u xP_iy, $(\forall j)(j \in N - \{i\} \to yP_jx)$, then $C_u(\{x, y\}) = \{y\}$. As before, let W be a smallest set pairwise decisive for one alternative against another, say x against y. Our assumption implies that W has at least two individuals, say 1 and 2. Partition W as $\{1, 2\} \cup W^*$. Consider a profile u_1 with restricted orderings

$$1: \quad xyz,$$
$$\{2\} \cup W^*: \quad zxy,$$
$$N - W: \quad yzx.$$

$C_{u_1}(\{x, y\}) = \{x\}$ by xPD_Wy. By our assumption, $C_{u_1}(\{x, z\}) = \{z\}$. By triple acyclicity, $z \in C_{u_1}(\{y, z\})$.

Now examine u_2 with restricted orderings

$$1: \quad xy,$$
$$2: \quad yx,$$
$$W^*: \quad xy,$$
$$N - W: \quad yx.$$

Since W is a smallest set decisive for one alternative against another, $y \in C_{u_2}(\{x, y\})$.

Next examine u_3 with restricted orderings

$$1: \quad (xyz),$$
$$2: \quad zyx,$$
$$W^*: \quad xzy,$$
$$N - W: \quad yxz.$$

Going from u_2 to u_3, positive responsiveness requires $C_{u_3}(\{x, y\}) = \{y\}$. Going from u_1 to u_3, positive responsiveness requires $C_{u_3}(\{y, z\}) = \{z\}$. Triple acyclicity then gives $z \in C_{u_3}(\{x, z\})$.

Next examine u_4 with restricted orderings

$$1: \quad zx,$$
$$2: \quad zx,$$
$$W^*: \quad xz,$$
$$N - W: \quad xz.$$

Going from u_3 to u_4, positive responsiveness requires $C_{u_4}(\{x, z\}) = \{z\}$. This says $xPD_{\{1,2\}}z$ and so $W = \{1, 2\}$.

Finally examine u_5 with restricted orderings

$$1: \quad xyz,$$
$$2: \quad zxy,$$
$$N - W: \quad yzx.$$

By xPD_Wy, $\{x\} = C_{u_5}(\{x, y\})$. Our assumption gives $C_{u_5}(\{y, z\}) = \{y\}$. By triple acyclicity, $x \in C_{u_5}(\{x, z\})$; but this contradicts our assumption. $\square$

Proof of Theorem 4-10   Let 1, x and y be an individual and a pair of alternatives with the properties described in the lemma. We will show 1 is a weak pairwise dictator. In the presence of positive pairwise responsiveness, this can be established by proving that for all $s, t \in E$,

$$sP_1t \quad \text{and} \quad (\forall j)(j \in N - \{i\} \to tP_js) \quad \text{imply} \quad s \in C_u(\{s, t\}). \quad (8)$$

We will prove only that for all $t \in E$

$$xP_1t \quad \text{and} \quad (\forall j)(j \in N - \{i\} \to tP_jx) \quad \text{imply} \quad x \in C_u(\{s, t\}). \quad (9)$$

The steps from (9) to (8) are sufficiently similar to the ones we use to establish (9) that they are left to the reader to complete.

To prove (9) we first examine u_1 with restricted orderings

$$
\begin{aligned}
1: &\quad xyt, \\
2: &\quad (xy)t, \\
3: &\quad ytx, \\
4: &\quad ytx, \\
N - \{1, 2, 3, 4\}: &\quad ytx.
\end{aligned}
$$

By the lemma and positive responsiveness, $C_{u_1}(\{x, y\}) = \{x\}$. By the weak pairwise Pareto condition, $C_{u_1}(\{y, t\}) = \{y\}$. By triple acyclicity, $x \in C_{u_1}(\{x, t\})$.

Now examine u_2 with restricted orderings

$$
\begin{aligned}
1: &\quad yxt, \\
2: &\quad yxt, \\
3: &\quad tyx, \\
4: &\quad y(xt), \\
N - \{1, 2, 3, 4\}: &\quad tyx.
\end{aligned}
$$

Going from u_1 to u_2, positive responsiveness requires $C_{u_2}(\{x, t\}) = \{x\}$. By the weak pairwise Pareto condition, $C_{u_2}(\{x, y\}) = \{y\}$. Triple acyclicity then gives $y \in C_{u_2}(\{y, t\})$.

Next we examine u_3 with restricted orderings

$$
\begin{aligned}
1: &\quad xyt, \\
2: &\quad ytx, \\
3: &\quad (xyt), \\
4: &\quad ytx, \\
N - \{1, 2, 3, 4\}: &\quad tyx.
\end{aligned}
$$

By the lemma and positive responsiveness, $C_{u_3}(\{x, y\}) = \{x\}$. Going from u_2 to u_3, positive responsiveness requires $C_{u_3}(\{y, t\}) = \{y\}$. Another application of triple acyclicity gives $x \in C_{u_3}(\{x, t\})$.

Next examine u_4 with restricted orderings

$$
\begin{aligned}
1: &\quad yxt, \\
2: &\quad tyx, \\
3: &\quad yxt, \\
4: &\quad tyx, \\
N - \{1, 2, 3, 4\}: &\quad tyx.
\end{aligned}
$$

Going from u_3 to u_4, positive responsiveness requires $C_{u_4}(\{x, t\}) = \{x\}$. The weak pairwise Pareto condition gives $C_{u_4}(\{x, y\}) = \{y\}$. Triple acyclicity yields $y \in C_{u_4}(\{y, t\})$.

Finally, consider u_5 with restricted orderings

$$
\begin{aligned}
1: &\quad xyt, \\
2: &\quad t(xy), \\
3: &\quad ytx, \\
4: &\quad (yt)x, \\
N - \{1, 2, 3, 4\}: &\quad tyx.
\end{aligned}
$$

Going from u_4 to u_5, positive responsiveness requires $C_{u_5}(\{y, t\}) = \{y\}$. By the lemma and positive responsiveness, $C_{u_5}(\{x, y\}) = \{x\}$. A final application of triple acyclicity yields $x \in C_{u_5}(\{x, t\})$. One application of independence of irrelevant alternatives then gives (9). $\square$

Referring back to the distinction we made in Chapter 3 between contraction-consistency conditions and expansion-consistency conditions, Sen [318] notes that all of the above impossibility theorems that rely on a regularity property rely on a contraction-consistency type (or on a condition such as transitive rationality that implies a contraction-consistency condition).

> There is a fundamental asymmetry in the ability of social decision procedures to cope with consistency conditions of two types. The "contraction-consistency properties" (e.g., α) cause problems even in the weakest form, while the "expansion-consistency properties" (e.g., β, γ, δ, ε) are easily accommodated even in their strongest form. [318, p. 81]

> So the basic question relating to this class of impossibility results is: Do we want any contraction-consistency property? If so, we are in trouble. If not, we can sail through easily, no matter how much expansion-consistency we want to incorporate in our social choices. [318, p. 74]

We will reconsider Sen's position in the next chapter.

The condition of transitive rationality has *not* been the only object of criticism in Arrow's second theorem. Independence of irrelevant alternatives· has probably been the principle target of critics. Of course we already have Sen's theorem on the impossibility of a Paretian liberal which uses neither IIA nor any regularity condition. Blau has proposed replacing IIA with the weaker and more defensible condition of *independence of single irrelevant alternatives*: If $E - B$ contains just a single alternative, then $u|_B = u'|_B$ implies $C_u(B) = C_{u'}(B)$.

Theorem 4-12   There is no collective choice rule f satisfying

   (i)   the standard domain constraint,
   (ii) $|E| < \infty$,
   (iii)   each $C_u = f(u)$ has a complete, reflexive, and transitive rationalization $R(u)$,
   (iv)   independence of single irrelevant alternatives,
   (v)   the weak pairwise Pareto condition,
   (vi)   general nondictatorship.

Proof   This is immediate from (Arrow's second impossibility) Theorem ˙ 4-3 and Theorem 3-15, which allow us to derive independence of irrelevant alternatives from k-ary independence and $|E| = k + 1$ as holds here by (ii) and (iv).   □

Of course this use of (iv) instead of IIA is just an *apparent* weakening: in the presence of (i)–(iii), Theorem 3-15 tells us that (iv) and IIA are logically equivalent. Clearly we can also develop this apparent weakening for Theorem 4-4 on quasi-transitive rationality or Theorem 4-8 on acyclic rationality. It is an open question whether or not we get an impossibility result if we substitute (ii) and (iv) for IIA in propositions such as Theorem 4-10 which use a regularity condition (Property α) weaker than rationality.

The one constraint that has been present in *all* our impossibility theorems so far is the weak pairwise Pareto condition. That we cannot simply point triumphantly at this condition and then ignore the impossibility theorem literature is brought out in the next result, due to Wilson [352]. In this theorem, a *pairwise dictator* is a single individual i such that i is globally pairwise decisive between all pairs of social states and an *inverse pairwise dictator* is an individual $i \in N$ such that if $xP_{iu}y$, then $C_u(\{x, y\}) = \{y\}$.

Theorem 4-13   There does not exist a collective choice rule f satisfying

   (i)   each $C_u = f(u)$ has a complete, reflexive, and transitive rationalization $R(u)$,
   (ii)   standard domain constraint (2),
   (iii)   independence of irrelevant alternatives,

(iv)   weak nonimposition: for all x, y there is a $u \in U$ such that $x \in C_u(\{x, y\})$,

(v)   no pairwise dictator,

(vi)   no inverse pairwise dictator,

(vii)   nonnull; it is not true that

$$C_u(v) = v \quad \text{for all} \quad u \in U \quad \text{and all} \quad v \in V.$$

Proof   By independence of irrelevant alternatives, $C_u(\{x, y\})$ is a function only of the ordered pair

$$(\{i/xR_{iu}y\}, \{i/yR_{iu}x\}).$$

By the standard domain constraint, we must examine this function for all elements of

$$A = \{(b, c)/b \subseteq N, c \subseteq N, b \cup c = N\}.$$

Now the Pareto condition (not assumed here) tells us that at $(N, \varnothing)$ we have $C_u(\{x, y\}) = \{x\}$. Without the Pareto condition, we still want to get the result that $x \in C_u(\{x, y\})$ when we are in situations similar to $(N, \varnothing)$. Our next job is to capture the right notion of similarity. For all *distinct* pairs of alternatives x, y, define

$$F(x, y) = \{(b, c) \,|\, (b, c) \in A \text{ and for all } u, \text{ if } \\ \{i \,|\, xR_{iu}y\} = b \text{ and } \{i/yR_{iu}x\} = c, \text{ then } \\ x \in C_u(\{x, y\}).$$

(iv) guarantees that $F(x, y)$ is not empty.

We next provide two lexicographic inclusion orderings on A:

$$(b, c)B_1(b', c') \quad \text{iff} \quad b \subsetneqq b' \quad \text{or} \quad b = b' \quad \text{and} \quad c \subsetneqq c',$$
$$(b, c)B_2(b', c') \quad \text{iff} \quad c \subsetneqq c' \quad \text{or} \quad c = c' \quad \text{and} \quad b \subsetneqq b'.$$

B_1 and B_2 are transitive but *not* complete. Since A is finite we are assured that there exist B_1-maximal and B_2-maximal elements of nonempty subsets of A.

We will be interested in local maximal sets

$$B_1{}^0(x, y) = \{(b, c) \,|\, (b, c) \in F(x, y) \text{ and there is no } (b', c') \\ \text{in } F(x, y) \text{ such that } (b', c')B_1(b, c)\},$$
$$B_2{}^0(x, y) = \{(b, c) \,|\, (b, c) \in F(x, y) \text{ and there is no } (b', c') \\ \text{in } F(x, y) \text{ such that } (b', c')B_2(b, c)\};$$

and in global maximal sets

$$B_1{}^0 = \{(b, c) \,|\, (b, c) \in \bigcup F(x, y) \text{ and there is no } (b', c') \\ \text{in } \bigcup F(x, y) \text{ such that } (b', c')B_1(b, c)\},$$

$$B_2{}^0 = \{(b,c)\,|\,(b,c) \in \bigcup F(x,y) \text{ and there is no } (b',c')$$
$$\text{in } \bigcup F(x,y) \text{ such that } (b',c')B_2(b,c)\}.$$

The elements of $B_1{}^0$ and $B_2{}^0$ are the pairs that are generally to behave "similar to" the way $(\varnothing, N)$ and $(N, \varnothing)$ behave for choice functions satisfying the Pareto condition.

With all this preparation, we can embark on the first and most important part of the proof, establishing that each global maximum is everywhere a local maximum, i.e., that

$$(b,c) \in B_1{}^0 \to (b,c) \in B_1{}^0(x,y) \qquad \text{for all distinct } x, y,$$
$$(b,c) \in B_2{}^0 \to (b,c) \in B_2{}^0(x,y) \qquad \text{for all distinct } x, y. \tag{10}$$

We will explicitly prove the result for $B_1{}^0$, the $B_2{}^0$ case can be dealt with similarly. Since $(b,c) \in B_1{}^0$, then $(b,c) \in B_1{}^0(x,y)$ for at least one pair (x,y). We will show that this implies $(b,c) \in B_1{}^0(x,z)$ for $z \notin \{x,y\}$. Let (b',c') be a member of $B_1{}^0(y,z)$. Consider a u satisfying the following:

	$i \in b - c$	$i \in b \cap c$	$i \in c - b$
$i \in b' - c'$:	xyz	$(xy)z$	yzx
$i \in b' \cap c'$:	$x(yz)$	(xyz)	$(zy)x$
$i \in c' - b'$:	zxy	$z(xy)$	zyx

Since $(b,c) \in F(x,y)$, $x \in C_u(\{x,y\})$; $(b',c') \in F(y,z)$ implies $y \in C_u(\{y,z\})$. Transitive rationality implies $x \in C_u(\{x,z\})$. Thus $F(x,z)$ contains

$$(b \cap b', (c \cap c') \cup [(c - b) \cap (b' - c')] \cup [(b - c) \cap (c' - b')]).$$

Since $(b,c) \in B_1{}^0$, we cannot have $b \cap b' \subsetneqq b$. Thus $b \subseteq b'$ and $b \cap b' = b$. Also $b \subseteq b'$ implies $[(b - c) \cap (c' - b')] = \varnothing$, so $F(x,z)$ contains

$$(b, (c \cap c') \cup [(c - b) \cap (b' - c')]).$$

Since $(b,c) \in B_1{}^0$, we cannot have $(c \cap c') \cup [(c - b) \cap (b' - c')] \subsetneqq c$. Hence $c \subseteq c'$ and

$$(c \cap c') \cup [(c - b) \cap (b' - c')] = c.$$

Thus $(b,c) \in F(x,z)$ and by its global maximality, $(b,c) \in B_1{}^0(x,z)$. An analogous argument allows us to derive $(b,c) \in B_1{}^0(w,y)$ for $w \notin \{x,y\}$. Linking these two proves $(b,c) \in B_1{}^0(w,z)$ for all distinct w, z as was to be shown.

Now suppose $(b,c) \in B_1{}^0$. Then by the above, $(b,c) \in B_1{}^0(w,x)$. The previous paragraph then shows that if $(b',c') \in F(x,y)$, then $b \subseteq b'$. Similarly, if $(b,c) \in B_2{}^0$, then $c \subseteq c'$ whenever $(b',c') \in F(x,y)$.

These last remarks enable us to get the first detailed information about members of $B_1{}^0$ and $B_2{}^0$:

$$(b,c) \in B_1{}^0 \to c = N - b, \qquad (b,c) \in B_2{}^0 \to b = N - c. \tag{11}$$

Again we will settle the B_1^0 case; the B_2^0 case follows analogously. $N - b \subseteq c$; if $N - b \neq c$, then we have

$$(b, N - b)B_1(b, c). \tag{12}$$

Since $(b, c) \in B_1^0$, then for every distinct pair x, y, $(b, c) \in B_1^0(x, y)$, and (12) then tells us $(b, N - b) \notin F(x, y)$. Completeness of the social relation then tells us $(N - b, b) \in F(y, x)$ and this holds for all (y, x). Since $(b, c) \in B_1^0$, $(b, c) \in B_1^0(y, x)$ and by the previous paragraph $b \subseteq N - b$, i.e., $b = \varnothing$ and, since $b \cup c = N, c = N = N - b$, contrary to our assumption that $n - b \neq c$. Thus our assumption is wrong and $c = N - b$.

This disjointness of the two components of any member of B_1^0 or B_2^0 can be combined with a voting paradox profile to get very deep information about those two sets:

$$(b, N - b) \in B_1^0 \rightarrow |b| \leq 1, \qquad (N - c, c) \in B_2^0 \rightarrow |c| \leq 1. \tag{13}$$

For suppose $|b| \geq 2$; let $b = b' \cup b''$ where b' and b'' are disjoint and nonempty and look at a profile u with orderings given by

$$b': \quad xyz,$$
$$b'': \quad zxy,$$
$$N - b: \quad yzx.$$

Since $(b, N - b) \in B_1^0$, $(b, N - b) \in B_1^0(x, y)$ and hence $xP(u)y$. If $yR(u)x$, then $(N - b, b) \in F(x, y)$ and so $b \subseteq N - b$, contrary to $|b| \leq 2$. Thus $xP(u)y$. If $xR(u)z$, $(b', N - b')$ would be in $F(x, z)$ and then $b \subseteq b'$, contrary to $b'' \neq \varnothing$. Similarly, $zR(u)y$ is ruled out. Thus $xP(u)y$, $zP(u)x$ and $yP(u)z$ contradicting transitivity. Thus $|b| \geq 2$ is false and the first part of (13) is proven. The second part is handled analogously.

B_1^0 must contain just a *single* element (Exercise: Prove this) either $(\varnothing, N)$ or $(\{j\}, N - \{j\})$ for some j. In the second case, suppose $xR(u)y$, then $(\{i/xR_{ui}y\}, (i/yR_{ui}x\}) \in F(x, y)$ so $b \subseteq \{i/xR_{ui}y\}$, i.e., $xR_{uj}y$. Equivalently, if $yP_{uj}x$, then $yP(u)x$, i.e., j is a dictator. Similarly, B_2^0 contains just a single element either $(N, \varnothing)$ or $(N - \{k\}, \{k\})$ for some k. In the second case, k is an inverse dictator. We are left with the case

$$B_1^0 = \{(\varnothing, N)\} \qquad \text{and} \qquad B_2^0 = \{(N, \varnothing)\}.$$

Let u be *any* profile, and let z be any alternative distinct from x and y. Examine u', derived from u by taking z to the bottom of everyone's ordering. Since $(\varnothing, N) \in B_1^0$, $(\varnothing, N) \in B_1^0(z, x) \subseteq F(z, x)$. Thus $zR(u)x$. Also $(N, \varnothing) \in B_2^0$ implies $(N, \varnothing) \in B_2^0(x, z) \subseteq F(x, z)$, so $xR(u)z$. Thus $xI(u)z$ and similarly $yI(u)z$. Transitivity then yields $xI(u)y$. For *any* profile, *all* pairs of alternatives are socially indifferent, i.e., $C_u(v) = v$ everywhere contrary to (vii). $\square$

Exercises

1. Show that Blau's collective choice rule satisfies all the conditions of Arrow's original version of Theorem 4-2.
2. Present a collective choice rule that satisfies all the conditions of Theorem 4-3 except independence of irrelevant alternatives.
3. Show that in Theorem 4-3 we could have relaxed the no-dictator condition (which ruled out an i where $\{i\}$ is globally decisive) to a condition ruling out any i where $\{i\}$ is locally decisive.
4. Show that in Theorem 4-4 the regularity condition can be changed to: each C_u can be rationalized by a semiorder. (A semiorder P is an asymmetric complete binary relation satisfying for all w, x, y, z:
   (a) wPx and $yPz \rightarrow wPz$ or yPx,
   (b) wPx and $xPy \rightarrow wPz$ or zPy.)
5. As called for in the proof of Theorem 4-13, show that $B_1{}^0$ must contain just a single element.

5 CONDITIONAL DECISIVENESS

This chapter introduces two new important conditions, neutrality and anonymity. They are both permutation conditions, neutrality involving permutations on alternatives while anonymity involves permutations on individuals.

Let θ be a permutation on E. Then if R is a binary relation on E, we define R^θ by

$$(x, y) \in R \Leftrightarrow (\theta(x), \theta(y)) \in R^\theta.$$

Then, if $u = (R_1, R_2, \ldots, R_n) \in \mathscr{R}_E^{\,n}$, we let

$$\theta(u) = (R_1^{\,\theta}, R_2^{\,\theta}, \ldots, R_n^{\,\theta}).$$

A collective choice rule f given by $f : u \mapsto C_u$ satisfies *neutrality* if, for every permutation θ on E,

$$C_{\theta(u)}(\theta(v)) = \theta(C_u(v)).$$

Neutrality is called a "conditional decisiveness" constraint because of the following:

Lemma 5-1 If a collective choice rule $f : u \mapsto C_u$ satisfies

    (i)   neutrality,
   (ii) independence of irrelevant alternatives,
  (iii) the standard domain constraint,

then, if S is (semi-) decisive for x against y, S is (semi-) decisive between any pair of distinct alternatives. [Here, "(semi-) decisive" can be interpreted as local or global, strong or weak, general or pairwise.]

Proof Exercise. □

This conditional decisiveness aspect shows how neutrality is antithetical to the combination of nondictatorship and liberalism conditions of Chapter 2. Suppose f satisfies neutrality and $\{i\}$ is globally decisive for x against y; then i is a dictator. Theorem 2 shows a conflict between a weakened liberalism requirement and a strengthened no-weak-dictator constraint. (Note that no Pareto condition is employed.)

Theorem 5-2   There is no collective choice rule f satisfying

   (i)   the standard domain constraint (2),
   (ii)   independence of irrelevant alternatives,
   (iii)   triple acyclicity of the base relation,
   (iv)   no individual is locally pairwise semidecisive between all pairs,
   (v)   neutrality,
   (vi)   there exists a set S of two individuals and a pair of alternatives x, y such that $xPD_S y$.

Proof   Consider a profile u with restricted orderings given by

$$1:\quad xyz,$$
$$2:\quad zxy,$$
$$N - \{1,2\}:\quad yzx,$$

where $S = \{1,2\}$ is the set specified in condition (vi). If $x \in C_u(\{x,z\})$, then, by IIA, $\{1\}$ is locally pairwise semidecisive for x against z and so, by Lemma 5-1, between any pair of alternatives. This contradicts (iv), so $C_u(\{x,z\}) = \{z\}$. Similarly, since $\{2\}$ is not to be locally pairwise semidecisive between all pairs, $C_u(\{y,z\}) = \{y\}$. Triple acyclity then implies $y \in C_u(\{x,y\})$, violating $xPD_{\{1,2\}}y$. □

As Lemma 5-1 suggests, neutrality plays its most important role when IIA is also assumed. These two conditions have been combined by Ferejohn and Grether [101]. A collective choice rule $f : u \mapsto C_u$ satisfies *neutrality-and-independence* if whenever $u = (R_1, \ldots, R_n)$ and $u' = (R_1', \ldots, R_n')$ are related by

$$(\forall i \in N)[(xR_i y \Leftrightarrow zR_i'w) \;\&\; (yR_i x \Leftrightarrow wR_i z)],$$

then

$$x \in C_u(\{x,y\}) \Leftrightarrow z \in C_{u'}(\{w,z\}) \qquad \text{and} \qquad y \in C_u(\{x,y\}) \Leftrightarrow w \in C_{u'}(\{w,z\}).$$

Lemma 5-3 If f satisfies (i) neutrality and (ii) independence of irrelevant alternatives, then f satisfies neutrality-and-independence. If f satisfies (i) neutrality-and-independence and (ii) rationality, then f satisfies both independence of irrelevant alternatives and neutrality.

    Proof Exercise. □

    In fact, as we shall soon see, neutrality is often also combined with a nonnegative responsiveness condition as well. Thus we follow Blau and Deb [51] in defining a collective choice rule $f : u \mapsto C_u$ to satisfy *NIM* (weak neutrality, independence, and monotonicity) if whenever $u = (R_1, R_2, \ldots, R_n)$ and $u' = (R_1', R_2', \ldots, R_n')$ are related by

$$(\forall i \in N)[(xP_i y \to zP_i'w) \mathbin{\&} (wP_i'z \to yP_i x)],$$

then

$$C_u(\{x, y\}) = \{x\} \to C_{u'}(\{w, z\}) = \{z\}.$$

Lemma 5-4 If f satisfies (i) neutrality, (ii) independence of irrelevant alternatives, and (iii) nonnegative pairwise responsiveness, then f satisfies NIM. If f satisfies NIM and rationality, then f satisfies each of (i) neutrality, (ii) independence of irrelevant alternatives, and (iii) nonnegative pairwise responsiveness.

    Proof Exercise. □

We now set about developing some impossibility results.

Theorem 5-5 (Blau and Deb [51], Sen [318]). There does not exist a collective choice rule satisfying

    (i)   the standard domain constraint,
    (ii) $|E| \geq n$,
    (iii) NIM,
    (iv) Property α,
    (v) no weak pairwise dictator.

    Proof Let i be an arbitrary individual. Since i is not a weak pairwise dictator, there is a pair x, y of alternatives and a profile u, such that $xP_{iu}y$ but $C_u(\{x, y\}) = \{y\}$. Now let u' be a profile that looks like u except that x is taken to the bottom of R_j for all $j \neq i$. By NIM, we must have $C_{u'}(\{x, y\}) = \{y\}$. A further application of NIM shows that if u'' is *any* profile for which $xP_{iu''}y$ and $yP_{ju''}x$ for all $j \neq i$, $C_{u''}(\{x, y\}) = \{y\}$. Again by NIM, this must be true for all pairs x, y and by the arbitrary nature of i, for all i. We have $N - \{i\}$ weakly, locally pairwise decisive between every pair of alternatives for all i and so by Property α, weakly locally *generally* decisive between every pair of alternatives. But by Theorem 2-2, such an f must fail somewhere [see the discussion of "(3) *All but one*" following the proof of Theorem 2-2]. $\square$

We now introduce the second of our permutation conditions. Let σ be a permutation on $N = \{1, 2, \ldots, n\}$ and for $u = (R_1, R_2, \ldots, R_n)$, define

$$\sigma(u) = (R_{\sigma(1)}, R_{\sigma(2)}, \ldots, R_{\sigma(n)}).$$

Then a collective choice rule $f : u \mapsto C_u$ satisfies *anonymity* if for all $u \in U$ and all $v \in V$, $C_u(v) = C_{\sigma(u)}(v)$. Anonymity is called a "conditional decisiveness" constraint because of the following lemma.

Lemma 5-6 If a collective choice rule $f : u \mapsto C_u$ satisfies

  (i) anonymity,
  (ii) the standard domain constraint,

then if a set S is pairwise (semi-) decisive for x against y, so is any set T with $|T| = |S|$. [Here, "(semi-) decisive" can be interpreted as local or global, strong, or weak.]

  Proof Exercise. $\square$

The conditions of neutrality and anonymity are combined in the following result, due to Hansson [155].

Theorem 5-7 There is no collective choice rule f satisfying

  (i) the standard domain constraint (2),
  (ii) each $C_u = f(u)$ has a complete, reflexive, and transitive rationalization $R(u)$,
  (iii) neutrality-and-independence,
  (iv) anonymity,
  (v) nonnull.

  Proof First we note that by Lemma 5-3, f satisfies independence of irrelevant alternatives and neutrality. We now show that Theorem 5-7 follows easily from:

Lemma 5-8 If a collective choice rule satisfies (i)–(iv) in the statement of Theorem 5-7, then for all $x, y \in E$ and all $u = (R_1, \ldots, R_n) \in U$,

$$(\forall i)(x P_{iu} y) \rightarrow x I(u) y.$$

Assuming the truth of Lemma 5-8, let u be any profile and x, y be any two alternatives. Construct a new profile u' by taking a third alternative z to the bottom of everyone's preference ordering. By the lemma, $x I(u') z$ and $y I(u') z$. By transitive rationality, $x I(u') y$, so that an application of IIA yields $x I(u) y$. Rationality then implies $C_u(v) = v$ for all u, v, contrary to (v). $\square$

All that remains is a proof of the lemma. We split our proof into two cases by the parity of n.

CASE 1: *n is even*; $n = 2m$. Consider a profile u', with

$$
\left.\begin{matrix}1\\ \vdots\\ m\end{matrix}\right\} rs,
$$

$$
\left.\begin{matrix}m+1\\ \vdots\\ n\end{matrix}\right\} sr.
$$

If $rP(u')s$, then, by neutrality and anonymity, $sP(u')r$ and both cannot hold by our rationality assumption. Similarly we rule out $sP(u')r$. Hence $rI(u')s$. Two alternatives are socially indifferent if half prefer the first to the second and half prefer the second to the first. Now consider any society u in which everyone strictly prefers x to y. We will get results about u by examining u^*, derived from u by taking a third alternative z to the bottom of half of the orderings and to the top of the other half:

$$
\left.\begin{matrix}1\\ \vdots\\ m\end{matrix}\right\} xyz,
$$

$$
\left.\begin{matrix}m+1\\ \vdots\\ n\end{matrix}\right\} zxy.
$$

As we have just shown, $zI(u^*)x$ and $zI(u^*)y$. By transitive rationality, $xI(u^*)y$ and thus $xI(u)y$ by independence of irrelevant alternatives.

CASE 2: *n is odd*; $n = 2m + 1$. Consider a profile u', with

$$
\left.\begin{matrix}1\\ \vdots\\ m+1\end{matrix}\right\} rs,
$$

$$
\left.\begin{matrix}m+2\\ \vdots\\ n\end{matrix}\right\} sr.
$$

Suppose $rP(u')s$. Then, by anonymity and neutrality, any set of $m + 1$ individuals is weakly, locally decisive between any pair of alternatives. But that would lead to trouble on u'', given by

$$
\begin{aligned}
&1:\quad xyz,\\
&2:\quad zxy,\\
&\left.\begin{array}{l}3\\ \vdots\\ m+1\end{array}\right\}\ xyz,\\
&m+2:\quad yzx,\\
&\left.\begin{array}{l}m+3\\ \vdots\\ n\end{array}\right\}\ zyx.
\end{aligned}
$$

Here, $m + 1$ individuals $(1, 3, 4, \ldots, m + 2)$ prefer y to z and all others prefer z to y, giving $yP(u'')z$. Also $m + 1$ individuals $(2, m + 2, m + 3, \ldots, n)$ prefer z to x with all others preferring x to z, giving $zP(u'')x$. But $m + 1$ individuals $(1, \ldots, m + 1)$ prefer x to y with all others preferring y to x. The result $xP(u'')y$ shows a violation of transitivity. Thus we must rule out $rP(u')s$. Similar analysis shows we must rule out $sP(u')r$. Hence $rI(u')s$. By anonymity and neutrality, if any set of $m + 1$ individuals prefer one alternative to another with everyone else opposed, we have social indifference between the alternatives.

Now consider any profile u in which everyone strictly prefers x to y. We will get results about u by examining u^*, derived from u by taking a third alternative z to the top of $m + 1$ orderings and to the bottom of the remainder:

$$
\begin{aligned}
&\left.\begin{array}{l}1\\ \vdots\\ m+1\end{array}\right\}\ zxy,\\
&\left.\begin{array}{l}m+2\\ \vdots\\ n\end{array}\right\}\ xyz.
\end{aligned}
$$

As we have just shown, $zI(u^*)x$ and $zI(u^*)y$. By transitive rationality, $xI(u^*)y$ and thus $xI(u)y$ by independence of irrelevant alternatives. $\square$

Theorem 5-7 has been interpreted by Hansson as a critique of the condition of independence of irrelevant alternatives [155]. Fishburn, on the other hand, sees this as a critique of the condition of transitive rationality [109].

In the previous chapter we saw that we could dramatically weaken the regularity condition if we introduced positive responsiveness. Here, the introduction of positive responsiveness allows us, in addition, to drop the nonnull requirement. Since rationality is not being assumed, Lemma 5-3 cannot be invoked and so IIA and neutrality are separately assumed. The resulting theorem is due, essentially, to May [216] who was establishing necessary and sufficient conditions that f correspond to simple majority voting.

Theorem 5-9   There is no collective choice rule satisfying

(i)   the standard domain constraint (2),
(ii)   neutrality,
(iii)   anonymity,
(iv)   independence of irrelevant alternatives,
(v)   positive pairwise responsiveness,
(vi)   triple acyclicity of the base relation.

Proof   Given a profile u and distinct alternatives x, y, we note that $|\{i\,|\,xP_{iu}y\}|, |\{i\,|\,yP_{iu}x\}|$, and $|\{i\,|\,xI_{iu}y\}|$ are, respectively, the number of orderings in u with $xP_{iu}y$, the number in u with $yP_{iu}x$ and the number in u with $xI_{iu}y$. By independence of irrelevant alternatives, anonymity, and neutrality, $C_u(\{x, y\})$ depends only on the magnitudes of $|\{i\,|\,xP_{iu}y\}|, |\{i\,|\,yP_{iu}x\}|$, and $|\{i\,|\,xI_{iu}y\}|$ (or since these numbers sum to n, $C_u(\{x, y\})$ depends only on the first two).

If $|\{i\,|\,xP_{iu}y\}| = |\{i\,|\,yP_{iu}x\}|$, then $C_u(\{x, y\}) = \{x, y\}$. For, if $C_u(\{x, y\}) = \{x\}$, say, anonymity and neutrality would imply $C_u(\{x, y\}) = \{y\}$ contrary to our assumption that x and y are distinct.

If $|\{i\,|\,xP_{iu}y\}| = |\{i\,|\,yP_{iu}x\}| + 1$, then, by the previous result and positive responsiveness, $C_u(\{x, y\}) = \{x\}$. Similarly, by induction, if $|\{i\,|\,xP_{iu}y\}| = |\{i\,|\,yP_{iu}x\}| + m$ for $m \geq 1$, we have $C_u(\{x, y\}) = \{x\}$.

Thus we have:

if $|\{i\,|\,xP_{iu}y\}| > |\{i\,|\,yP_{iu}x\}|$,   then $C_u(\{x, y\}) = \{x\}$;

if $|\{i\,|\,yP_{iu}x\}| > |\{i\,|\,xP_{iu}y\}|$,   then $C_u(\{x, y\}) = \{y\}$;

if $|\{i\,|\,xP_{iu}y\}| = |\{i\,|\,yP_{iu}x\}|$,   then $C_u(\{x, y\}) = \{x, y\}$.

Now consider a profile u satisfying

$$1: \quad xyz,$$
$$2: \quad yzx,$$
$$3: \quad zxy,$$
$$\left.\begin{matrix} 4 \\ \vdots \\ n \end{matrix}\right\} (xyz).$$

By the above, $C_u(\{x, y\}) = \{x\}, C_u(\{y, z\}) = \{y\}$, but $C_u(\{x, z\}) = \{z\}$, violating triple acyclicity.   □

A result of Ferejohn and Grether [100] can be reinterpreted as showing that we can also relax the regularity condition of Hansson's theorem to acyclic rationality and maintain a kind of nonnegative responsiveness if we pay for this by requiring many alternatives and both no-weak-dictator and the *strong* Pareto condition. Of course, both conditions imply a nonnull restraint and so the latter can be dropped from our list. When IIA, neutrality, and anonymity are all assumed, $C_u(\{x, y\})$ depends only on $|\{i\,|\,xP_{iu}y\}|$, $|\{i\,|\,yP_{iu}x\}|$, and $|\{i\,|\,xI_{iu}y\}|$. These values are then used in the definition of ratio responsiveness. A collective choice rule $f : u \mapsto C_u$ satisfies *ratio responsiveness* if for all $x, y \in E$, whenever u and u' are related by

$$\frac{|\{i\,|\,xP_{iu'}y\}|}{|\{i\,|\,xP_{iu'}y\}| + |\{i\,|\,yP_{iu'}x\}|} \geqq \frac{|\{i\,|\,xP_{iu}y\}|}{|\{i\,|\,xP_{iu}y\}| + |\{yP_{iu}x\}|}.$$

then

$$C_u(\{x, y\}) = \{x\} \to C_{u'}(\{x, y\}) = \{x\},$$
$$C_u(\{x, y\}) = \{x, y\} \to x \in C_{u'}(\{x, y\}).$$

Lemma 5-10 If $f : u \mapsto C(u)$ is a collective choice rule satisfying

   (i)   the standard domain constraint (2),
   (ii)   acyclic rationality,
  (iii) neutrality-and-independence,
   (iv) anonymity,
   (v)   the strong Pareto condition,
   (vi) ratio responsiveness,

then there is an α, $0 \leq \alpha < 1$, such that

$$C_u(\{x, y\}) = \{x\} \quad \text{iff} \quad |\{i\,|\,xP_{iu}y\}| > \alpha[|\{i\,|\,xP_{iu}y\}| + |\{i\,|\,yP_{iu}x\}|].$$

Proof See Ferejohn and Grether [100], Theorem 10 for a proof.   □

Theorem 5-11 There is no collective choice rule f satisfying

    (i)   the standard domain constraint,
   (ii) $|E| \geq n$,
   (iii) acyclic rationality,
   (iv) neutrality-and-independence,
   (v)   anonymity,
   (vi) the strong Pareto condition,
  (vii) ratio responsiveness,
 (viii) no weak pairwise dictator.

Proof By Lemma 5-10, there is an α satisfying for all $x, y \in E$,

$$0 \leq \alpha < 1$$

and

$$C_u(\{x, y\}) = \{x\} \qquad \text{iff} \quad |\{i \,|\, xP_{iu}y\}| > \alpha[|\{i \,|\, xP_{iu}y\}| + |\{i \,|\, yP_{iu}x\}|].$$

Let A be the set of all α satisfying these conditions. Then $\alpha^* = \inf A$ satisfies $0 \le \alpha^* < 1$.

CASE 1: $\alpha^* < (n - 1)/n$. Then any set of all individuals but one is locally pairwise weakly decisive between all pairs of alternatives. By rationality, we can change "pairwise" to "generally." But then Theorem 2-2, together with $|E| \ge n$, ensures an inconsistency.

CASE 2: $\alpha^* \ge (n - 1)/n$. Then

$$xP(u)y \qquad \text{iff} \quad (\forall i)(xP_{iu}y).$$

But for such an f, each individual is a weak dictator. $\square$

Before we close this chapter it will be useful to reconsider Sen's claims about the role of "expansion-consistency" and "contraction-consistency" regularity conditions.

In the proof of Theorem 5-9 we showed that if f satisfies the standard domain constraint (2), neutrality, anonymity, independence of irrelevant alternatives, and positive responsiveness, then the base relation is determined by simple majority vote:

$$xR(u)y \qquad \text{iff} \quad x \in C_u(\{x, y\}) \qquad \text{iff} \quad |\{i \,|\, xP_{iu}y\}| \ge |\{i \,|\, yP_{iu}x\}|.$$

Bordes [60] has shown that if f also satisfies the expansion-consistency condition, Property $\beta(+)$:

$$x \in C(S) \;\&\; y \in S \subseteq T \to [\, y \in C(T) \to x \in C(T)\,],$$

then on any larger agenda v, $C_u(v)$ is the set of $R(u, v)$-best elements of v, where $R(u, v)$ is the transitive closure of $R(u)|_v$, the restriction to v of the base relation. Such an f clearly satisfies the *pairwise* weak Pareto condition.

This f is the source of Sen's acceptance of expansion-consistency conditions: it satisfies the standard domain constraint, neutrality, IIA, positive responsiveness, and the pairwise weak Pareto condition, and generates choice functions satisfying Property $\beta(+)$.

However, consider the case where $n = 3$ and u is given, in part, by

1: $xyzw$,

2: $yzwx$,

3: $zwxy$.

Then for $v = \{x, y, z, w\}$, $R(u, v)$ is the relation of universal indifference on v so $C_u(v) = v$. Thus $w \in C_u(v)$ even though $z \in v$ and $zP_{iu}w$ for *all* i. The general, not pairwise, version of the weak Pareto condition is violated. This argument yields:

Theorem 5-12   There is no collective choice rule f satisfying

   (i)   the standard domain constraint,
  (ii)   neutrality,
 (iii)   anonymity,
  (iv)   independence of irrelevant alternatives,
   (v)   positive pairwise responsiveness,
  (vi)   each $C_u = f(u)$ satisfies Property $\beta(+)$,
 (vii)   the general weak Pareto condition.

Since the general weak Pareto condition seems as desirable as the pairwise version, the use of expansion-consistency conditions alone does not ensure avoidance of disturbing impossibility results. Sen, of course, has recognized this:

"But an exclusive reliance on $\beta(+)$ is problematic when there are cyclical choices involving the Pareto relation ... a choice function satisfying $\beta(+)$, but no contraction consistency, can exist only by putting Pareto-inferior states in the choice set for the alternatives over which the cycle holds" [318, p. 75].

The conditional decisiveness constraints of neutrality and anonymity will appear once more, in Chapter 8. However, a condition very similar to neutrality will play a crucial role in theorems by Park and by Kemp and Ng in Chapter 7.

Exercises

1. Prove Lemma 5-3.
2. Prove Lemma 5-4.
3. Prove Lemma 5-6.
4. Prove that if a collective choice rule $f: u \mapsto C_u$ satisfies (i)–(vi), then f satisfies neutrality:
    (i)   the standard domain constraint,
    (ii)   independence of irrelevant alternatives,
    (iii) each C_u can be rationalized by a reflexive, complete, and quasi-transitive binary relation $R(u)$,
    (iv)   the strong Pareto condition: N is strongly, globally decisive on all pairs of alternatives,
    (v)   If $xI_{iu}y$ for all $i \in N$, then $xI(u)y$,

(vi)   monotonicity: suppose $u = (R_1, \ldots, R_{i-1}, R_i, R_{i+1}, \ldots, R_n)$ and
$u' = (R_1, \ldots, R_{i-1}, R_i', R_{i+1}, \ldots, R_n)$; then for all x, y in E,
   (a)   if xI_iy, $xP(u)y$, and $xP_i'y$, then $xP(u')y$,
   (b)   if xI_iy, $xR(u)y$, and $xP_i'y$, then $xR(u')y$,
   (c)   if yP_ix, $xP(u)y$, and $xR_i'y$, then $xP(u')y$,
   (d)   if yP_ix, $xR(u)y$, and $xR_i'y$, then $xR(u')y$.
(Cf. Guha [150] and Blau [50].)

5.   Prove the following conditional decisiveness impossibility result (Allingham [2]): There is no collective choice rule $f : u \mapsto C_u$ satisfying
   (i)   the standard domain constraint,
   (ii)   the strong Pareto condition,
   (iii)   each C_u has a reflexive, complete, and transitive rationalization $R(u)$,
   (iv)   if $xI_{iu}y$ for all $i \in N$, then $xI(u)y$,
   (v)   independence of irrelevant alternatives,
   (vi)   impersonality: if there is some $i \in N$ such that $\{i\}$ is a weak dictator, then everyone is a weak dictator.

6 STRATEGY-PROOFNESS

Early in the discussion of the importance of Arrow's theorem, Weldon remarked: "The social welfare function and the institutional mechanism are rarely completely analogous, for the latter depends on expressed and not on actual preferences [343, p. 453]." Arrow raised the issue of divergence between actual and expressed preferences only to dismiss it from consideration [8, p. 7]. But concern over this issue goes back far in the history of social choice theory. C. L. Dodgson (Lewis Carroll) is quoted by Farquharson [97] as referring to the tendency of voters to adopt a

> principle of voting which makes an election more of a game of skill than a real test of the wishes of the electors and . . . my own opinion is that it is better for elections to be decided according to the wishes of the majority than of those who happen to have most skill at the game.

Of even greater vintage is a remark of Jean-Charles de Borda. Satterthwaite [298, p. 188] quotes Black [40, p. 182] quoting Borda's "vexed retort 'My scheme is only intended for honest men!' which . . . Borda . . . made when a colleague pointed out how easily his Borda count can be manipulated by sophisticated strategies."

Collective choice rules for which there is no incentive to express preferences other than true ones are called "strategy-proof" (also cheatproof, nonmanipulable, straightforward, stable, or unique). Strategy-proofness has become a focus of interest in social choice theory because it is closely related to "mainstream" economic theory issues of evaluating resource allocation mechanisms with respect to incentive compatibility (cf. Hurwicz [168]) and because it seems a desirable constraint for some interpretations:

> There may be nothing wrong with lying as a political strategy, but one would not, I assume, wish to give a systematic advantage to liars. (Riker [279])

Shortly after the appearance of Arrow's book, Dummett and Farquharson [93] and Vickrey [338] made some informal conjectures about the difficulty of designing strategy-proof choice procedures. Additional investigations on strategy-proofness were conducted by Majumdar [210], Murakami [232], Sen [309], and Pattanaik [248, 250–253]. The first formal impossibility result along these lines is a theorem, independently obtained by Gibbard [142] and Satterthwaite [297, 298],[1] that no collective choice rule exists satisfying strategy-proofness and several other constraints. We begin with their result.

The first constraints on the social choice function in the Gibbard–Satterthwaite theorem are domain restrictions. They admit only one agenda, $V = \{E\}$, and then require the collective choice rule to work for all societies, $U = R_E{}^n$.

The most important constraint they use is *single-valuedness*: for each v in V, $C(v)$ contains exactly one element. Of course, there is only one v, namely E, in the Gibbard–Satterthwaite analysis. The importance of this constraint stems from its use in the rest of the problem; single-valuedness is used in their method of formalizing both strategy-proofness and a nondictatorial condition.

Let us deal first with the nondictatorial constraint. Using single-valuedness, we let $\overline{C_u(v)}$ be the unique member of $C_u(v)$. Then a collective choice rule f is *nondictatorial* if for no i, $i = 1, \ldots, n$, is it true that for all $(R_1, \ldots, R_n) = u \in U$ and for all $x \neq \overline{C_u(v)}$ in the range [i.e., for which there is some u' in U with $x = \overline{C_{u'}(E)}$] $\overline{C_u(E)}P_{iu}x$. Finally, we turn to strategy-proofness. A collective choice rule is *strategy-proof* at (v, u) if it is not manipulable at (v, u). f is *manipulable* at (v, u) if, when $u = (R_1, R_2, \ldots, R_n)$, there is a $u' = (R_1, \ldots, R_{i-1}, R_i', R_{i+1}, \ldots, R_n)$ such that $\overline{C_{u'}(v)}P_i\overline{C_u(v)}$, where $C_u = f(u)$ and $C_{u'} = f(u')$.

The Gibbard–Satterthwaite theorem then is:

Theorem 6-1 There is no collective choice rule $f : u \mapsto C_u$ satisfying on V, U

> (i) domain,
>> (a) $V = \{E\}$, $|E| \geq 3$,
>> (b) there is an n, $3 \leq n < \infty$, with $U = R_E{}^n$,
>> (c) f is total on V, U,

---

[1] Niemi and Riker [237] give independent credit to Satish Jain.

(ii) single-valuedness,
(iii) strategy-proof for all $(v, u) \in V \times U$,
(iv) there are at least three elements of E having the property that there is a $u \in U$ such that the element is in $C_u(E)$,
(v) the nondictatorial constraint.

Our proof of Theorem 6-1 follows very closely an approach of Schmeidler and Sonnenschein [300]. That approach requires first establishing a related result. To state this other result, let Q_E be the set of complete, asymmetric, and transitive relations on E (these are *strict* preference orderings).

Lemma 6-2 There is no collective choice rule, $f : u \mapsto C_u$ on V, U satisfying

(i) domain,
    (a) $V = \{E\}, |E| \geq 3$,
    (b) there is an n, $3 \leq n < \infty$, with $U = Q_E{}^n$,
    (c) f is total on V, U,
(ii) single-valuedness,
(iii) the nondictatorial constraint,
(iv) strategy-proof for all $(v, u) \in V \times U$,
(v) there are at least three elements of E having the property that there is a $u \in U$ such that the element is in $C_u(E)$.

The proof of Lemma 6-2 in turn will be based on the following result:

Theorem 6-3 There is no collective choice rule $f : u \mapsto C_u$ on V, U satisfying

(i) domain,
    (a) $|E| \geq 3$,
    (b) V is the set of all finite members of $2^E - \{\varnothing\}$,
    (c) there is an n, $3 \leq n < \infty$, with $U = Q_E{}^n$,
    (d) f is total on V, U,
(ii) Each $C = f(u)$ has a complete, reflexive, and transitive rationalization $R(u)$,
(iii) independence of irrelevant alternatives,
(iv) the weak Pareto condition,
(v) nondictatorship.

Proof This is just Theorem 4-3 (Arrow's second impossibility theorem) with $U = Q_E{}^n$ replacing $U = R_E{}^n$. Noting that the proof given in Chapter 4 nowhere requires use of a profile in $R_E{}^n$ not in $Q_E{}^n$ suffices to confirm this result. □

Proof of Lemma 6-2 (Schmeidler and Sonnenschein) We will show that if there were an f satisfying the five conditions of Lemma 6-2, there would be an f^* satisfying the five conditions of Theorem 6-3. Suppose

$f : u \to C_u$ satisfies the conditions of Lemma 6-2. Let $E^* = \{x \mid (\exists u)(\{x\} = C_u(E))\}$, the set of alternatives chosen by the images of f. By condition (v) of Lemma 6-2, $|E^*| \geq 3$. Let Q be an arbitrary complete, asymmetric, and transitive relation on $E - E^*$. Given $u^* = (P_1^*, \ldots, P_n^*) \in Q_{E^*}^n$, and $x, y \in E^*$, define $u^*(x, y) = (P_1, \ldots, P_n)$ by the rules

- (a) $xP_i y$ iff $xP_i^* y$,
- (b) for all w, z in $E^* - \{x, y\}$,
  - (i) $xP_i w$ and $yP_i w$,
  - (ii) $wP_i z$ iff $wP_i^* z$,
- (c) for all r, s in $E - E^*$,
  - (i) $t \in E^* \to tP_i r$,
  - (ii) $rP_i s$ iff rQs.

Thus $u^*(x, y)$ is derived from u^* by bringing x and y to the top of each ordering, preserving relations within $\{x, y\}$ and within $E^* - \{x, y\}$, and then appending $E - E^*$, ordered by Q, on the bottom. Define a binary relation $R^*(u^*)$ on E^* by

$$xR^*(u^*)y \qquad \text{iff} \qquad C_{u^*(x,y)}(E) = \{x\}.$$

Where v is a finite member of $2^{E^*} - \{\varnothing\}$, define

$$C_{n^*}^*(v) = \{x \in v \mid xR^*(u^*)y \text{ for all } y \in v\},$$

and define f^* as the function on $U = Q_{E^*}^n$ that maps u^* to $C_{u^*}^*$. We show that f^* satisfies the conditions of Theorem 6-3.

$C_{u^*}^*$ is clearly rational, via $R^*(u^*)$ and $R^*(u^*)$ is reflexive and antisymmetric. If f^* satisfies the weak Pareto condition, then $R^*(u^*)$ is complete. If $R^*(u^*)$ is also transitive, f^* is total. It remains to prove that

- (1) f^* satisfies the weak Pareto condition,
- (2) f^* satisfies independence of irrelevant alternatives,
- (3) $R^*(u^*)$ is transitive,
- (4) f^* satisfies nondictatorship.

To establish (1), assume x and y are in E^* and let $u^* = (P_1^*, \ldots, P_n^*)$ satisfy $xP_i^* y$ for all i. We need to show $xP^*(u^*)y$. If not, $C_{u^*(x,y)}(E) = \{r\}$ for some $r \neq x$, and $u^*(x, y) = (P_1, \ldots, P_n)$ satisfies the condition that everyone strictly prefers x to all other alternatives. Since $x \in E^*$, there is a $u' = (P_1', \ldots, P_n')$ such that $C_{u'}(E) = \{x\}$. Let

$$u_j = (P_1', \ldots, P_j', P_{j+1}, \ldots, P_n),$$

and let i be the smallest j with $C_{u_j}(E) = \{x\}$. We have $0 < i \leq n$,

$$C_{u_{i-1}}(E) = \{z\} \neq \{x\} \qquad \text{with} \quad u_{i-1} = (P_1', \ldots, P_{i-1}', P_i, P_{i+1}, \ldots, P_n),$$

$$C_{u_i}(E) = \{x\} \qquad \text{with} \quad u_i = (P_1', \ldots, P_{i-1}', P_i', P_{i+1}, \ldots, P_n),$$

where xP_iz. Thus f is manipulable at u_{i-1}. Therefore $C_{u^*(x,y)}(E) = \{x\}$ and the weak Pareto condition holds for f^*. As noted, this also tells us $R^*(u^*)$ is complete.

To establish (2), independence of irrelevant alternatives, let $u^* = (P_1^*, \ldots, P_n^*)$ and $\underline{u}^* = (\underline{P}_1^*, \ldots, \underline{P}_n^*)$ be two profiles in $Q_{E^*}^n$ with $u^*|_v = \underline{u}^*|_v$. We wish to show that $R^*(u^*)$ and $R^*(\underline{u}^*)$ restricted to v are equal. Suppose not, i.e., for distinct $x, y \in v$, $xR^*(u^*)y$ and $yR^*(\underline{u}^*)x$, so that by antisymmetry, $xP^*(u^*)y$ and $yP^*(\underline{u}^*)x$. With $u^*(x,y) = (P_1, \ldots, P_n)$ and $\underline{u}^*(x,y) = (\underline{P}_1, \ldots, \underline{P}_n)$, we have $C_{u^*(x,y)}(E) = \{x\}$ and $C_{\underline{u}^*(x,y)}(E) = \{y\}$. Define

$$u_j = (\underline{P}_1, \ldots, \underline{P}_j, P_{j+1}, \ldots, P_n), \qquad j = 0, \ldots, n.$$

Let i be the least integer with $C_{u_j}(E) \neq \{x\}$. Then $0 < i \leq n$ and, by the weak Pareto condition, $C_{u_i}(E) = \{y\}$. Thus we have

$$C_{u_{i-1}}(E) = \{x\} \quad \text{with} \quad u_{i-1} = (\underline{P}_1, \ldots, \underline{P}_{i-1}, P_i, P_{i+1}, \ldots, P_n),$$
$$C_{u_i}(E) = \{y\} \quad \text{with} \quad u_i = (\underline{P}_1, \ldots, \underline{P}_{i-1}, \underline{P}_i, P_{i+1}, \ldots, P_n),$$

and xP_iy iff $x\underline{P}_iy$. If xP_iy, f is manipulable at u_i; if yP_ix, f is manipulable at u_{i-1}.

We now need to establish (3), transitivity of $R^*(u^*)$. If transitivity did not hold, there would be a triple $\{x, y, z\} \in E^*$ and a society u^* with

$$C_{u^*(x,y)}(E) = \{x\}, \qquad C_{u^*(y,z)}(E) = \{y\}, \qquad C_{u^*(x,z)}(E) = \{z\}.$$

Let $u' = (P_1', \ldots, P_n') \in Q_E^n$ be constructed from u^* as follows: bring $\{x, y, z\}$ to the top of each R_i' ordering, preserving the P_i^* relations within $\{x, y, z\}$ and within $E^* - \{x, y, z\}$, then append $E - E^*$, ordered by Q, at the bottom. We first show that the element in $C_{u'}(E)$ is in $\{x, y, z\}$. Suppose not; let $u^*(x,y) = (P_1, \ldots, P_n)$ and define

$$u_j = (P_1, \ldots, P_j, P_{j+1}', \ldots, P_n'), \qquad j = 0, \ldots, n.$$

Let i be the least integer j such that $C_{u_j}(E) \subseteq \{x, y, z\}$; then $0 < i \leq n$. Then

$$C_{u_{i-1}}(E) \subseteq E^* - \{x, y, z\} \quad \text{where} \quad u_{i-1} = (P_1, \ldots, P_{i-1}, P_i', P_{i+1}', \ldots, P_n'),$$
$$C_{u_i}(E) \subseteq \{x, y, z\} \quad \text{where} \quad u_i = (P_1, \ldots, P_{i-1}, P_i, P_{i+1}', \ldots, P_n').$$

But every element in $\{x, y, z\}$ is strictly preferred to each element in $E^* - \{x, y, z\}$ according to P_i'. Thus f is manipulable at u_{i-1}.

Now there are three possible values of $C_{u'}(E)$. We will treat $C_{u'}(E) = \{x\}$, and the other two possibilities can be dealt with similarly. Let $u'(x, z)$ be the result of taking x and z to the top of each ordering, preserving the P_i' relations within $\{x, z\}$ and within $E - \{x, z\}$:

$$C_{u'(x,z)}(E) = C_{u'|E^*}^*(\{x, z\})$$
$$= C_{u^*}^*(\{x, z\}) \quad \text{by independence of irrelevant alternatives,}$$
$$= C_{u^*(x,z)}(E) = \{z\}.$$

With $u'(x, z) = (P_1^0, \ldots, P_n^0)$, consider

$$u_j^0 = (P_1^0, \ldots, P_j^0, P'_{j+1}, \ldots, P_n'), \qquad j = 0, \ldots, n.$$

Let i be the least integer j such that $C_{u_j^0}(E) \neq \{x\}$. Since $w \notin \{x, y, z\}$ implies xP_k^0w and $xP_k'w$ for all k, we can show as before $w \notin C_{u_i^0}(E)$, i.e., $C_{u_i^0}(E) \subseteq \{x, y, z\}$. Since $C_{u_i^0}(E)$ is not $\{x\}$, there are two cases. Note $0 < i \leq n$.

CASE 1: $C_{u_i^0}(E) = \{y\}$. But $C_{u_{i-1}^0}(E) = \{x\}$ and xP_i^0y. Therefore f is manipulable at u_i^0.

CASE 2: $C_{u_i^0}(E) = \{z\}$. Again $C_{u_{i-1}^0}(E) = \{x\}$. Now xP_i^0z iff $xP_i'z$. If xP_i^0z, f is manipulable at u_i^0; if zP_i^0x, f is manipulable at u_{i-1}^0.

In each case we have a violation of strategy-proofness, so $R^*(u^*)$ is transitive.

Finally, we suppose f^* violates nondictatorship, via individual 1, and show that f must violate the nondictatorial condition via 1. If not, there is a $u = (P_1, \ldots, P_n) \in Q_E^n$ with $C_u(E) = \{y\}$, xP_1y, and $x \in E^*$. Let $u' = (P_1', \ldots, P_n')$ be the result of raising $\{x, y\}$ to the top and retaining the p_i orderings within $\{x, y\}$ and within $E^* - \{x, y\}$, and then appending $E - E^*$, ordered by Q, at the bottom. Since 1 is a dictator for f^*,

$$C_{u'|E^*}^*(\{x, y\}) = \{x\}.$$

Thus $C_{u'}(E) = \{x\}$. Define

$$u_j = (P_1', \ldots, P_{j-1}', P_j', P_{j+1}, \ldots, P_n), \qquad j = 0, \ldots, n.$$

Let i be the least integer j such that $C_{u_j}(E) \neq \{y\}$. Now $0 < i \leq n$, so we have

$$C_{u_{i-1}}(E) = \{y\}, \qquad u_{i-1} = (P_1', \ldots, P_{i-1}', P_i, P_{i+1}, \ldots, P_n),$$
$$C_{u_i}(E) \neq \{y\}, \qquad u_i = (P_1', \ldots, P_{i-1}', P_i', P_{i+1}, \ldots, P_n).$$

CASE 1. $C_{u_i}(E) = \{x\}$. If xP_iy, f is manipulable at u_{i-1}; if yP_ix, then $yP_i'x$ and f is manipulable at u_i.

CASE 2: $C_{u_i}(E) = \{w\}$, $w \notin \{x, y\}$. Then $yP_i'w$ and f is manipulable at u_i. $\square$

Proof of Theorem 6-1 (Schmeidler and Sonnenschein) Suppose f satisfies conditions (i)–(iv) of Theorem 6-1. Let f' be the restriction of f to Q_E^n. f' then certainly satisfies the domain, single-valuedness, and strategy-proof conditions of Lemma 6-2. It can also be shown (Exercise: Do it) that the three-element range condition must also be satisfied. Then Lemma 6-2 tells us that the nondictatorial condition is violated, say, by individual 1. We need only show 1 violates the nondictatorial condition on the full R_E^n domain. Suppose not; there is a $u = (R_1, \ldots, R_n) \in R_E^n$ with $C_u(E) = \{y\}$ and an x in the range of some C_u in the range of f with xP_1y. Let $u' = (P_1',$

$\ldots, P_n') \in Q_E{}^n$ be a profile in which x is at the top of P_1' while y is at the top of each P_i' for $i \neq 1$. Since 1 violates the nondictatorial condition on $Q_E{}^n$, $C_{u'}(E) = \{x\}$. Define

$$u_j = (R_1, \ldots, R_{j-1}, R_j, P'_{j+1}, \ldots, P_n'), \qquad j = 0, \ldots, n,$$

and let i be the least integer such that $C_{u_j}(E) = \{y\}$.

Now $0 < i \leq n$, so we have

$$C_{u_{i-1}}(E) \neq \{y\}, \qquad u_{i-1} = (R_1, \ldots, R_{i-1}, P_i', P'_{i+1}, \ldots, P_n'),$$
$$C_{u_i}(E) = \{y\}, \qquad u_i = (R_1, \ldots, R_{i-1}, R_i, P'_{i+1}, \ldots, P_n').$$

If $i > 1$, y is at the top of P_i' and f is manipulable at u_{i-1}. If $i = 1$, f is manipulable by 1 at u_1. $\square$

Pattanaik [253, p. 1] suggests that under some circumstances we may want to weaken the concept of strategy-proofness:

> In actual life the stability of a given voting situation (i.e., the absence of any strategic manipulation by any coalition, which will disrupt the voting situation) is often the result of counterbalancing of "threats" and "counter-threats" . . .

Instead of ruling out manipulable situations, Pattanaik develops some different formulations of the idea that manipulable situations will not be exploited because of coalitions presenting counterthreats. From among his formulations, we present one: a collective choice rule f satisfies *strategy-proofness by counterthreats* if whenever f is manipulable at (u, v) by i, i.e., when $u = (R_1, \ldots, R_{i-1}, R_i, R_{i+1}, \ldots, R_n)$ and there is a u' (called a "threat"), $u' = (R_1, \ldots, R_{i-1}, R_i', R_{i+1}, \ldots, R_n)$ such that $\overline{C_{u'}(v)} P_i \overline{C_u(v)}$, then there is a coalition $S \subset N - \{i\}$ such that for each $j \in S$, there is an R_j'' such that if u'' is the profile (called a "counterthreat") which assigns

$$R_j'' \text{ to } j \in S, \qquad R_i' \text{ to } i, \qquad R_k \text{ to } k \in N - (S \cup \{i\}),$$

then $\overline{C_{u''}(v)} P_j \overline{C_{u'}(v)}$ for all $j \in S$ and $\overline{C_u(v)} P_i \overline{C_{u''}(v)}$.

This weaker strategy-proofness will be combined with a larger class of admissible agenda and a much-strengthened nondictatorship condition. f will be said to have a *triple dictator* if there is an $i \in N$ and an agenda $v \in V$ of cardinality 3 such that for all x in v, whenever at u $xP_{iu}y$ for all $y \in v - \{x\}$, then $\overline{C_u(v)} = x$.

Theorem 6-4 (Pattanaik) There is no collective choice rule $f: u \mapsto C_u$ satisfying

   (i)   the standard domain constraint (3),
   (ii) independence of irrelevant alternatives,
   (iii) single-valuedness,

(iv)   nonnegative responsiveness,
(v)   nonimposed,
(vi)   no triple dictator,
(vii) strategy-proof by counterthreats.

Proof   As in the Schmeidler–Sonnenschein proof of the Gibbard–Satterthwaite theorem, we show that any f satisfying the conditions of Theorem 6-4 yields an f^* satisfying the conditions of Theorem 6-3.

Select from E a three-element subset E^*. Let $u^* = (P_1^*, \ldots, P_n^*) \in Q_{E^*}^n$ be given and let Q be an arbitrary connected, antisymmetric, and transitive relation on $E - E^*$. Then for $x, y \in E^*$, $u^*(x, y)$ is defined by

(a) $xP_i y$ iff $xP_i^* y$,
(b)   for $z \in E^* - \{x, y\}$, $xP_i z$ and $yP_i z$,
(c)   for all r, s in $E - E^*$,
    (i) $t \in E^* \rightarrow tP_i r$,
    (ii) $rP_i s$ iff rQs.

Define a binary relation $R^*(u^*)$ on E^* by

$$xR^*(u^*)y \qquad \text{iff} \quad x = y \quad \text{or} \quad C_{u^*(x,y)}(E^*) \neq \{y\}.$$

$R^*(u^*)$ is clearly reflexive, complete, and antisymmetric. Temporarily, we shall assume the truth of the following:

CLAIM: If $E^* = \{x, y, z\}$ and, with $x \neq y$, profiles $u^* = (P_1^*, \ldots, P_n^*) \in Q_{E^*}^n$ and $u' = (R_1', \ldots, R_n') \in R_E^n$ are related by

(a)   for all i, not $xI_i'y$, and
(b) $yP_i^*x \rightarrow P_i^* = R_i'|_{E^*}$,

then

$$yR^*(u^*)x \rightarrow C_{u'(x,y,z)}(E^*) \neq \{x\},$$

where $u'(x, y, z) \in Q_E^n$ is constructed from u' by putting E^* at the top of each ordering, preserving the P_i' relations within E^*, and ordering $E - E^*$ (below E^*) by Q.

We shall first use this claim to prove transitivity of $R^*(u^*)$ and nondictatorship. Suppose $xR^*(u^*)y$ and $yR^*(u^*)z$. If either of these is due to equality, $xR^*(u^*)z$ is immediate. Hence we can assume $x, y,$ and z are distinct, that $\{x, y, z\}$ is a triple. Let u' be chosen so that $u'|_{E^*} = u^*$. Then, using the claim,

$$\overline{C_{u'(x,y,z)}(E^*)} \neq y \qquad \text{and} \qquad \overline{C_{u'(x,y,z)}(E^*)} \neq z.$$

Hence

$$\overline{C_{u'(x,y,z)}(E^*)} = x.$$

This, with the claim, implies $zR^*(u^*)x$ is false, and completeness gives $xR^*(u^*)z$ as we sought.

Defining

$$C^*_{u^*}(v) = \{x \in v/xR^*(u^*)y \text{ for all } y \in v\}$$

for $v \in V^* = 2^{E^*} - \{ \ ^+\}$ and f^* by $f^*(u^*) = C^*_{u^*}$, we have transitive rationality and so totality on $U^* = Q^n_{E^*}$. It is an exercise to check that f^* inherits the properties of IIA, nonnegative responsiveness and nonimposition from f. Theorem 3-18 then applies, so that f^* satisfies the weak Pareto condition.

The remaining condition to verify for f^* is nondictatorship. We will show that if 1 were a dictator for f^*, then 1 would be a triple dictator for f. Suppose $xP_{1u}y$ and $xP_{1u}z$ at $u = (R_1, \dots, R_n) \in R_E^n$ and $x \neq \overline{C_u(E^*)}$, say by $\overline{C_u(E^*)} = y$. We seek a contradiction. By IIA, we must have $\overline{C_{u(x,y,z)}(E^*)} = y$, where $u(x, y, z)$ is constructed from u by putting E^* on the top of each ordering, preserving the R_{iu} relations within E^*, then ordering $E - E^*$ below by Q. By nonnegative responsiveness, $\overline{C_{u'}(E^*)} = y$, where $u' = (R_1', \dots, R_n') \in R_E^n$ differs from $u(x, y, z)$ if at all only in that y is advanced above z (but still below x) in R_1' (so $xP_1'yP_1'z$) and y is put at the top of each $R_i', i \neq 1$. Looking at $u^* = (R_1^*, \dots, R_n^*)$ in $Q^n_{E^*}$ defined by

$$1: \quad xyz,$$
$$N - \{1\}: \quad yxz,$$

we see by 1's dictatorship for f^* that $xR^*(u^*)y$. By the claim, $\overline{C_{u'}(E^*)} \neq y$, the contradiction we seek.

What remains is to prove the claim. For the claim to fail, there must be a $u^* \in Q^n_{E^*}$ and $u' \in R_E^n$ with $xI_i'y$ for no i and $yP_i'x \to P_i^* = P_i'|_{E^*}, yR^*(u^*)x$, and $C_{u'(x,y,z)}(E^*) = \{x\}$.

Partition N into $N_1 = \{i|xP_i'y\}$ and $N_2 = \{i|yP_i'x\}$. Without loss of generality, let $N_1 = \{1, \dots, m\}$, $N_2 = \{m+1, \dots, n\}$. Define $\hat{u}^*$ in $Q^n_{E^*}$ by the rule

(1) if $i \in N_1$, put x on top and order y and z by P_i',
(2) if $i \in N_2$, $P_i^* = P_i^*P_i'|_{E^*}$.

Then $\hat{u}$ is defined by putting E^* on top, ordered as in $\hat{u}^*$, and $E - E^*$ below, ordered by Q. Since $C_{u'(x,y,z)}(E^*) = \{x\}$, nonnegative responsiveness yields $C_u(E^*) = \{x\}$. Let $\bar{u}$ be defined by

(i) x, y is at the top of $\bar{P}_i$, ordered as in P_i^*,

(ii) z is next,

(iii) $E - E^*$ is below ordered by Q.

Finally, define $u_j = (\hat{P}_i, \ldots, \hat{P}_j, \bar{P}_{j+1}, \ldots, \bar{P}_n), j = 0, \ldots, n$. Then $u_0 = \bar{u}$ and

$$C_{u_0}(E^*) = C_u(E^*) = \{y\},$$

while $u_n = \hat{u}$ and

$$C_{u_n}(E^*) = C_{\hat{u}}(E^*) = \{x\}.$$

If we let i be the largest integer such that $C_{u_j}(E^*) \neq x$, then i satisfies $0 \leq i < n$. We are now left with

$$C_{u_i}(E^*) \neq \{x\}, \qquad u_i = (\hat{P}_1, \ldots, \hat{P}_{i-1}, \hat{P}_i, \bar{P}_{i+1}, \ldots, \bar{P}_n),$$
$$C_{u_{i+1}}(E^*) = \{x\}, \qquad u_{i+1} = (\hat{P}_i, \ldots, \hat{P}_{i-1}, \hat{P}_i, \hat{P}_{i+1}, \bar{P}_{i+2}, \ldots, \bar{P}_n).$$

CASE 1: $C_{u_i}(E^*) = \{z\}$.   Since $x\bar{P}_{i+1}z$, we have a violation of strategy-proofness at u_i unless there is a coalition $S \subseteq N - \{i + 1\}$ which can present a counterthreat. But since $x\bar{P}_{i+1}z$ and $y\bar{P}_{i+1}z$, nothing S can do would yield an outcome from E^* worse than z as seen by $i + 1$ with ordering $\bar{P}_{i+1}$. Accordingly, f fails strategy-proofness by counterthreats at u_i via $i + 1$.

CASE 2: $C_{u_i}(E^*) = \{y\}$.

SUBCASE 1: $i + 1 \leq m$.   Since $i + 1 \leq m$, $x\bar{P}_{i+1}y$, so we have a violation of strategy-proofness at u_i unless there is a coalition $S \subseteq N - \{i + 1\}$ which can present a counterthreat. But to stop $i + 1$, the counterthreat profile would have to make z chosen and for S to act, its members must prefer z to x. But at u_i, *everyone* prefers x to z. Accordingly, at u_i, f fails strategy-proofness by counterthreats.

SUBCASE 2: $i + 1 > m$. $y\hat{P}_{i+1}x$, so we have a violation of strategy-proofness at u_{i+1} unless there is a coalition $S \subseteq N - \{i + 1\}$ which can present a counterthreat. Since $\bar{P}_{i+1}$ has $y\bar{P}_{i+1}x\bar{P}_{i+1}z$, $\hat{P}_{i+1}$ would be the same as $\bar{P}_{i+1}$ if $xP_{i+1}z$ and then $i + 1$ could not force a change by shifting to $\bar{P}_{i+1}$. Hence $zR_{i+1}x$. Thus there is nothing in E^* worse than x for $i + 1$ with P_{i+1}, so no counterthreat can be established.

For each case a violation of strategy-proofness with counterthreats has been found. Hence we were wrong in assuming the claim could fail. □

This proof goes through largely on the strength of the no-triple-dictator condition. In the presence of Property α and the other conditions of Theorem 4, no-triple-dictator could be shown to be equivalent to nondictatorship. (Exercise: Show this.) But that is just another way of displaying the great power of Property α.

The results presented so far in this chapter have depended heavily on the assumption of single-valuedness. Since we start with the assumption that "alternative" will be interpreted in such a way that any two alternatives must be incompatible, it seems obvious that any group of individuals in making a collective choice must finally choose just a single alternative. We accept this, but it does *not* constitute a defense of the single-valuedness criterion. While accepting the idea that social choices must be made in conformity with individual preferences, this should not preclude the use of additional information. This was the basis for our distinguishing, in Chapter 1, between the function $Ch(v, x)$, defined on $V \times X$, and $C(v) = \bigcup_{x \in X} Ch(v, x)$, defined on V. Single-valuedness says that there is enough information in individual preference orderings *alone* so that making a choice "in conformity with" them completely determines the appropriate choice. But if, for example, everyone is indifferent between x and y but vastly prefers both to any other alternative, then those preferences suffice only to determine that the final outcome should be either x or y (but not both). Additional information, such as (but *not* necessarily restricted to) a random device (coin toss) might be invoked to help choose between x and y. The demand by most impossibility theorems that the social choice function work for a wide variety of situations (e.g., requiring $U = R_E^n$) is here seen as a demand that $C_u(v)$ be defined for at least some situations in which u and v do not give enough information to narrow the appropriate outcomes down to just a single alternative. In the remainder of this chapter we present the consequences of abandoning the single-valuedness requirement.

However, it is important to observe that we cannot just ask if there is a collective choice rule satisfying all the conditions of the Gibbard–Satterthwaite theorem except single-valuedness. For, as noted, the conditions of nondictatorship and strategy-proofness have been defined *only* for those rules which are known to satisfy single-valuedness. Before we ask about impossibility results, we must provide natural generalizations of those conditions so that they make sense for social choice functions which allow nonsingleton image sets.

For nondictatorship, we dealt in Chapter 2 with the generalization we need here. We shall say that a collective choice rule f is *nondictatorial* if for no i, $i = 1, \ldots, n$, is it true that for all $u = (R_1, \ldots, R_n) \in U$ and all x, y in E

$$xP_iy \rightarrow [x \in v \rightarrow y \notin C_u(v)],$$

i.e., no individual is weakly, globally decisive between all pairs of alternatives.

Natural generalizations of strategy-proofness are harder to find. We will retain the idea that f is strategy-proof at (v, u) only if it is not manipulable there. We then want to say that f is manipulable at (v, u) if, for some i, changing u to u' by changing only R_i to R_i' results in changing C_u to $C_{u'}$ such that, based on R_i, i finds $C_{u'}(v)$ to be more desirable that $C_u(v)$, i.e., i has an incentive to make the change. In general, this incentive question is very difficult. When we accept the Gibbard–Satterthwaite condition of single-valuedness, the complexities melt away. When $C_u(v) = \{x\}$ and $C_{u'}(v) = \{y\}$, i has the incentive to change just when yP_ix. In the absence of single-valuedness, unclear cases can arise. Suppose $C_u(v) = \{x, y\}$ and $C_{u'}(v) = \{z\}$:

(i) If xI_iz and yP_iz, then i can gain nothing and may lose by forcing the change to u'. Here we are sure f *is not* manipulable at (v, u).

(ii) If xI_iz and zP_iy, then i can lose nothing and may gain by forcing the change. Here we are sure f *is* manipulable at (v, u).

(iii) If xP_iz and zP_iy, we are at a loss. Individual i may gain (if y would have resulted) or may lose (if it was to be x).

We would have to know more about the procedure by which final choices are made from that set of alternatives selected only on the information in the preference orderings. (For an analysis where the only additional information used is the value of a random variable and where individuals choose on an expected value criterion, see Gibbard [144] where an impossibility theorem may be found.)

Without a detailed examination of final selection procedures (and a theory of how individuals make "rational" decisions in the face of those procedures), the best we can do is to focus on the clear-cut cases. f is *clearly manipulable* at (v, u) if there is some i such that $u = (R_1, \ldots, R_{i-1}, R_i, R_{i+1}, \ldots, R_n)$, $u' = (R, \ldots, R_{i-1}, R_i', R_{i+1}, \ldots, R_n)$, and if

(1) for all x and y, $x \in C_{u'}(v)$ and $y \in C_u(v)$ implies xR_iy, and
(2) there is at least one $x \in C_{u'}(v)$ and one $y \in C_u(v)$ with xP_iy.

f is *weakly strategy-proof* at (v, u) if it is not clearly manipulate there.[2]

Now we can raise our questions about the Gibbard–Satterthwaite impossibility result. Are there any collective choice rules which are weakly strategy-proof but not dictatorial? To make this a serious problem we must deal with domain restrictions. We continue to require $U = R_E{}^n$. We will also require flexibility with respect to agenda: V contains all finite subsets of E. A collective choice rule satisfying both these requirements plus nondictatorship and weak strategy-proofness is f^0, a constant function, assigning C^0 to each u where $C^\circ(v) = v$. While this function does have a varied range (e.g., with more than three members), it is very insensitive to u. The three-member-range condition of the Gibbard–Satterthwaite theorem must be seen in light of the fact that their choice function was working on just a single agenda E.

---

[2] An alternative strategy-proofness criterion is given by Gärdenfors [133], where the reader will find an impossibility theorem that also invokes neutrality and anonymity conditions.

What is required is a varied range for each agenda. So let us impose a strong sensitivity requirement: f is *nonimposed* if for each finite agenda v, if v^* is a nonempty subset of v, there must be at least one society u with $C_u(v) = v^*$.

Are there any collective choice rules which are weakly strategy-proof, nondictatorial, and nonimposed? Suppose E is finite so that, by our domain restriction, $V = 2^E - \{\varnothing\}$. Let $M_i(v, u)$ be the R_i-best elements of v, i.e.,

$$M_i(v, u) = \{x \in v \mid \text{for all } y \text{ in } v, xR_iy\}.$$

Then consider f_M which assigns to u the choice function[3]

$$C_u(v) = \bigcup_{i=1}^{n} M_i(v, u).$$

(i)   Given $v^* \subseteq v$, $v^* \neq \varnothing$, define u^* by the following rule: for every i,

xP^iy if x and y are both in v^* or both in $E - v^*$,

xP_iy if x is in v^* and y is in $E - v^*$.

Then $C_{u^*}(v) = v^*$. Therefore, f_M is nonimposed.

(ii)   Suppose, in u, xP_iy. Let $j \in N - \{i\}$. If, in u, y is R_j-best in E, then $y \in v \to y \in C_u(v)$. Thus i is not a dictator.

(iii)   Suppose f_M is clearly manipulable at $u = (R_1, \ldots, R_{i-1}, R_i, R_{i+1}, \ldots, R_n)$ because there is an R_i' so that with

$$u' = (R_1, \ldots, R_{i-1}, R_i', R_{i+1}, \ldots, R_n),$$

$C_u(v)$ and $C_{u'}(v)$ satisfy the condition that there exist alternatives x and y with $x \in C_{u'}(v)$ and $y \in C_u(v)$, and xP_iy while either $x \notin C_u(v)$ or $y \notin C_{u'}(v)$.

CASE 1: $y \notin C_{u'}(v)$.   Then y is not R_j-best for $j \neq i$. Since $y \in C_u(v)$, y must be R_i-best. But this contradicts xP_iy.

CASE 2: $y \in C_{u'}(v)$, but $x \notin C_u(v)$.   Since $x \notin C_u(v)$, x is not R_i-best. Let z be R_i-best. Then zP_ixP_iy and $z \in C_u(v)$. But then zP_iy, $z \in C_u(v)$, and $y \in C_{u'}(v)$ contradict the manipulability assumption.

Since clear manipulability of f_M leads in each case to a contradiction f_M is weakly strategy-proof.

A more familiar social choice function which is strategy-proof, nondictatorial, and nonimposed is f_P, mapping u onto C_u^P where $C_u^P(v)$ is the set of Pareto-optimal alternatives in v. Establishing strategy-proofness for f_P, however, is not as simple as with f_M.

---

[3] f_M is essentially the random dictator discussed by Zeckhauser [356] and Gibbard [144].

These two examples reduce the impact of the Gibbard–Satterthwaite theorem. That theorem depends on an assumption (of single-valuedness) which is not desirable and which, if abandoned, allows the construction of (reinterpreted) nondictatorial, (reinterpreted) strategy-proof collective choice rules which are still sensitive to preferences.

This does not deny the possibility of a disturbing impossibility result based on strategy-proofness when large image sets are allowed. There are two obvious routes toward such impossibility theorems. One involves simply strengthening one of the present conditions, while the other involves adding one or more conditions of a type different from those already used.

Taking the strengthening route first, we will focus on the nondictatorship condition. Strengthening the nonimposed requirement seems implausible while strengthening the strategy-proofness requirement sensibly would seem to require detailed information about the interpretation of "alternative" and of "individual" as well as details about how $C_u(v)$ is narrowed down to the unique final outcome. As noted earlier, some work of this latter sort has been done by Gibbard [144]. Nondictatorship, however, is a very weak condition; the only strengthening that has played any serious role in the social choice literature up to this date deals with weak pairwise dictators. An individual i is a *weak pairwise dictator* if, for every x and y in E, whenever u has xP_iy then $x \in C_u(\{x, y\})$. In both our examples, f_M and f_P, introduced previously, *everyone* is a weak pairwise dictator. Are there any collective choice rules which are weakly strategy-proof, nonimposed, and for which there are no weak pairwise dictators?

It can easily be checked that these conditions are all satisfied by f^* which we define for the case of three individuals and three alternatives as the rule taking u to C_u^*, where

$$C_u^*(\{x\}) = \{x\}, \qquad C_u^*(\{y\}) = \{y\}, \qquad C_u^*(\{z\}) = \{z\},$$

$$C_u^*(\{x, y, z\}) = \bigcup_{i=1}^{n} M_i(\{x, y, z\}, u),$$

$$C_u^*(\{x, y\}) = \begin{cases} \{x\} & \text{if} \quad xP_1y, \\ \{y\} & \text{if} \quad yR_ix \text{ for all } i \text{ and } yP_ix \\ & \qquad \text{for at least one } i, \\ \{x, y\} & \text{otherwise,} \end{cases}$$

$$C_u^*(\{y, z\}) = \begin{cases} \{y\} & \text{if} \quad yP_2z, \\ \{z\} & \text{if} \quad zR_iy \text{ for all } i \text{ and } zP_iy \\ & \qquad \text{for at least one } i, \\ \{y, z\} & \text{otherwise,} \end{cases}$$

$$C_u^*(\{x, z\}) = \begin{cases} \{z\} & \text{if } zP_3x, \\ \{x\} & \text{if } xR_iz \text{ for all } i \text{ and } xP_iz \\ & \qquad \text{for at least one } i, \\ \{x, z\} & \text{otherwise.} \end{cases}$$

f^* suffers from a malady closely related to weak dictatorship. While no individual is weakly pairwise decisive between all pairs of alternatives, each pair of alternatives has an individual weakly pairwise decisive between *that* pair. It is an open question as to how far nondictatorship can be strengthened in this sort of direction and still avoid impossibility results.

The second interesting route is the addition of new conditions unrelated to nonimposition, nondictatorship, and strategy-proofness. If we confine our attention to conditions already used in the social choice literature, we can quickly reduce the amount of work. The function f^* used above satisfies two of the most commonly used conditions: independence of irrelevant alternatives and the *weak* general Pareto condition [that if xP_iy for all i, then $x \in v$ implies $y \notin C_u(v)$]. The other main class of conditions that might be employed are the regularity conditions. Of these, one of the most interesting for our purposes is independence of path,

$$C(v_1 \cup v_2) = C(C(v_1) \cup C(v_2))$$

for all admissible v_1, v_2, and u. This condition ensures that in choosing from a large set $v_1 \cup v_2$, the outcome is not influenced by the way we break the set into pieces v_1 and v_2 for separate consideration, making our final choice from the union of the elements chosen separately from the pieces. In effect then, path independence is another kind of strategy-proofness, dealing not with manipulation of preferences but with manipulation of agenda. An impossibility result using path independence would seem to reflect an inconsistency between two varieties of nonmanipulability.

Do there exist collective choice rules satisfying weak strategy-proofness, nonimposition, no weak pairwise dictator, and path independence? f^* does not qualify because if u is given by

$$1: \quad xyz,$$
$$2: \quad yzx,$$
$$3: \quad zxy,$$

then $C_u^*(\{x, y, z\}) = \{x, y, z\}$, while

$$C_u^*(C_u^*(\{x, y\}) \cup C^*(\{z\})) = C_u^*(\{x\} \cup \{z\}) = \{z\}.$$

We shall prove that the answer is "no" even if we reduce the independence of path condition to the weaker requirement of quasitransitivity of the base relation:

$$C(\{x,y\}) = \{x\} \quad \text{and} \quad C(\{y,z\}) = \{y\} \quad \text{imply} \quad C(\{x,z\}) = \{x\}.$$

Theorem 6-5   There is no collective choice rule satisfying

    (i)   the standard domain constraint,
    (ii) weak strategy-proofness,
    (iii) nonimposition,
    (iv) no weak pairwise dictators,
    (v) quasitransitivity of the base relation.

Proof   In the manner in which Schmeidler and Sonnenschein reduce the Gibbard–Satterthwaite theorem to a strict preference version of Arrow's second theorem, we shall show that any f satisfying all the conditions of this theorem would, on the restriction to Q_E^n, contradict the following result:

Theorem 6-6   There is no collective choice rule f satisfying

    (i)   the standard domain constraint, except $U = Q_E^n$,
    (ii) the weak pairwise Pareto condition,
    (iii) binary independence of irrelevant alternatives: if u, restricted to $\{x,y\}$, equals u', restricted to $\{x,y\}$, then $C_u(\{x,y\}) = C_{u'}(\{x,y\})$,
    (iv) no weak pairwise dictators,
    (v) quasitransitivity of the base relation.

Proof   This is just Theorem 4-6 with $U = Q_E^n$ replacing $U = R_E^n$. Noting that the proof of Theorem 4-6 nowhere requires the use of a profile in R_E^n not in Q_E^n suffices to confirm the result.

Proof of Theorem 6-5   Our task now is simply to prove that (i)–(v) of Theorem 6-5 imply the Pareto condition and binary independence of irrelevant alternatives (for the case of strong preferences).

Suppose $u = (P_1, \ldots, P_n)$ satisfies xP_iy for all i and $C_u(\{x,y\}) \neq \{x\}$. By nonimposition, there is some $u' = (R_1', \ldots, R_n')$ with $C_{u'}(\{x,y\}) = \{x\}$. Define

$$u_j = (R_1', \ldots, R_{j-1}', P_j, P_{j+1}, \ldots, P_n), \qquad j = 0, 1, \ldots, n.$$

Let i be the least value of j for which $C_{u_j}(\{x,y\}) = \{x\}$. By our discussion of u and u', $0 < i \leq n$. Since $C_{u_{i-1}}(\{x,y\}) \neq \{x\}$, $C_{u_i}(\{x,y\}) = \{x\}$, and xP_iy, f is clearly manipulable at u_{i-1} contrary to weak strategy-proofness. Hence $C_u(\{x,y\}) = \{x\}$ and the Pareto condition is established.

Now suppose $u = (P_1, \ldots, P_n)$ and $u' = (P_1', \ldots, P_n')$ are two elements of P_E^n with xP_iy if and only if $xP_i'y$. Suppose $C_u(\{x,y\}) \neq C_{u'}(\{x,y\})$. Define

$$u_i = (P_1', \ldots, P_j', P_{j+1}, \ldots, P_n), \qquad j = 0, 1, \ldots, n.$$

We let i be the least value of j for which $C_{u_j}(\{x, y\}) \neq C_{u_0}(\{x, y\})$. Clearly $0 < i \leq n$.

$$u_i = (P_1', \ldots, P_{i-1}', P_i', P_{i+1}, \ldots, P_n),$$
$$u_{i-1} = (P_1', \ldots, P_{i-1}', P_i, P_{i+1}, \ldots, P_n),$$
$$C_{u_i} = (\{x, y\}) \neq C_{u_{i-1}}(\{x, y\}) = C_{u_0}(\{x, y\}).$$

Since P_i and P_i' agree on $\{x, y\}$ and do not display indifference between x and y, f is clearly manipulable at either u_{i-1} or u_i. Suppose, for example, $x P_i y$ and $x P_i' y$ while

$$C_{u_{i-1}}(\{x, y\}) = \{x\}, \qquad C_{u_i}(\{x, y\}) = \{x, y\};$$

then f is clearly manipulable at u_i. All other cases can be handled similarly. $\square$

Impossibility results obtained by Barbera that combine regularity conditions with weak-strategy-proofness are given in one of the exercises.

Exercises

1. Illustrate the power of the single-valuedness assumption by showing that it implies the equivalence of the contraction-consistency condition Property α and the expansion-consistency condition Property $\beta(+)$.
2. Prove: If a collective choice rule satisfies
   (i) the standard domain restriction (except $U = Q_E^n$),
   (ii) single-valuedness,
   (iii) the weak Pareto condition,
   (iv) independence of irrelevant alternatives,
   (v) each C_u has a complete, reflexive, and transitive rationalization,
   then it is strategy-proof.
3. In the proof of Theorem 6-1, show that the three-element range condition is satisfied by f', the restriction of f to Q_E^n.
4. In the proof of Theorem 6-4, show that the induced collective choice rule f^* inherits the properties of independence of irrelevant alternatives, nonnegative responsiveness, and nonimposition from f.
5. Prove: In the presence of Property α and conditions (i)–(v) of Theorem 6-4, no-triple-dictator is equivalent to the usual nondictatorship.
6. (Muller and Satterthwaite) For a collective choice rule on Q_E^n satisfying single-valuedness, strategy-proofness is equivalent to the condition of strong nonnegative responsiveness:
   For all x, if $u = (P_1, \ldots, P_n)$ and $u' = (P_1', \ldots, P_n')$ are profiles satisfying, for all $y \in E$, $x P_i y \to x P_i' y$, then

$$C_u(v) = \{x\} \to C_{u'}(v) = \{x\}.$$

7. (Barbera)   There is no collective choice rule $f : u' \to C_u$ satisfying
    (i)   the standard domain constraint,
    (ii)   each C_u has a complete, reflexive, and acyclic rationalization,
    (iii)   nonimposition,
    (iv)   weak strategy-proofness,
    (v)   no oligarchy.

[Barbera has also shown that if the weak Pareto condition and positive responsiveness are added, condition (v) can be weakened to nondictatorship.]

7 DOMAIN: PART I

If we can hope that a social choice procedure need be prepared to cope with only a small subset of the set V of admissible agenda indicated in the standard domain restriction, or if individual preferences are interrelated in some way that eliminates the need for an aggregating procedure to work over *all* of R_E^n, then perhaps "good" collective choice rules can be found.

Some limits on this hope are established by results presented in earlier chapters. When impossibility theorems on strategy-proofness were being developed, it was noted that for Arrow's second impossibility theorem (Theorem 4-3) and for a result on base quasitransitivity (Theorem 4-6) the set of admissible profiles could be confined to Q_E^n without affecting the proofs. Also, we noted that the Gibbard–Satterthwaite theorem (Theorem 6-1) used a very small set of admissible agenda, $V = \{E\}$.

The first few domain contractions we discuss are related to issues raised by Arrow in *Social Choice and Individual Values*. As we noted in Chapter 4, Arrow's original theorem worked not with $U = R_E^n$ but with the existence of a "free triple," a subset S of E with $|S| = 3$, and $\{u|_S \mid u \in U\} = R_S^n$. Blau's counterexample led to corrections by Blau and Arrow, which invoked the standard domain constraint. But an alternative correction, by Murakami [231], retains Arrow's domain contraction and instead strengthens the nondictatorship requirement. For Murakami, the problem with Blau's counterexample is that individual 1 is a dictator, not on *all* alternatives, but on the free triple. This observation leads to:

Theorem 7-1 (*Murakami variant*) There is no collective choice rule f: $u \mapsto C_u$ satisfying

(i) domain,

(a)   there is a subset $S \subseteq E$ with $|S| = 3$ and

$$\{u|_S \mid u \in U\} = R_S^n \qquad \text{for some} \quad n \geq 3,$$

(b) $V \supseteq 2^S - \{\varnothing\}$,

(ii)   independence of irrelevant alternatives,

(iii)   each $C_u = f(u)$ has a complete, reflexive, and transitive rationalization $R(u)$,

(iv)   the weak Pareto condition,

(v)   no one is a pairwise dictator on S.

Proof   Exercise. $\square$

Another domain restriction dealt with in detail by Arrow was a restriction on profiles called "single-peaked preferences," a condition first developed by Black [40] and used by him as a description of domains over which a simple majority voting collective choice rule works. Let S be an irreflexive, connected, and transitive binary relation on the triple $\{x, y, z\}$. Then by $S(x, y, z)$ we mean xSy and ySz or zSy and ySx; $S(x, y, z)$ captures the idea that y is between x and z in the S ordering. $S(z, x, y)$ and $S(x, z, y)$ are defined analogously. A profile $u = (R_1, \ldots, R_n)$ is *single-peaked on triples* if, for each triple $\{x, y, z\}$ there is an irreflexive, connected, and transitive binary relation S on the triple such that for $\alpha, \beta, \gamma \in \{x, y, z\}$ it is true for all $i = 1, \ldots, n$ that

$$\alpha R_i \beta \quad \text{and} \quad S(\alpha, \beta, \gamma) \rightarrow \beta P_i \gamma.$$

It can be shown [8, Chapter VII] that if n is odd, u is single-peaked on triples, and f is the collective choice rule determined by simple majority vote, then $C_u = f(u)$ has a reflexive, complete, and transitive rationalization. Since f also satisfies independence of irrelevant alternatives, nondictatorship, and the weak Pareto condition, this collective choice rule satisfies Arrow's constraints on a narrowed domain.

There are two main problems with simple majority vote on profiles exhibiting single-peakedness as a route around the problems raised by Arrow's impossibility theorem. First, the domain contraction is a *very* stringent one. Only a very small fraction of profiles satisfy single-peakedness. Some evidence related to this will be mentioned later when we discuss evidence on the fraction of profiles yielding choice functions with transitive rationalizations.

Secondly, even though Arrow's other conditions are satisfied by simple majority vote, that is an extremely incomplete list of desiderata for collective choice rules. Other criteria must also be examined. Dummett and Farquharson [93] examine simple majority vote restricted to profiles satisfying a variant of single-peakedness and find strategy-proofness satisfied. Liberalism conditions, however, are clearly violated by majority vote even on the restricted domain. For a quite different sort of criterion that runs into trouble when voting operates on single-peaked profiles, we look at continuity issues [188]. Suppose E is the unit interval $[0, 1]$, with the usual topology. In Figure 7-1, individual preference orderings R_i are represented by (uniformly) continuous functions U_i, so that higher function values correspond to more preferred alternatives. All but one individual have the common preference relation whose representation peaks at $x = \frac{2}{3}$. If n is odd, simple majority vote yields a choice function C_u with a reflexive, complete, and transitive rationalization $R(u)$. We consider the criterion that $R(u)$ have a continuous representation $U(\cdot)$, such that $U(x) \geqq U(y)$ iff $xR(u)y$. Look at some sequence of values converging to b from below, say $b - (1/2)$, $b - (1/3)$, ..., $b - (1/m)$, ... For suitably large M, $m > M$ implies $U_1(b - (1/m)) < U_1(a)$ while $U_i(b - (1/m)) > U_i(a)$ for $i = 2, \ldots, n$. Thus $(b - (1/m))$ $P(u)a$, so $U(b - (1/m)) > U(a)$. Continuity of U would yield $U(b) \geqq U(a)$. But $U_1(b) < U_1(a)$, while $U_i(b) = U_i(a)$ for $i = 2, \ldots, n$ so that $aP(u)b$ and $U(a) > U(b)$. Looking at a similar sequence such as $a + (1/2)$, $a + (1/3)$, ..., $a + (1/m)$, ... will convince us that $U(\cdot)$ cannot be continuous at a either. Only at $x = 0$, $x = \frac{2}{3}$, or $x = 1$ does this simple sort of examination fail to reveal a discontinuity. Uniformly continuous, single-peaked orderings aggregate to a social ordering for which any "utility" function representation must be discontinuous almost everywhere.

An important observation related to the use of majority voting on single-peaked profiles has been made by Inada [169]. He shows that if we slightly enlarge the domain so that all individuals *but one* satisfy single-peakedness while one individual is free to order E in any way, then Arrow's theorem still holds. (Inada's analysis was completed before Blau's counterexample appeared, but it can be adapted to one of the revised versions of Arrow's theorem.)

Responding to the first issue, the extreme restrictiveness of single-peakedness, a series of theories sought broader domains over which majority

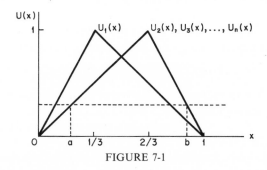

FIGURE 7-1

voting might still work. This search led to an interest in the conditions of value restriction, extremal restriction, and limited agreement. Given a profile u and a triple of alternatives, we say that u satisfies *limited agreement* on the triple if there are alternatives x, y in the triple with xR_iy for all i. Given the triple $\{x, y, z\}$, we can choose an ordered triple (x, y, z); the ordered triple satisfies *extremal restriction* if the existence in u of an i with the ordering

$$i: \quad xyz$$

implies that anyone finding z uniquely best must find x to be uniquely worst. Profile u satisfies *extremal restriction* on $\{x, y, z\}$ if every ordered triple obtainable from $\{x, y, z\}$ satisfies extremal restriction. Define an individual i to be *concerned* at u on a triple if there is at least one pair x, y in the triple with xP_iy. Then u satisfies *value restriction* on a triple if there is some element, say x, in the triple such that all individuals concerned at u on the triple agree that x is not best, or agree it is not worst, or agree it is not medium. For simple majority voting, if u satisfies extremal restriction on every triple, $C_u = f(u)$ has a reflexive, complete, and transitive rationalization; if for u every triple satisfies at least one of limited agreement, value restriction, or extremal restriction, C_u has a reflexive, complete, and acyclic rationalization [309, but see also 190].

With respect to these results, the first remark to be made is that the domains implied are still very narrow. There has been extensive research on the fraction of R_E^n on which simple majority vote yields acyclic, quasi-transitive, or transitive rationalizations (Black [40], Guilbaud [151], Riker [279], Klahr [200], Campbell and Tullock [75, 76] Williamson and Sargent [345], Garman and Kamien [137], Niemi and Weisberg [238], Gleser [147], DeMeyer and Plott [90], May [219], Kelly [189]). The results so far suggest that this fraction is quite small, especially for large numbers of alternatives.

The second point to be made is that even on these narrow domains, difficulties are to be found with respect to liberalism conditions. A collective choice rule $f : u \mapsto C_u$ satisfies *pairwise federalism* if there is a nonempty subset S_1 of N and two alternatives x, y such that S_1 is weakly globally, pairwise decisive between x and y and there is a nonempty subset S_2 of N_1 disjoint from S_1, and two alternatives, w, z, such that S_2 is weakly, globally, pairwise decisive between w and z. This is a pairwise version of the minimal federalism of Chapter 2.

Theorem 7-2 (Batra and Pattanaik [31]) There is no collective choice rule $f : u \mapsto C_u$ satisfying

    (i)   domain,
        (a) V contains all finite subsets of E,

(b) U contains all societies $u \in R_E^n$ ($n \geq 3$) satisfying both single-peakedness and limited agreement over every triple of alternatives,

(c) f is total on V, U,

(ii)   the weak *general* Pareto condition,

(iii)   pairwise federalism,

(iv)   regularity: for all u, v, x, y,

$$C_u(\{x, y\}) = \{x\} \rightarrow [y \in C_u(v) \rightarrow x \in C_u(v)].$$

Proof   The proof follows an outline similar to that of Sen's analysis of the impossibility of a Paretian liberal. Let x, y be the alternatives between which S_1 is decisive while S_2 is decisive between w and z.

CASE 1: $\{x, y\} = \{w, z\}$, *say* $x = w$ *and* $y = z$.   A society u can be found that satisfies the domain constraint such that we have

$$S_1: \quad xy,$$
$$N - S_1: \quad yx.$$

By the decisiveness of S_1, $y \notin C_u(\{x, y\})$; by the decisiveness of $S_2 \subset N - S_1$, $x \notin C_u(\{x, y\})$. Thus totality is violated.

CASE 2: $\{x, y\} \cap \{w, z\}$ *contains a single element, say* $x = w$.   A society u can be found that satisfies the domain constraint such that we have

$$S_1: \quad zyx,$$
$$N - S_1: \quad xzy.$$

Then by the decisiveness of S_1, $C_u(\{x, y\}) = \{y\}$; by the decisiveness of $S_2 \subseteq N - S_1$, $C_u(\{x, z\}) = \{x\}$. Now consider $C_u(\{x, y, z\})$. y is not in this set by an application of the Pareto condition. If $x \in (\{x,\ y,\ z\})$, then the regularity condition implies $y \in C_u(\{x, y, z\})$, which is false. Thus $x \notin C_u(\{x, y, z\})$. If $z \in C_u(\{x, y, z\})$, the regularity condition implies $x \in C_u(\{x, y, z\})$, which is false. Thus $C_u(\{x, y, z\}) = \emptyset$, violating the totality condition.

CASE 3: $\{x, y\} \cap \{w, z\} = \emptyset$.   A society u can be found that satisfies the domain constraint such that we have

$$S_1: \quad zyxw,$$
$$N - S_1: \quad xwzy.$$

By the Pareto condition, neither w nor y can be in $C_u(\{w, x, y, z\})$. Note that the decisiveness conditions yield $C_u(\{x, y\}) = \{y\}$ and $C_u(\{w, z\}) = \{w\}$. If $x \in C_u(\{w, x, y, z\})$, then so is y by the regularity condition. If $z \in C_u(\{w, x, y, z\})$, then so is w by the regularity constraint.   □

A second theorem using the same domain constraint and pairwise federalism will now be developed. The weak general Pareto condition will be relaxed to the pairwise version. In compensation, we require f to satisfy two other conditions. The first is an *extreme* strengthening of the nonnull requirement to $|v| > 2 \to C_u(v) \neq v$. The second is a regularity condition stronger than that of Batra and Pattanaik, developed by Schwartz [302]. Given a binary relation R on E, we have discussed choice functions based on R where the R-best elements are chosen:

$$C(v) = \{x \in v \mid xRy \text{ for all } y \text{ in } v\}.$$

The obvious difficulty is that $C(v)$ may be empty when R contains P-cycles. Schwartz proposes that $C(v)$ be obtained from R as the union of those smallest sets B such that nothing in $v - B$ stands in a P relation to anything in B. For this theorem, we use this proposal where R is the base relation.

Theorem 7-3 (Ramachandra [270])   There is no collective choice rule f: $u \mapsto C_u$ satisfying

    (i)   domain,
        (a) V contains all finite subsets of E,
        (b) U contains all societies $u \in R_E^n$ ($n \geq 2$) satisfying both single-peakedness and limited agreement over every triple of alternatives,
        (c) f is total on V, U,
   (ii) the weak pairwise Pareto condition,
  (iii) pairwise federalism,
  (iv) $|v| > 2 \to C_u(v) \neq v$,
   (v) regularity: $C_u(v)$ is the union of all sets B such that
        (a) $B \subseteq v$,
        (b) $x \in v - B \ \& \ y \in B \to [C_u(\{x, y\}) \neq \{x\}]$, all x, y,
        (c)   there is no nonempty $B' \subsetneqq B$ such that

$$x \in v - B' \ \& \ y \in B \to [C_u(\{x, y\}) = \{x\}] \text{ for all } x, y.$$

Proof   Let x, y be the alternatives between which S_1 is decisive while S_2 is decisive between w and z.

CASE 1: $\{x, y\} = \{w, z\}$.   An analysis just like that of Batra and Pattanaik yields a contradiction.

CASE 2: $\{x, y\} \cap \{w, z\}$ *contains a single element, say* $x = w$.   A society u can be found that satisfies the domain constraint such that we have

$$S_1: \quad zyx,$$
$$N - S_1: \quad xzy.$$

By the Pareto condition, $C_u(\{z, y\}) = \{z\}$. By the decisiveness conditions, $C_u(\{x, y\}) = \{y\}$ and $C_u(\{x, z\}) = \{x\}$. For $v = \{x, y, z\}$, a check of all possible sets B for the regularity condition will show that only $B = v$ satisfies all the requirements. $C_u(\{x, y, z\}) = \{x, y, z\}$, contrary to constraint (iv).

CASE 3: $\{x, y\} \cap \{w, z\} = \varnothing$. A society u can be found that satisfies the domain constraint such that we have

$$S_1: \quad zyxw,$$

$$N - S_1: \quad xwzy.$$

By the Pareto condition, $C_u(\{z, y\}) = \{z\}$ and $C_u(\{x, w\}) = \{x\}$. By the decisiveness conditions, $C_u(\{x, y\}) = \{y\}$ and $C_u(\{w, z\}) = \{w\}$. For $v = \{w, x, y, z\}$, a check of all possible sets B for the regularity condition will show that only $B = v$ satisfies all the requirements, contradicting (iv). □

The last of the domain contractions Arrow dealt with in the first edition of *Social Choice and Individual Values* involved the "individualistic assumptions." Here, elements of E are endowed with "economic" structure and certain assumptions are made about individual preference orderings. In the simplest case, an element of E is an $n \cdot m$ element vector $x = (x_{11}, \ldots, x_{nm})$, where x_{ij} specifies the amount of the jth commodity consumed by the ith individual. The preference relation for the ith individual is constrained so that if x and y agree on components $i1$ through im we have xI_iy. Further, monotonicity is assumed so that xP_iy if each $x_{ij} \geq y_{ij}$ for $j = 1, \ldots, m$ with strict inequality for at least one j. Arrow believed his theorem went through for this case, but Blau's counterexample could be adapted to a counterexample for the "individualistic" version [46]. Blau corrected Arrow's theorem by invoking $U = R_E{}^n$. The corresponding individualistic version is trivial because nonimposition is violated: if x assigns all commodities to individual 1 and none to anyone else and y does the same to individual 2, there is only one possible social ordering of these two alternatives. Murakami's use of a stronger nondictatorship condition *can* be adapted to yield an impossibility theorem. Details of such an adaptation are left to the reader.

The next contractions we consider relate to the critique given by Samuelson mentioned at the end of Chapter 1. If f is going to be applied just once, now, and the prevailing u is known, f need cope only with this one u. Parks and, independently, Kemp and Ng have developed impossibility theorems where U is a singleton set. Of course, if all individuals have identical preferences, social choice is much simpler. This says simply that we shall not obtain impossibility theorems for *all* singleton U's. The heart of each of the next few theorems is the specification of a class of u's for which $U = \{u\}$ serves as the basis for an impossibility result.

$u \in R_E{}^n$ satisfies *diversity* if for a three-element set T, then for each element u^* of $Q_T{}^n$, there is an injective map $\sigma: T \to E$ such that $u|_{\sigma(T)} = \sigma^{(u^*)}$.

Theorem 7-4 (Parks) There is no collective choice rule $f: u \mapsto C_u$ satisfying

　(i)　domain,
　　　(a)　V contains all finite elements of $2^E - \{\varnothing\}$,
　　　(b)　$U = \{u\}$, where $u \in R_E{}^n$ satisfies diversity, $n > 2$,
　　　(c)　f is total on U, V,
　(ii)　the weak Pareto condition,
　(iii)　neutrality-and-independence,
　(iv)　C_u has a complete, reflexive, and transitive rationalization $R(u)$,
　(v)　nondictatorship.

Proof　Let $V^* = 2^T - \{\varnothing\}$ and $U^* = Q_T{}^n$. Define $f^*: u^* \mapsto C_{u^*}$ by

$$C_{u^*}(v^*) = \sigma^{-1}(\{x \in \sigma(T) \,|\, xR(u)y \text{ for all } y \in \sigma(T)\}).$$

We will show that if an f exists satisfying the conditions of this theorem, then f^* would satisfy the conditions of Theorem 7-1. The condition of neutrality-and-independence guarantees that f^* is well defined, i.e., if σ and φ are two injections from T into E with

$$u|_{\sigma(T)} = \sigma(u^*), \qquad u|_{\varphi(T)} = \varphi^{(u^*)},$$

then

$$\sigma^{-1}(\{x \in \sigma(T)/xR(u)y \text{ for all } y \in \sigma(T)\})$$
$$= \varphi^{-1}(\{x \in \varphi(T)/xR(u)y \text{ for all } y \in \varphi(T)\}).$$

Neutrality-and-independence also implies that f^* satisfies independence of irrelevant alternatives. That f^* satisfies the weak Pareto condition and non-dictatorship is immediate from the corresponding properties of f. Finally, $C_{u^*} = f^*(u^*)$ is rationalized by the complete, reflexive-and-transitive relation $R^*(u^*)$, where

$$xR^*(u^*)y \qquad \text{iff} \qquad \sigma(x)R(u)\sigma(y). \qquad \square$$

In the next theorem, the class of profiles is substantially widened. The price to be paid for this is a strengthening of the weak Pareto condition to the strong version and a substantial strengthening of nondictatorship and neutrality-and-independence to a condition that incorporates an anonymity constraint.

$u \in R_E{}^n$ satisfies *variety* if there are three alternatives x, y, z in E and two individuals j, k such that

　(i)　all individuals other than j and k are indifferent at u among all of x, y, z,

(ii) R_j and R_k restricted to $\{x, y, z\}$ are antisymmetric,

(iii) for *exactly* one pair of distinct alternatives from $\{x, y, z\}$, R_j and R_k restricted to this pair are identical.

A collective choice rule $f : u \mapsto C_u$ satisfies *invariance* at u if for any permutation σ on N, and any w, x, y, z,

$$wR_i x \qquad \text{iff} \quad yR_{\sigma(i)}z \quad \text{for all } i$$

implies

$$w \in C_u(\{w, x\}) \qquad \text{iff} \quad y \in C_u(\{y, z\}).$$

Theorem 7-5 (Kemp and Ng) There is no collective choice rule $f : u \mapsto C_u$ satisfying

(i) domain,

    (a) V contains all elements of $2^E - \{\emptyset\}$ of cardinality less than or equal to 2,

    (b) $U = \{u\}$, where $u \in R_E^n$ satisfies variety, $n > 2$,

    (c) f is total on U, V,

(ii) the strong pairwise Pareto condition,

(iii) invariance,

(iv) C_u has a complete, reflexive, and transitive rationalization $R(u)$.

Proof Let $\{x, y, z\}$ be a set of the sort guaranteed by the variety condition and j, k be the corresponding pair of individuals. Without loss of generality, we can say we are in one of two cases:

CASE 1:

$$j: \quad xyz,$$
$$k: \quad zxy,$$
$$N - \{j, k\}: \quad (xyz).$$

CASE 2:

$$j: \quad xyz,$$
$$k: \quad yzx,$$
$$N - \{j, k\}: \quad (xyz).$$

We will treat Case 1, leaving Case 2 as an exercise. By invariance, $C_u(\{x, z\}) = \{x, z\}$ and $C_u(\{y, z\}) = \{y, z\}$. By transitive rationality, $C_u(\{x, y\}) = \{x, y\}$. But this contradicts the strong pairwise Pareto condition. $\square$

In an unusual tradeoff, we relax considerably the regularity condition (to Sen's Property β) and pay by changing the Pareto condition from a pairwise to a general version.

Theorem 7-6 (Kemp and Ng) There is no collective choice rule $f : u \mapsto C_u$ satisfying

  (i) domain,
   (a) V contains all elements of $2^E - \{\varnothing\}$ of cardinality less than or equal to 3,
   (b) $U = \{u\}$, where $u \in R_E{}^n$ satisfies variety, $n > 2$,
   (c) f is total on U, V,
  (ii) the strong general Pareto condition,
  (iii) invariance,
  (iv) C_u satisfies Property β:

$$\text{if } A \subseteq B \text{ and } \{x, y\} \subseteq C_u(A), \text{ then } x \in C_u(B) \text{ iff } y \in C_u(B).$$

Proof With $\{x, y, z\}$ and j, k given by the variety condition, we have the same two cases as in the proof of Theorem 7-5. We again treat just Case 1. By invariance and totality,

$$C_u(\{x, z\}) = \{x, z\}, \qquad C_u(\{y, z\}) = \{y, z\}.$$

By Property β,

$$
\begin{aligned}
x \in C_u(\{x, y, z\}) & \quad \text{iff} \quad z \in C_u(\{x, y, z\}), \\
y \in C_u(\{x, y, z\}) & \quad \text{iff} \quad z \in C_u(\{x, y, z\}).
\end{aligned}
$$

Totality then implies $C_u(\{x, y, z\}) = \{x, y, z\}$. But $y \in C_u(\{x, y, z\})$ violates the strong general Pareto condition. $\square$

So far we have examined the effects of narrowing U. Now we turn our attention to narrowing V. What makes most of our proofs go through is the presence in V of all sets of pairs of alternatives. In our first theorem, many pairs of alternatives are still known to be admissible agenda, but this is not known about *all* pairs.

Theorem 7-7 (Fishburn [123]) There is no collective choice rule $f : u \mapsto C_u$ satisfying

  (i) domain,
   (a) there is an n, $3 \leq n < \infty$ with $U \supseteq Q_E{}^n$,
   (b) $E = E_1 \cup E_2$, $E_1 \cap E_2 = \varnothing$, $|E_1| \geq 2$, $|E_2| \geq 2$, and $v \in V$ if v contains an $x \in E_1$ and a $y \in E_2$,
   (c) f is total on V, U,
  (ii) the Pareto condition: if $\{x, y\} \in V$ and xP_iy for all i at u, then $C_u(\{x, y\}) = \{x\}$,
  (iii) 2-ary independence,
  (iv) for $i \in N$, there is an $\{a, b\} \in V$ and $u \in U$ with aP_ib at u and $b \in C_u(\{a, b\})$,

(v) regularity: for every $u \in U$ and $v = \{x_1, \ldots, x_m\} \in V$, if $\{x_i, x_{i+1}\} \in V$ for $i = 1, \ldots, m - 1$, if $x_1 \in C_u(\{x_1, x_2\})$, $x_2 \in C_u(\{x_2, x_3\}), \ldots,$ $x_{m-1} \in C_u(\{x_{m-1}, x_m\})$, and if $\{x_1, x_m\} \in V$, then $x_1 \in C_u(\{x_1, x_m\})$; further, if at least one of $C_u(\{x_i, x_{i+1}\})$ is a singleton,

$$C_u(\{x_1, x_m\}) = \{x_1\}.$$

Proof Fishburn's original proof shows the other conditions contradict the finite n assumption. We will give a classical Arrow-type proof, showing a contradiction of the nondictatorship conditions (iv). Modifying slightly our earlier terminology, we shall say xD_Sy if $\{x, y\} \in V$ and when xP_iy for $i \in S$ at u while yP_jx for $j \in N - S$, we have $C_u(\{x, y\}) = \{x\}$. We write $x\bar{D}_Sy$ if we do not require yP_jx for all $j \in N - S$. As a first stage in this proof we show that if xD_Sy for any x, y, then $a\bar{D}_Sb$ and $b\bar{D}_Sa$ for all $a \in E_1, b \in E_2$. So suppose xD_Sy. If both x and y are in the same E_i, say E_1, let $z \in E_2$ and examine a $u \in U$ with

$$S: \quad xyz,$$
$$N - S: \quad yzx.$$

By xD_Sy, $C_u(\{x, y\}) = \{x\}$. By the domain constraint, $\{y, z\} \in V$, and $C_u(\{y, z\}) = \{y\}$ by the Pareto condition. The regularity condition then yields $C_u(\{x, z\}) = \{x\}$ since $\{x, z\}$ and $\{x, y, z\}$ are both in V. Independence then yields xD_Sz. Hence we can assume x and y come from different E_i's, say $x \in E_1$ and $y \in E_2$. To prove $a\bar{D}_Sb$ and $b\bar{D}_Sa$, we consider three cases.

CASE 1: $\{x, y\} \cap \{a, b\} = \varnothing$. Let u be a profile with

$$S: \quad ba,$$
$$N - S: \quad [ab],$$

and consider u_1 with

$$S: \quad bxya,$$
$$N - S: \quad y[ab]x.$$

We have $\{x, y\}, \{b, x\}, \{a, y\}$, and $\{b, x, y, a\}$ in V with $C_{u_1}(\{b, x\}) = \{b\}$ and $C_{u_1}(\{y, a\}) = \{y\}$ by the Pareto condition and $C_{u_1}(\{x, y\}) = \{x\}$ by xD_Sy. Regularity yields $C_{u_1}(\{a, b\}) = \{b\}$ and independence implies $C_u(\{a, b\}) = \{b\}$. Thus $b\bar{D}_Sa$. We next show xD_Sb. Let u_2 be a profile

$$S: \quad xyab,$$
$$N - S: \quad [ya]bx.$$

We have $\{x, y\}, \{y, a\}, \{a, b\}$, and $\{y, b, a, x\}$ in V with $C_{u_2}(\{x, y\}) = \{x\}$ by xD_Sy, $C_{u_2}(\{y, a\}) = \{y\}$ and $C_{u_2}(\{a, b\}) = \{a\}$ by the Pareto condition, regularity gives $C_{u_2}(\{x, b\}) = \{x\}$ and independence yields xD_Sb. This implies

$y\bar{D}_S a$ in the same way $xD_S y$ implied $b\bar{D}_S a$. Now let u_3 be a profile with

$$S: \quad yabx,$$

$$N - S: \quad ab[xy].$$

Since $y\bar{D}_S a$, $C_{u_3}(\{a, y\}) = \{y\}$. By the Pareto condition, $C_{u_3}(\{a, b\}) = \{a\}$ and $C_{u_4}(\{b, x\}) = \{b\}$. Regularity then gives $C_{u_3}(\{y, x\}) = \{y\}$, and independence yields $y\bar{D}_S x$. This implies $a\bar{D}_S b$ in the same way $xD_S y$ implied $b\bar{D}_S a$.

CASE 2: *Exactly one of $a = x$ and $b = y$ holds.* We will treat $a = x$, leaving $b = y$ to be dealt with by the reader. Let u be a profile with

$$S: \quad ab,$$

$$N - S: \quad [ab],$$

and consider u_1 with

$$S: \quad aywb,$$

$$N - S: \quad yw[ab],$$

where w is some second alternative in E_1. We have $\{a, y\}$, $\{y, w\}$, $\{w, b\}$, and $\{a, y, w, b\}$ all in V with $C_{u_1}(\{a, y\}) = \{a\}$ by $xD_S y$, $C_{u_1}(\{y, w\}) = \{y\}$ and $C_{u_1}(\{w, b\}) = \{w\}$ by the Pareto condition. Hence $C_{u_1}(\{a, b\}) = \{a\}$, so $C_u(\{a, b\}) = \{a\}$ by independence and so $a\bar{D}_S b$. $b\bar{D}_S w$ is obtained from $aD_S y$ as in Case 1, and this result is used to establish $b\bar{D}_S a$ from u_2 with

$$S: \quad bwya,$$

$$N - S: \quad wy[ab].$$

CASE 3: *$a = x$ and $b = y$.* Pick $w \in E_1$ and $z \in E_2$. From applications of Case 1,

$$xD_S y \rightarrow z\bar{D}_S w \rightarrow zD_S w \rightarrow [a\bar{D}_S b \text{ and } b\bar{D}_S a].$$

Now any set S such that for some x and y we have $xD_S y$ will be called a decisive set. Let W be a smallest decisive set. If W contains more than one individual, pick $i \in W$ and consider u with

$$i: \quad xbya,$$

$$W - \{i\}: \quad abxy,$$

$$N - W: \quad yabx,$$

where $a, x \in E_1$ and $b, y \in E_2$. $C_u(\{x, y\}) = \{x\}$ since W is decisive. If $C_u(\{a, y\}) = \{a\}$, then $W - \{i\}$ would be decisive, contrary to our choice of W. Thus $y \in C_u(\{a, y\})$. If $C_u(\{a, b\}) = \{b\}$, then $\{i\}$ would be decisive, contrary to our choice of W. Thus $a \in C_u(\{a, b\})$. Regularity implies $C_u(\{x, b\}) = \{x\}$, and this would make $\{i\}$ decisive, a contradiction. Hence W contains just one individual, j. We show j's power violates condition (iv). Let $\{a, b\} \in V$ and $u \in U$ with

aP_jb at u. If a and b are from different E_i's, $C_u(\{a, b\}) = \{a\}$ from the first part of this proof. If $a, b \in E_1$, say, go from u with

$$S: \quad ab,$$
$$N - S: \quad [ab],$$

to u_1 with

$$S: \quad ayb,$$
$$N - S: \quad [ab]y,$$

where $y \in E_2$. By the first part of this proof, $C_{u_1}(\{a, y\}) = \{a\}$ and $C_{u_1}(\{y, b\}) = \{y\}$. Regularity yields $C_{u_1}(\{a, b\}) = \{a\}$, and independence gives $C_u(\{a, b\}) = \{a\}$. Thus j violates condition (iv). $\square$

In the same way that Theorem 7-7 is analogous to Arrow's second theorem, the next two theorems are analogous to Theorem 4-4 on quasitransitivity and Theorem 4-8 on acyclicity. Proofs are left as exercises.

Theorem 7-8   (Fishburn [123])   There is no collective choice rule $f : u \mapsto C_u$ satisfying

   (i)   domain,
      (a)   there is an n, $3 \leq n < \infty$, with $U \supseteq Q_E{}^n$,
      (b) $E = E_1 \cup E_2$, $E_1 \cap E_2 = \varnothing$, $|E_1| \geq 2$, $|E_2| \geq 2$, and $v \in V$ if v contains an $x \in E_1$ and a $y \in E_2$,
      (c) f is total on V, U,
   (ii)   the Pareto condition: if $\{x, y\} \in V$ and xP_iy for all i at u, then $C_u(\{x, y\}) = \{x\}$,
   (iii)   2-ary independence,
   (iv)   for each $i \in N$, there is an $\{a, b\} \in V$ and $u \in U$ with aP_ib at u and $C_u(\{a, b\}) = \{b\}$,
   (v)   regularity: for every $u \in U$ and $v = \{x_1, \dots, x_m\} \in V$, if $\{x_i, x_{i+1}\} \in V$ for $i = 1, \dots, m - 1$, if $C_u(\{x_1, x_2\}) = \{x_1\}$, $C_u(\{x_2, x_3\}) = \{x_2\}, \dots, C_u(\{x_{m-1}, x_m\}) = \{x_{m-1}\}$, and if $\{x_1, x_m\} \in V$, then $C_u(\{x_1, x_m\}) = \{x_1\}$.

This theorem relaxes the regularity constraint and strengthens the no-dictator condition. The regularity condition is further relaxed in the next theorem, where the cost comes in changing $n \geq 3$ to $n \geq 4$ and introducing a positive responsiveness condition.

Theorem 7-9   (Fishburn [123])   There is no collective choice rule $f : u \mapsto C_u$ satisfying

   (i)   domain,
      (a)   there is an n, $4 \leq n < \infty$, with $U \supseteq Q_E{}^n$,
      (b) $E = E_1 \cup E_2$, $E_1 \cap E_2 = \varnothing$, $|E_1| \geq 2$, $|E_2| \geq 2$, and $v \in V$ if v

contains an $x \in E_1$ and a $y \in E_2$,

  (c) f is total on V, U,

  (ii) the Pareto condition: if $\{x, y\} \in V$ and xP_iy for all i at u, then $C_u(\{x, y\}) = \{x\}$,

  (iii) 2-ary independence,

  (iv) for each $i \in N$, there is an $\{a, b\} \in V$ and $u \in U$ with aP_ib at u and $C_u(\{a, b\}) = \{b\}$,

  (v) regularity: for every $u \in U$ and $v = \{x_1, \ldots, x_m\} \in V$, if $\{x_i, x_{i+1}\} \in V$ for $i = 1, \ldots, m - 1$, if $C_u(\{x_1, x_2\}) = \{x_1\}$, $C_u(\{x_2, x_3\}) = \{x_2\}, \ldots, C_u(\{x_{m-1}, x_m\}) = \{x_{m-1}\}$, and if $\{x_1, x_m\} \in V$, then $x_1 \in C_u(\{x_1, x_m\})$.

  (vi) responsiveness: for every x, y and every u, u', if there is an $i \in N$ such that

  (a) $yP_{iu'}x$,

  (b) $xP_{iu}y$,

  (c) for $j \in N - \{i\}$, the jth components of u and u' are identical,

then, if $x \in C_{u'}(\{x, y\})$, we must have $C_u(\{x, y\}) = \{x\}$.

So far, although not *all* two-element subsets of E are in V, many such subsets must still be admissible agenda. The next two theorems do not require any two-element agenda. The first uses just a single admissible agenda; like another theorem with that kind of agenda constraint (by Gibbard and Satterthwaite on strategy-proofness), a new f^* is constructed from f based on transformations of profiles.

Theorem 7-10 (Hansson [156]) There is no collective choice rule $f : u \mapsto C_u$ satisfying

  (i) domain,

   (a) there is an n, $3 \leqq n < \infty$, with $U = Q_E{}^n$,

   (b) there is a finite subset T of E with $|T| \geqq 3$ and $T \in V$,

  (ii) if $x \in T$ and xP_iy for all i at u, then $y \notin C_u(T)$,

  (iii) there is no i such that $x \in T$ and xP_iy at u implies $y \notin C_u(T)$,

  (iv) for each $u \in U$, there is a reflexive and transitive binary relation $R(u)$ such that the set of $R(u)$-maximal elements of v,

$$\{x \in v \,|\, \text{there is no } y \in v \text{ with } yP(u)x\},$$

is a subset of $C_u(v)$,

  (v) if $u, u' \in U$, $v \in V$, $u|_v = u'|_v$, v contains at least one $R(u)$-maximal element and at least one $R(u')$-maximal element, then x is $R(u)$-maximal in v iff it is $R(u')$-maximal in v.

 Proof Let $U^* = Q_T{}^n$ and $V^* = 2^T - \{\emptyset\}$. We will define an f^* on $Q_T{}^n$ into $\mathscr{C}_{V^*}$ and show that if there were an f satisfying the conditions of this theorem, f^* would satisfy the conditions of Theorem 6-3. Let Z be an arbitrary complete, reflexive, antisymmetric, and transitive binary relation on $E - T$. Given $u^* = (R_1{}^*, \ldots, R_n{}^*) \in U^*$ and a nonempty subset S of T, then by $u^*(S)$ we mean the element of U whose i-th component R_i is determined by the rules

(a) if $x, y \in S$ or $x, y \in T - S$, then $xR_i y$ iff $xR_i{}^* y$,
(b) if $x \in S$ and $y \in E - S$ or $x \in T$ and $y \in E - T$, then $xP_i y$,
(c) if $x, y \in E - T$, then $xR_i y$ iff xZy.

Then f^* will map u^* to $C_{u^*}^*$, which takes S to the set of $R(u^*(S))$-maximal elements of S.

Since S is finite and $R(u^*(S))$ is transitive, $C_{u^*}^*(S)$ is nonempty, so f^* is total and satisfies the domain conditions for Theorem 6-3. Conditions (ii) and (iv) ensure f^* satisfies the weak general Pareto condition. Condition (v) implies f^* satisfies IIA, and conditions (iii) and (iv) imply f^* satisfies nondictatorship.

It remains to show that each $C_{u^*}^*$ has a complete, reflexive, and transitive rationalization. We will do this by going through Theorem 3-10 of Sen, showing that it is sufficient to prove $C_{u^*}^*$ satisfies both Properties α and β. For Property α, suppose $v \subseteq v' \subseteq T$ and $x \in C_{u^*}^*(v') \cap v$. From the latter, x is $R(u^*(v'))$-maximal in v. From $u^*(v')|_v = u^*(v)|_v$, the independence condition tells us x is $R(u^*(v))$-maximal in v, i.e., $x \in C_{u^*}^*(v)$. Thus

$$C_{u^*}^*(v') \cap v \subseteq C_{u^*}^*(v),$$

and Property α is confirmed.

We turn to Property β:

$$v \subseteq v' \to [C(v) \cap C(v') \neq \varnothing \to C(v) \subseteq C(v')].$$

Suppose $v \subseteq v' \subseteq T$, $C_{u^*}^*(v) \cap C_{u^*}^*(v') \neq \varnothing$, and $x \in C_{u^*}^*(v)$. Since $v \subseteq v'$, $u^*(v')|_v = u^*(v)|_v$. Since $C_{u^*}^*(v) \cap C_{u^*}^*(v') \neq \varnothing$, v contains an $R(u^*(v))$-maximal element and an $R^*(u^*(v'))$-maximal element. By independence, the set $C_{u^*}^*(v)$ of $R(u^*(v))$-maximal elements of v equals the set $C_{u^*}^*(v') \cap v$ of $R(u^*(v'))$-maximal elements of v. Thus $x \in C_{u^*}^*(v')$, confirming Property β. □

As a technical note, observe that no totality condition is included. Constraint (iv) guarantees $C_u(v) \neq \varnothing$ sufficiently often for our purposes.

Our final theorem in this chapter is Fishburn's adaptation of the Mas-Colell and Sonnenschein theorem on acyclicity to the case in which all agenda of size m are admissible, but where m no longer need be as small as 2. Any m larger than 2 but strictly less than $|E|$ will do.

Theorem 7-11 (Fishburn [122]) There is no collective choice rule $f : u \mapsto C_u$ satisfying

(i) domain,

(a)   there is an n, $3 \leq n < \infty$, with $U \supseteq Q_E^n$,

(b)   there is an m, $3 \leq m < \infty$, with $|E| > m$ and such that if $|v| = m$ and $v \subseteq E$, then $v \in V$,

(c) f is total on V, U,

(ii) m-ary independence,

(iii)   the m-ary Pareto condition: if $|v| = m$ and xP_iy for all i at u, then $x \in v \to y \notin C_u(v)$,

(iv)   the m-ary no-weak-dictator condition: for every $i \in N$, there is a v, $|v| = m$, such that at u, xP_iy for all $y \in v - \{x\}$ and $x \notin C_u(v)$,

(v) m-ary positive responsiveness: suppose $x \in v$ and $|v| = m$, and that $u = (R_1, \ldots, R_n)$ and $u' = (R_1', \ldots, R_n')$ in U satisfy the following conditions where $i \in N$:

(a)   for $j \in N - \{i\}$, $R_j|_v = R_j'|_v$,

(b) $R_i|_{v-\{x\}} = R_i'|_{v-\{x\}}$,

(c)   for some $y \in v$, yP_ix at u' but xP_iy at u, then, if $x \in C_u(v)$, $C_u(v) = \{x\}$,

(vi) m-ary rationality: if $|v| \geq m$ and $v \in V$, then

$$C_u(v) = \{x \in v \,|\, \text{for all } z \subseteq v, x \in z \in V, |z| = m \to x \in C_u(z)\}.$$

Proof   We will follow closely Fishburn's proof to display for the reader the delicate shifts from profile to profile and agenda to agenda he uses to bring out the properties of f. As in Fishburn's proof of Arrow's theorem (see Chapter 4), we show the other properties of f contradict $n < \infty$.

The first step, as usual, is to prove a contagious property of f; if a set S has a little decisiveness, it must have a broad power among alternatives. We write $D_S(a_1, \ldots, a_m)$ to mean that if at u

$$S: \quad a_1 a_2 \cdots a_m,$$
$$N - S: \quad a_2 \cdots a_m a_1,$$

then $a_1 \in C_u(\{a_1, \ldots, a_m\})$. We write $\bar{D}_S(v)$ for v with $|v| = m$ if at u, when $x \in v$ and xP_iy for all $i \in S$ and all $y \in v - \{x\}$, then $x \in C_u(v)$. If $\bar{D}_S(v)$ for all v with $|v| = m$, we say S is m-ary decisive. Our first step is to show that if $|S| \leq n - 2$ and $D_S(a_1, \ldots, a_m)$ for some $a_1, \ldots, a_m$, then S is m-ary decisive. Without loss of generality, we suppose $S = \{1, \ldots, r\}$ while $N - S = \{r + 1, \ldots, n\}$.

We start from the knowledge that $a_1 \in C_u(\{a_1, \ldots, a_m\})$ when u satisfies

$$
\begin{array}{rl}
1: & a_1 a_2 \cdots a_m, \\
& \vdots \\
r: & a_1 a_2 \cdots a_m, \\
r+1: & a_2 \cdots a_m a_1, \\
& \vdots \\
n: & a_2 \cdots a_m a_1,
\end{array}
\tag{1}
$$

and wish to show $x \in C_{u'}(\{x, x_1, \ldots, x_{m-1}\})$ when u' satisfies

$$
\begin{aligned}
1&: \quad x[x_1 \cdots x_{m-1}], \\
&\;\vdots \\
r&: \quad x[x_1 \cdots x_{m-1}], \\
r+1&: \quad [x_1 \cdots x_{m-1}]x, \\
&\;\vdots \\
n&: \quad [x_1 \cdots x_{m-1}]x,
\end{aligned}
\tag{2}
$$

for then $\bar{D}_S(\{x, x_1, \ldots, x_{m-1}\})$ follows by positive responsiveness. From (1), we get u_1 by inverting $a_m a_1$ to $a_1 a_m$ for $r+1$. Then $C_{u_1}(\{a_1, \ldots, a_m\}) = \{a_1\}$. Insert x_1 after a_2 in each relation to obtain u_2 with

$$
\begin{aligned}
1&: \quad a_1 a_2 x_1 a_3 \cdots a_m, \\
&\;\vdots \\
r&: \quad a_1 a_2 x_1 a_3 \cdots a_m, \\
r+1&: \quad a_2 x_1 a_3 \cdots a_{m-1} a_1 a_m, \\
r+2&: \quad a_2 x_1 a_3 \cdots a_{m-1} a_m a_1, \\
&\;\vdots \\
n&: \quad a_2 x_1 a_3 \cdots a_{m-1} a_m a_1.
\end{aligned}
$$

Totality and rationality require that some *one* element be chosen from *every* m-element agenda in which it appears. $x_1, a_3, \ldots, a_m$ are ruled out by the m-ary Pareto condition. a_2 is ruled out by independence:

$$
C_{u_2}(\{a_1, \ldots, a_m\}) = C_{u_1}(\{a_1, \ldots, a_m\}) = \{a_1\}.
$$

Hence $a_1 \in C_{u_2}(\{x_1, a_1, \ldots, a_{m-1}\})$, and so $a_1 \in C_{u_3}(\{x_1, a_1, \ldots, a_{m-1}\})$ for any u_3 satisfying

$$
\begin{aligned}
1&: \quad a_1 a_2 x_1 a_3 \cdots a_{m-1}, \\
&\;\vdots \\
r&: \quad a_1 a_2 x_1 a_3 \cdots a_{m-1}, \\
r+1&: \quad a_2 x_1 a_3 \cdots a_{m-1} a_1, \\
r+2&: \quad a_2 x_1 a_3 \cdots a_{m-1} a_1, \\
&\;\vdots \\
n&: \quad a_2 x_1 a_3 \cdots a_{m-1} a_1,
\end{aligned}
\tag{3}
$$

by independence. From (3), we get u_4 by inverting $a_{m-1} a_1$ to $a_1 a_{m-1}$ for $r+1$. Responsiveness implies $C_{u_4}(\{x_1, a_1, \ldots, a_{m-1}\}) = \{a_1\}$. Pick $x_2 \in E - \{x_1, a_1, \ldots, a_{m-1}\}$ and insert it between a_2 and a_3 in each relation to get

u_5 with

$$1: \quad a_1a_2[x_1x_2]a_3 \cdots a_{m-2}a_{m-1},$$

$$\vdots$$

$$r: \quad a_1a_2[x_1x_2]a_3 \cdots a_{m-2}a_{m-1},$$

$$r+1: \quad a_2[x_1x_2]a_3 \cdots a_{m-2}a_1a_{m-1},$$

$$r+2: \quad a_2[x_1x_2]a_3 \cdots a_{m-2}a_{m-1}a_1,$$

$$\vdots$$

$$n: \quad a_2[x_1x_2]a_3 \cdots a_{m-2}a_{m-1}a_1.$$

Totality, rationality, Pareto, and independence again yield $\{a_1\} = C_{u_5}(\{x_1, x_2, a_1, a_2, \ldots, a_{m-1}\})$. Hence $a_1 \in C_{u_5}(\{x_1, x_2, a_1, a_2, \ldots, a_{m-2}\})$, and so $C_{u_6}(\{x_1, x_2, a_1, a_2, \ldots, a_{m-2}\})$ for any u_6 satisfying

$$1: \quad a_1a_2[x_1x_2]a_3 \cdots a_{m-2},$$

$$\vdots$$

$$r: \quad a_1a_2[x_1x_2],$$

$$r+1: \quad a_2[x_1x_2]a_3 \cdots a_{m-2}a_1,$$

$$r+2: \quad a_2[x_1x_2]a_3 \cdots a_{m-2}a_1,$$

$$\vdots$$

$$n: \quad a_2[x_1x_2]a_3 \cdots a_{m-2}a_1.$$

Continuing in this manner, we determine $a_1 \in C_{u_7}(\{x_1, \ldots, x_{m-2}, a_1, a_2\})$ for any u_7 satisfying

$$1: \quad a_1a_2[x_1x_2 \cdots x_{m-2}],$$

$$\vdots$$

$$r: \quad a_1a_2[x_1x_2 \cdots x_{m-2}],$$

$$r+1: \quad a_2[x_1x_2 \cdots x_{m-2}]a_1,$$

$$\vdots$$

$$n: \quad a_2[x_1x_2 \cdots x_{m-2}]a_1.$$

$$(4)$$

In particular, $a_1 \in C_{u_8}(\{x_1, \ldots, x_{m-2}, a_1, a_2\})$, where u_8 satisfies

$$1: \quad a_1a_2[x_1x_2 \cdots x_{m-3}]x_{m-2},$$

$$\vdots$$

$$r: \quad a_1a_2[x_1x_2 \cdots x_{m-3}]x_{m-2},$$

$$r+1: \quad a_2[x_1x_2 \cdots x_{m-3}]x_{m-2}a_1,$$

$$\vdots$$

$$n: \quad a_2[x_1x_2 \cdots x_{m-3}]x_{m-2}a_1.$$

$$(5)$$

From (5) we get u_9 by inverting $x_{m-2}a_1$ to $a_1 x_{m-2}$ for $r + 1$. Responsiveness implies $C_{u_9}(\{x_1, \ldots, x_{m-2}, a_1, a_2\}) = \{a_1\}$. Pick $y \in E - \{x_1, \ldots, x_{m-2}, a_1, a_2\}$ and insert it just before a_1 in each relation to get u_{10} satisfying

$$
\begin{aligned}
1&: \quad ya_1, a_2[x_1 x_2 \cdots x_{m-3}]x_{m-2}, \\
&\vdots \\
r&: \quad ya_1 a_2[x_1 x_2 \cdots x_{m-3}]x_{m-2}, \\
r+1&: \quad a_2[x_1 x_2 \cdots x_{m-3}]ya_1 x_{m-2}, \\
r+2&: \quad a_2[x_1 x_2 \cdots x_{m-3}]x_{m-2}ya_1, \\
&\vdots \\
n&: \quad a_2[x_1 x_2 \cdots x_{m-3}]x_{m-2}ya_1.
\end{aligned}
$$

Totality, rationality, Pareto, and independence yield $\{y\} = C_{u_{10}}(\{y, x_1, \ldots, x_{m-2}, a_1, a_2\})$. Hence $y \in C_{u_{10}}(\{y, x_1, \ldots, x_{m-2}, a_2\})$, and so $y \in C_{u_{11}}(\{y, x_1, \ldots, x_{m-2}, a_2\})$ for any u_{11} satisfying

$$
\begin{aligned}
1&: \quad ya_2[x_1 x_2 \cdots x_{m-3}]x_{m-2}, \\
&\vdots \\
r&: \quad ya_2[x_1 x_2 \cdots x_{m-3}]x_{m-2}, \\
r+1&: \quad a_2[x_1 x_2 \cdots x_{m-3}]yx_{m-2}, \\
r+2&: \quad a_2[x_1 x_2 \cdots x_{m-3}]x_{m-2}y, \\
&\vdots \\
n&: \quad a_2[x_1 x_2 \cdots x_{m-3}]x_{m-2}y.
\end{aligned}
\tag{6}
$$

From (6), we get u_{12} by inverting $x_{m-2}y$ to yx_{m-2} for $r + 2$ so that $C_{u_{12}}(\{y, x_1, \ldots, x_{m-2}, a_2\}) = \{y\}$. Then insert $t \in E - \{y, x_1, \ldots, x_{m-2}, a_2\}$ after a_2 and before x_{m-2} and, where appropriate, before y to get u_{13} satisfying

$$
\begin{aligned}
1&: \quad ya_2[tx_1 x_2 \cdots x_{m-3}]x_{m-2}, \\
&\vdots \\
r&: \quad ya_2[tx_1 x_2 \cdots x_{m-3}]x_{m-2}, \\
r+1&: \quad a_2[tx_1 x_2 \cdots x_{m-3}]yx_{m-2}, \\
r+2&: \quad a_2[tx_1 x_2 \cdots x_{m-3}]yx_{m-2}, \\
r+3&: \quad a_2[tx_1 x_2 \cdots x_{m-3}]x_{m-2}y, \\
&\vdots \\
n&: \quad a_2[tx_1 x_2 \cdots x_{m-3}]x_{m-2}y.
\end{aligned}
$$

As before, totality, rationality, Pareto, and independence yield $\{y\} = C_{u_{13}}(\{y, x_1, \ldots, x_{m-2}, a_2, t\})$, and so $y \in C_{u_{13}}(\{y, x_1, \ldots, x_{m-3}, a_2, t\})$. Independence then yields $y \in C_{u_{14}}(\{y, x_1, \ldots, x_{m-3}, a_2, t\})$ for any u_{14} satisfying

$$
\begin{aligned}
1: &\quad ya_2[tx_1x_2 \cdots x_{m-3}], \\
&\quad \vdots \\
r: &\quad ya_2[tx_1x_2 \cdots x_{m-3}], \\
r+1: &\quad a_2[tx_1x_2 \cdots x_{m-3}]y, \\
&\quad \vdots \\
n: &\quad a_2[tx_1x_2 \cdots x_{m-3}].
\end{aligned} \tag{7}
$$

Going back to (5), we again get u_9 by inverting $x_{m-2}a_1$ to a_1x_{m-2} for $r+1$. $C_{u_9}(\{x_1, \ldots, x_{m-2}, a_1, a_2\}) = \{a_1\}$. Insert y from $E - \{x_1, \ldots, x_{m-2}, a_1, a_2\}$ just after a_2 to get u_{15} satisfying

$$
\begin{aligned}
1: &\quad a_1a_2y[x_1x_2 \cdots x_{m-3}]x_{m-2}, \\
&\quad \vdots \\
r: &\quad a_1a_2y[x_1x_2 \cdots x_{m-3}]x_{m-2}, \\
r+1: &\quad a_2y[x_1x_2 \cdots x_{m-3}]a_1x_{m-2}, \\
r+2: &\quad a_2y[x_1x_2 \cdots x_{m-3}]x_{m-2}a_1, \\
&\quad \vdots \\
n: &\quad a_2y[x_1x_2 \cdots x_{m-3}]x_{m-2}a_1.
\end{aligned}
$$

The usual techniques give $\{a_1\} = C_{u_{15}}(\{y, x_1, \ldots, x_{m-2}, a_1, a_2\})$ and $a_1 \in u_{16}(\{y, x_1, \ldots, x_{m-2}, a_1\})$ for any u_{16} satisfying

$$
\begin{aligned}
1: &\quad a_1y[x_1x_2 \cdots x_{m-3}]x_{m-2}, \\
&\quad \vdots \\
r: &\quad a_1y[x_1x_2 \cdots x_{m-3}]x_{m-2}, \\
r+1: &\quad y[x_1x_2 \cdots x_{m-3}]a_1x_{m-2}, \\
r+2: &\quad y[x_1x_2 \cdots x_{m-3}]x_{m-2}a_1, \\
&\quad \vdots \\
n: &\quad y[x_1x_2 \cdots x_{m-3}]x_{m-2}a_1.
\end{aligned}
$$

Inverting $x_{m-2}a_1$ to a_1x_{m-2} in $r+2$, inserting $t \in E - \{a_1, y, x_1, \ldots, x_{m-2}\}$ after y but, where appropriate, before a_1, evaluation, and dropping of x_{m-2} gives $a_1 \in C_{u_{17}}(\{a_1, y, t, x_1, \ldots, x_{m-3}\})$ for any u_{17} satisfying

$$
\begin{aligned}
1: &\quad a_1y[tx_1x_2 \cdots x_{m-3}], \\
&\quad \vdots \\
r: &\quad a_1y[tx_1x_2 \cdots x_{m-3}], \\
r+1: &\quad y[tx_1x_2 \cdots x_{m-3}]a_1, \\
n: &\quad y[tx_1x_2 \cdots x_{m-3}]a_1.
\end{aligned} \tag{8}
$$

The results for (7) and (8) are two cases of the following result, the other cases of which can be determined from (5) in the same manner: For any distinct $x, y, x_1, \ldots, x_{m-2}$ in E, $x \in C_{u_{19}}(\{x, y, x_1, \ldots, x_{m-2}\})$ for any profile u_{18} satisfying

$$
\begin{array}{rl}
1: & xy[x_1 x_2 \cdots x_{m-2}], \\
& \vdots \\
r: & xy[x_1 x_2 \cdots x_{m-2}], \\
r+1: & y[x_1 x_2 \cdots x_{m-2}]x, \\
& \vdots \\
n: & y[x_1 x_2 \cdots x_{m-2}]x.
\end{array} \tag{9}
$$

We show next that this result for (9) proves the result we want for (2). To do this, we consider two possibilities: $m = 3$ and $m > 3$. If $m = 3$, consider a u_{19} satisfying

$$
\begin{array}{rl}
1: & x[x_1 x_2]y, \\
& \vdots \\
r: & xy[x_1 x_2 \cdots x_{m-2}], \\
r+1: & [x_1 x_2]xy, \\
r+2: & [x_1 x_2]yx, \\
& \vdots \\
n: & [x_1 x_2]yx.
\end{array} \tag{10}
$$

Using the result for (9) plus responsiveness, we have $C_{u_{19}}(\{x, x_1, y\}) = \{x\} = C_{u_{19}}(\{x, x_2, y\})$. Then $C_{u_{19}}(\{x, x_1, x_2, y\}) = \{x\}$, so $C_{u_{19}}(\{x, x_1, x_2\})$ contains x, and this confirms the $m = 3$ result for (2).

Now suppose $m > 3$ and look at a profile u_{20} satisfying

$$
\begin{array}{rl}
1: & xy[x_1 x_2 \cdots x_{m-2}]a, \\
& \vdots \\
r: & xy[x_1 x_2 \cdots x_{m-2}]a, \\
r+1: & y[x_1 x_2 \cdots x_{m-2}]xa, \\
r+2: & y[x_1 x_2 \cdots x_{m-2}]ax, \\
& \vdots \\
n: & y[x_1 x_2 \cdots x_{m-2}]ax.
\end{array}
$$

By the result for (9) plus responsiveness, we have $C_{u_{20}}(\{x, y, x_2, x_3, \ldots, x_{m-2}, a\}) = \{x\} = C_{u_{20}}(\{x, y, x_1, x_3, \ldots, x_{m-2}, a\})$. Then $C_{u_{20}}(\{x, y, x_1, x_2, x_3, \ldots, x_{m-2}, a\}) = \{x\}$, so $x \in C_{u_{20}}(\{x, x_1, x_2, x_3, \ldots, x_{m-2}, a\})$ and thus

$x \in C_{u_{21}}(\{x, x_1, x_2, \ldots, x_{m-2}, a\})$ for any u_{21} satisfying

$$
\begin{aligned}
1: &\quad x[x_1 x_2 \cdots x_{m-2}]a, \\
&\quad\ \vdots \\
r: &\quad x[x_1 x_2 \cdots x_{m-2}]a, \\
r+1: &\quad [x_1 x_2 \cdots x_{m-2}]xa, \\
r+2: &\quad [x_1 x_2 \cdots x_{m-2}]ax, \\
&\quad\ \vdots \\
n: &\quad [x_1 x_2 \cdots x_{m-2}]ax.
\end{aligned}
\tag{11}
$$

From (11) we construct u_{22} by inverting ax to xa for $r + 2$. By responsiveness, $C_{u_{22}}(\{x, x_1, \ldots, x_{m-2}, a\}) = \{x\}$. From u_{22} we get u_{23} by inserting $x_{m-1} \in E - \{x, x_1, \ldots, x_{m-2}, a\}$ within $[x_1, \ldots, x_{m-2}]$ in each relation:

$$
\begin{aligned}
1: &\quad x[x_1 x_2 \cdots x_{m-1}]a, \\
&\quad\ \vdots \\
r: &\quad x[x_1 x_2 \cdots x_{m-1}]a, \\
r+1: &\quad [x_1 x_2 \cdots x_{m-1}]xa, \\
r+2: &\quad [x_1 x_2 \cdots x_{m-1}]xa, \\
r+3: &\quad [x_1 x_2 \cdots x_{m-1}]ax, \\
&\quad\ \vdots \\
n: &\quad [x_1 x_2 \cdots x_{m-1}]ax.
\end{aligned}
$$

The usual analysis gives $\{x\} = C_{u_{23}}(\{x, x_1, \ldots, x_{m-1}, a\})$ and so, by independence and rationality, $x \in C_{u_{24}}(\{x, x_1, \ldots, x_{m-1}\})$ for any u_{24} satisfying

$$
\begin{aligned}
1: &\quad x[x_1 x_2 \cdots x_{m-1}], \\
&\quad\ \vdots \\
r: &\quad x[x_1 x_2 \cdots x_{m-1}], \\
r+1: &\quad [x_1 x_2 \cdots x_{m-1}]x, \\
&\quad\ \vdots \\
n: &\quad [x_1 x_2 \cdots x_{m-1}]x.
\end{aligned}
$$

But this is just the confirmation for (2) we were seeking. Thus if $|S| \leqq n - 2$ and $D_S(a_1, \ldots, a_m)$ for some $a_1, \ldots, a_m$, then S is m-ary decisive.

Now let W be a smallest set with $D_W(a_1, \ldots, a_m)$ for some $a_1, \ldots, a_m$. The m-ary Pareto condition ensures the existence of W and $W \neq \varnothing$. By the no-weak-dictator condition and our previous result, $|W| \geqq 2$. Choose $i \in W$. Partition W as $\{i\}$ and $W - \{i\} \neq \varnothing$. We seek to show that $|N|$ exceeds any finite limit and this will be done by showing $|N - W| > 0$ and $|N - W| \geqq |W|$, in such a way that the series can clearly be continued as

$$|N - W| \geq |W| + 1, \quad |N - W| \geq |W| + 2, \quad |N - W| \geq |W| + 3, \ldots.$$

First, then, we show $|N - W| > 0$. If not, $N - W = \varnothing$, and we look at profile u_{25} satisfying

$$i: \quad a_1 \cdots a_{m-1}x,$$
$$W - \{i\}: \quad xa_1 \cdots a_{m-1}.$$

By the definition of W, $x \notin C_{u_{25}}(\{a_1, \ldots, a_{m-1}, x\})$. Using the Pareto condition, $C_{u_{25}}(\{a_1, \ldots, a_{m-1}, x\}) = \{a_1\}$. This gives $D_{\{i\}}(a_1, \ldots, a_{m-1}, x)$, contrary to the definition of W.

Next we wish to show $|N - W| \geq |W|$. Examine u_{26} satisfying

$$i: \quad yxa_1 \cdots a_{m-1},$$
$$W - \{i\}: \quad xa_1a_2ya_3 \cdots a_{m-1},$$
$$N - W: \quad a_1ya_2 \cdots a_{m-1}x.$$

We shall need as an intermediate result $C_{u_{26}}(\{x, y, a_1, \ldots, a_{m-1}\}) = \{a_1\}$. That no a_i is chosen for $i > 1$ is seen by the Pareto condition. We must rule out x and y. Here we will treat y, leaving the calculation for x as an exercise.

Suppose $y \in C_{u_{26}}(\{x, y, a_1, \ldots, a_{m-1}\})$. Then by rationality, responsiveness, and independence, $C_{u_{27}}(\{x, y, a_1, \ldots, a_{m-1}\}) = \{y\}$ for any u_{27} satisfying

$$i: \quad ya_1a_2 \cdots a_{m-1},$$
$$W - \{i\}: \quad a_1ya_2a_3 \cdots a_{m-1},$$
$$N - W: \quad a_1ya_2 \cdots a_{m-1}.$$

We get u_{28} by inserting $z \in E - \{y, a_1, \ldots, a_{m-1}\}$ after a_1 in each relation:

$$i: \quad ya_1za_2 \cdots a_{m-1},$$
$$W - \{i\}: \quad a_1zya_2a_3 \cdots a_{m-1}, \tag{12}$$
$$N - W: \quad a_1zya_2 \cdots a_{m-1}.$$

$z \notin C_{u_{28}}(\{z, y, a_1, \ldots, a_{m-1}\})$ by the Pareto condition; rationality and independence exclude everything else but y. Therefore $C_{u_{28}}(\{z, y, a_1, \ldots, a_{m-1}\}) = \{y\}$. Another application of rationality and independence yields $y \in C_{u_{29}}(\{z, y, a_1, \ldots, a_{m-2}\})$ for any u_{29} satisfying

$$i: \quad ya_1za_2 \cdots a_{m-2},$$
$$W - \{i\}: \quad a_1zya_2 \cdots a_{m-2}, \tag{13}$$
$$N - W: \quad a_1zya_2 \cdots a_{m-2}.$$

By independence and responsiveness, $C_{u_{30}}(\{y, z, a_1, \ldots, a_{m-2}\}) = \{y\}$ for u_{30} satisfying

$$
\begin{array}{ll}
i\colon & ya_1za_2 \cdots a_{m-2}, \\
W - \{i\}\colon & a_1yza_2 \cdots a_{m-2}, \\
N - W\colon & a_1zya_2 \cdots a_{m-2}.
\end{array}
$$

Insert t after a_1 to get u_{31} satisfying

$$
\begin{array}{ll}
i\colon & ya_1tza_2 \cdots a_{m-2}, \\
W - \{i\}\colon & a_1tyza_2 \cdots a_{m-2}, \\
N - W\colon & a_1tzya_2 \cdots a_{m-2}.
\end{array}
$$

By the usual analysis, $C_{u_{31}}(\{y, t, z, a_1, \ldots, a_{m-2}\}) = \{y\}$. Hence $y \in C_{u_{31}}(\{y, t, z, a_1, \ldots, a_{m-3}\})$, so $y \in C_{u_{32}}(\{y, t, z, a_1, \ldots, a_{m-3}\})$ for any u_{32} satisfying

$$
\begin{array}{ll}
i\colon & ya_1tza_2 \cdots a_{m-3}, \\
W - \{i\}\colon & a_1tyza_2 \cdots a_{m-3}, \\
N - W\colon & a_1tzya_2 \cdots a_{m-3}.
\end{array}
$$

Invert zy to yz and use independence and responsiveness to get $C_{u_{33}}(\{y, t, z, a_1, \ldots, a_{m-3}\})$, where u_{33} satisfies

$$
\begin{array}{ll}
i\colon & ya_1tza_2 \cdots a_{m-3}, \\
W - \{i\}\colon & a_1tyza_2 \cdots a_{m-3}, \\
N - W\colon & a_1tyza_2 \cdots a_{m-3}.
\end{array}
$$

Insert p after a_1 to get u_{34} satisfying

$$
\begin{array}{ll}
i\colon & ya_1ptza_2 \cdots a_{m-3}, \\
W - \{i\}\colon & a_1ptyza_2 \cdots a_{m-3}, \\
N - W\colon & a_1ptyza_2 \cdots a_{m-3}.
\end{array}
$$

Again the usual analysis is applied to get $C_{u_{34}}(\{y, p, t, z, a_1, \ldots, a_{m-3}\}) = \{y\}$, and so $y \in C_{u_{35}}(\{y, p, t, a_1, \ldots, a_{m-3}\})$ for any u_{35} satisfying

$$
\begin{array}{lll}
i\colon & ya_1pta_2 \cdots a_{m-3}, & \\
W - \{i\}\colon & a_1ptya_2 \cdots a_{m-3}, & \text{(14)} \\
N - W\colon & a_1ptya_2 \cdots a_{m-3}. &
\end{array}
$$

Looking at (13) and (14), we see that we keep y among the chosen elements as we move y down the lists for everyone in $N - \{i\}$. Eventually we find

$y \in C_{u_{36}}(\{y, a_1, p, t, \ldots, r, s\})$, where u_{36} satisfies

$$i: \quad ya_1pt \cdots rs,$$
$$W - \{i\}: \quad a_1pt \cdots rsy,$$
$$N - W: \quad a_1pt \cdots rsy.$$

Hence $D_{\{i\}}(y, a_1, p, t, \ldots, r, s)$, contrary to our choice of W. Hence going back to our last assumption, we get $y \notin C_{u_{26}}(\{x, y, a_1, \ldots, a_{m-1}\})$. As we observed, x can be similarly excluded so that $C_{u_{26}}(\{x, y, a_1, \ldots, a_{m-1}\}) = \{a_1\}$. Then $a_1 \in C_{u_{37}}(\{x, y, a_1, a_3, \ldots, a_{m-1}\})$, where u_{37} satisfies

$$i: \quad yxa_1a_3 \cdots a_{m-1},$$
$$W - \{i\}: \quad xa_1ya_3 \cdots a_{m-1},$$
$$N - W: \quad a_1ya_3 \cdots a_{m-1}x.$$

Invert xa_1 to a_1x for i, getting $C_{u_{38}}(\{y, x, a_1, a_3, \ldots, a_{m-1}\}) = \{a_1\}$, where

$$i: \quad ya_1xa_3 \cdots a_{m-1},$$
$$W - \{i\}: \quad xa_1ya_3 \cdots a_{m-1},$$
$$N - W: \quad a_1ya_3 \cdots a_{m-1}x.$$

Now obtain u_{39} by inserting $p_1 \in E - \{x, y, a_1, a_3, \ldots, a_{m-1}\}$:

$$i: \quad yp_1a_1xa_3 \cdots a_{m-1},$$
$$W - \{i\}: \quad p_1xa_1ya_3 \cdots a_{m-1},$$
$$N - W: \quad a_1ya_3 \cdots a_{m-1}xp_1.$$

We want to show $C_{u_{39}}(\{x, y, p_1, a_1, a_3, \ldots, a_{m-1}\}) = \{a_1\}$. All but a_1 and p_1 are ruled out by rationality and the Pareto condition. Suppose $p_1 \in C_{u_{39}}(\{x, y, p_1, a_1, a_3, \ldots, a_{m-1}\})$, so $p_1 \in C_{u_{40}}(\{x, y, a_3, \ldots, a_{m-1}, p_1\})$ for any u_{40} satisfying

$$i: \quad yp_1xa_3 \cdots a_{m-1},$$
$$W - \{i\}: \quad p_1xya_3 \cdots a_{m-1},$$
$$N - W: \quad ya_3 \cdots a_{m-1}xp_1.$$

Inverting xp_1 to p_1x for $N - W$ gives u_{41}:

$$i: \quad yp_1xa_3 \cdots a_{m-1},$$
$$W - \{i\}: \quad p_1xya_3 \cdots a_{m-1},$$
$$N - W: \quad ya_3 \cdots a_{m-1}p_1x,$$

with $C_{u_{41}}(\{x, y, p_1, a_3, \ldots, a_{m-1}\}) = \{p_1\}$. Get u_{42} by inserting p_2 after y in each ordering:

$$
\begin{aligned}
i: \quad & y p_2 p_1 x a_3 \cdots a_{m-1}, \\
W - \{i\}: \quad & p_1 x y p_2 a_3 \cdots a_{m-1}, \\
N - W: \quad & y p_2 a_3 \cdots a_{m-1} p_1 x.
\end{aligned}
$$

The usual analysis has $\{p_1\} = C_{u_{42}}(\{x, y, p_1, p_2, a_3, \ldots, a_{m-1}\})$, and so $p_1 \in C_{u_{43}}(\{y, p_1, p_2, a_3, \ldots, a_{m-1}\})$ for any u_{43} satisfying

$$
\begin{aligned}
i: \quad & y p_2 p_1 a_3 \cdots a_{m-1}, \\
W - \{i\}: \quad & p_1 y p_2 a_3 \cdots a_{m-1}, \\
N - W: \quad & y p_2 a_3 \cdots a_{m-1} p_1.
\end{aligned}
$$

By responsiveness, $C_{u_{44}}(\{y, p_1, p_2, a_3, \ldots, a_{m-1}\}) = \{p_1\}$ for u_{44} satisfying

$$
\begin{aligned}
i: \quad & y p_2 p_1 a_3 \cdots a_{m-1}, \\
W - \{i\}: \quad & p_1 y p_2 a_3 \cdots a_{m-1}, \\
N - W: \quad & y p_2 p_1 a_3 \cdots a_{m-1}.
\end{aligned}
\tag{15}
$$

But comparing (15) and (12) we see that having p_1 chosen here would lead to $D_{W-\{i\}}(p_1, y, p_2, a_3, \ldots, a_{m-1})$, contrary to our choice of W. Going back to our last assumption, this contradiction rules out $p_1 \in C_{u_{39}}(\{x, y, p_1, a_1, a_3, \ldots, a_{m-1}\})$. Hence $C_{u_{39}}(\{x, y, p_1, a_1, a_3, \ldots, a_{m-1}\}) = \{a_1\}$. Dropping y and inverting $x a_1$ to $a_1 x$ for $W - \{i\}$ gives $C_{u_{45}}(\{x, p_1, a_1, a_3, \ldots, a_{m-1}\}) = \{a_1\}$ for any u_{45} satisfying

$$
\begin{aligned}
i: \quad & p_1 a_1 x a_3 \cdots a_{m-1}, \\
W - \{i\}: \quad & p_1 a_1 x a_3 \cdots a_{m-1}, \\
N - W: \quad & a_1 a_3 \cdots a_{m-1} x p_1.
\end{aligned}
$$

As in the usual analysis, p_2 is inserted after p_1 in each relation and x is dropped, giving $a_1 \in C_{u_{46}}(\{p_1, p_2, a_1, a_3, \ldots, a_{m-1}\})$ for u_{46} satisfying

$$
\begin{aligned}
W: \quad & p_1 p_2 a_1 a_3 \cdots a_{m-1}, \\
N - W: \quad & a_1 a_3 \cdots a_{m-1} p_1 p_2.
\end{aligned}
\tag{16}
$$

Following our procedures, we can operate on (16) to lower a_1 in W orderings, keeping a_1 chosen, ultimately leading to $D_{N-W}(a_1, z_1, \ldots, a_{m-1})$ for suitable z_i's. The choice of W then guarantees $|N - W| \geq |W|$. Since then $|N - W| \geq 2$, we can split $N - W$ up as $\{j\}$ and Z and show $|Z| \geq |W|$ or $|N - W| \geq |W| + 1$ and continue until $|N - W|$ is shown to exceed any specified finite bound. For more details, the reader is referred to Fishburn [122]. $\square$

Exercises

1. Prove Theorem 7-1.
2. State and prove an adaptation of Theorem 7-1 to include a restriction of admissible profiles to those satisfying the individualistic conditions of selfishness and monotonicity.
3. Treat Case 2 in the proofs of Theorems 7-5 and 7-6.
4. Prove Theorem 7-8.
5. Prove Theorem 7-9.
6. Extend the proof of Theorem 7-11 to $|N - W| \geqq |W| + 1$.

8 DOMAIN: PART II

In this chapter we consider the effects of four different revisions of the domain for a collective choice rule, none of which is a contraction revision like those of the previous chapter. In the first revision, the set N of individuals is no longer constrained to be finite. As noted in Chapter 4, this revision permits construction of collective choice rules which satisfy all Arrow's conditions. However, an impossibility result by Kirman and Sondermann can be shown to hold for the infinite N case.

The second revision considers populations of different sizes. Each profile has only finitely many orderings, but not all profiles have the same number of orderings. We present some investigations (motivated by a study by Smith) on impossibility results for such situations. The third revision has collective choice operating on "cardinal" utilities rather than preference preorderings.

The largest part of this chapter is devoted to collective choice rules on profiles that represent "extended" preferences of the form: individual i would rather be individual j in social state x than be individual k in social state y. The extra information available in such orderings does not enable us to bypass the kinds of theorems we have already obtained for "regular" preferences.

Infinite N

The case in which the set of individuals is no longer constrained to be finite is best studied by means of filters and ultrafilters. We now turn to a digression on filter theory.

A *filter* $\mathcal{F}$ on a set N (not necessarily finite) is a subset of 2^N having the properties

   (i) $N \in \mathcal{F}$,
   (ii) $\varnothing \notin \mathcal{F}$,
   (iii) $A \in \mathcal{F}\ \&\ A \subseteq B \subseteq N \to B \in \mathcal{F}$,
   (iv) $A, B \in \mathcal{F} \to A \cap B \in \mathcal{F}$.

If $\mathcal{F}$ and $\mathcal{F}'$ are two filters on N, $\mathcal{F}'$ is said to be strictly *finer* than $\mathcal{F}$ when $\mathcal{F} \subsetneq \mathcal{F}'$. An ultrafilter U on N is a filter on N such that there is no filter on N strictly finer than U. Let X be the set of all filters at least as fine as $\mathcal{F}$ and let Q be any nonempty ascending chain of elements of X. Then

$$\bigcup_{Y \in Q} Y$$

is easily seen to be a filter on N at least as fine as $\mathcal{F}$. Zorn's lemma (see Mathematical Appendix) may then be invoked to prove that there is a filter U on N in X which is maximal with respect to the $\subseteq$-ordering. U is clearly an ultrafilter. Thus, for every filter $\mathcal{F}$ on N, there is an ultrafilter U on N at least as fine as $\mathcal{F}$.

Lemma 8-1   A filter $\mathcal{F}$ on N is an ultrafilter on N iff for every subset S of N, either S or $N - S$ is an element of $\mathcal{F}$.

   Proof   Suppose $\mathcal{F}$ is an ultrafilter. Consider

$$\mathcal{F}' = \mathcal{F} \cup \{S \cap A \,|\, A \in \mathcal{F}\} \qquad \text{and} \qquad \mathcal{F}'' = \mathcal{F} \cup \{(N - S) \cap A \,|\, A \in \mathcal{F}\}.$$

First we show that one of these is a filter. Clearly both satisfy (i), (iii), and (iv) of the definition. If $\mathcal{F}'$ is not a filter, the reason must be that $S \cap A = \varnothing$ for some A in $\mathcal{F}$. Let B be any element of $\mathcal{F}$. If $(N - S) \cap B = \varnothing$, then we would have $A \subseteq N - S$ and $B \subseteq S$, so $A \cap B = \varnothing \notin \mathcal{F}$, contrary to (iv). Therefore $(N - S) \cap B \neq \varnothing$ for all $B \in \mathcal{F}$, so $\mathcal{F}''$ satisfies (ii) and is a filter. If $\mathcal{F}''$ is a filter, it is finer than $\mathcal{F}$ and, since $\mathcal{F}$ is maximal, $\mathcal{F} = \mathcal{F}''$, so $(N - S) = (N - S) \cap N \in \mathcal{F}$. If $\mathcal{F}'$ is a filter, $S \in \mathcal{F}$. Therefore either S or $N - S$ is in $\mathcal{F}$.

Now suppose $\mathcal{F}$ satisfies the condition that S or $N - S$ is in $\mathcal{F}$ for every $S \in 2^N$. If $\mathcal{F} \subsetneq \mathcal{F}'$, where $\mathcal{F}'$ is a filter, let T be an element of $\mathcal{F}'$ not in $\mathcal{F}$. Then $N - T \in \mathcal{F}$, so $N - T \in \mathcal{F}'$ and then $\varnothing = T \cap (N - T) \in \mathcal{F}'$, contrary to the assumption that $\mathcal{F}'$ is a filter. Thus no such $\mathcal{F}'$ exists and $\mathcal{F}$ is an ultrafilter. $\square$

We now provide some examples. Clearly $\{N\}$ alone is a filter on N. Also, if x and y are distinct elements of N, $\{S \,|\, \{x, y\} \subseteq S \subseteq N\}$ is a filter on N. If $|N| > 1$, the first is not an ultrafilter. The second is not an ultrafilter since neither $\{x\}$ nor $N - \{x\}$ are in N. If $x \in N$, then $\{S \,|\, x \in S \subseteq N\}$ *is* an ultrafilter on N. For finite N, this is the typical case.

Lemma 8-2 If $|N| < \infty$ and U is an ultrafilter on N, there is an $x \in N$ such that $U = \{S \mid x \in S \subseteq N\}$.

Proof Since N is finite, there are only finitely many elements of U. Successive application of (iv) says

$$\bigcap_{A \in U} A \in U.$$

By (ii), $\bigcap_{A \in U} A \neq \varnothing$. Let x be an element of $\bigcap_{A \in U} A$; every $S \in U$ satisfies $x \in S \subseteq N$. If $y \neq x$ and $y \in \bigcap_{A \in U} A$, then neither $\{x\}$ nor $N - \{x\}$ is in U, contrary to Lemma 8-1. Therefore $\bigcap_{A \in U} A = \{x\}$. Hence $\{x\} \in U$, and then (iii) tells us that every S satisfying $x \in S \subseteq N$ must be in U. $\square$

Closely related to Lemma 8-2 is the following terminology. A filter $\mathscr{F}$ is *free* if $\bigcap_{A \in \mathscr{F}} A = \varnothing$; otherwise $\mathscr{F}$ is *fixed*. If there is a nonempty set T such that $\mathscr{F} = \{S \mid T \subseteq S \subseteq N\}$, then $\mathscr{F}$ is called *principal* and T is the *base* of $\mathscr{F}$. Clearly $\mathscr{F}$ is fixed if and only if it is principal. Lemma 8-2 tells us that any ultrafilter on a finite set is fixed and has a singleton base. Again it is clear that *if* an *ultrafilter* has a base, it must be a singleton base. However, when N is not finite, some ultrafilters have no base.

Lemma 8-3 If N is infinite, there exist free ultrafilters on N.

Proof Let $\mathscr{F}$ be the set of all subsets S of N such that the cardinality of $N - S$ is finite, i.e., $\mathscr{F}$ is the set of "cofinite" sets. $\mathscr{F}$ is a filter but, by Lemma 1, not an ultrafilter. However, as we noted earlier, Zorn's lemma tells us the existence of an ultrafilter U finer than $\mathscr{F}$. If U were fixed, it would have a base T which, as we have seen, must be a singleton $T = \{x\}$. But $N - \{x\} \in \mathscr{F} \subseteq U$, and so $\{x\}$ cannot be a base for U. Thus U is free. $\square$

We will now present the connection between ultrafilters and social choice theory. Given a collective choice rule f on U, V, let $\mathscr{F}_f$ be the set of all sets of individuals that are weakly, globally pairwise decisive between every pair of alternatives. We will confirm that, for certain collective choice rules, $\mathscr{F}_f$ satisfies the properties of an ultrafilter. This series of results is due to Hansson [158] and, independently, to Kirman and Sondermann [199].

Lemma 8-4 If $A \in \mathscr{F}_f$ and $A \subseteq B$, then $B \in \mathscr{F}_f$.

Proof This is immediate from the definition of weak, global pairwise decisiveness. $\square$

Lemma 8-5 If f satisfies the weak pairwise Pareto condition, $N \in \mathscr{F}_f$.

Proof The weak pairwise Pareto condition is precisely the statement that N is weakly, globally pairwise decisive between every pair of alternatives. $\square$

Lemma 8-6 If U contains a profile u such that for some x, $y \in E$, $xP_{iu}y$ for all $i \in N$ and if f satisfies the weak Pareto condition, then $\varnothing \notin \mathscr{F}_f$.

Proof For the profile u of the lemma, everyone in $\varnothing$ strictly prefers $\dot{y}$ to x and $C(\{x, y\}) = \{x\}$ by the Pareto condition. Thus $\varnothing$ is not weakly pairwise decisive for y against x and so $\varnothing \notin \mathscr{F}$. $\square$

Lemma 8-7 Suppose f on U, V satisfies the conditions

(i) domain,
    (a) V contains all finite members of $2^E - \{\varnothing\}$,
    (b) $|E| \geq 3$,
    (c) $U = (R_E)^N$, the set of all functions from N to R_E,
    (d) f is total on U, V,
(ii) quasitransitivity of the base relation,
(iii) independence of irrelevant alternatives.

Then if A, $B \in \mathscr{F}_f$, we have $A \cap B \in \mathscr{F}_f$.

Proof Let u be any profile with restricted orderings

$$A \cap B: \quad xy,$$
$$N - (A \cap B): \quad [xy].$$

Consider u_1 with orderings

$$A \cap B: \quad xzy,$$
$$A - B: \quad [xy]z,$$
$$N - A: \quad z[xy].$$

By $xPD_A z$, $C_{u_1}(\{x, z\}) = \{x\}$. By $zPD_B y$, $C_{u_1}(\{z, y\}) = \{z\}$. Base quasitransitivity yields $C_{u_1}(\{x, y\}) = \{x\}$, and independence of irrelevant alternatives then gives $C_u(\{x, y\}) = \{x\}$. Thus $xPD_{A \cap B} y$. But x and y were arbitrary, so $A \cap B \in \mathscr{F}_f$. $\square$

The domain condition of Lemma 8-7 is just the standard domain restriction relaxed to allow infinite N.

Lemma 8-8 Suppose f on U, V satisfies

(i) domain, as in Lemma 8-7,
(ii) transitivity of the base relation,
(iii) independence of irrelevant alternatives.

Then if $A \subseteq N$, either $A \in \mathscr{F}_f$ or $N - A \in \mathscr{F}_f$.

Proof We first show that

$$\neg yPD_{N-A}x \to xPD_A z \quad \text{for all} \quad z \text{ not in } \{x, y\}. \tag{1}$$

Consider any u with

$$A: \quad xz,$$
$$N - A: \quad [xz].$$

From $\neg yPD_{N-A}x$ there is a profile u_1 with

$$A: \quad [xy],$$
$$N - A: \quad yx,$$

and $x \in C_{u_1}(\{x, y\})$. Finally, look at profile u_2 with

$$A: \quad [xy]z,$$
$$N - A: \quad y[xz].$$

By independence, $x \in C_{u_2}(\{x, y\}) = C_{u_1}(\{x, y\})$. By the Pareto condition, $C_{u_2}(\{y, z\}) = \{y\}$. By transitivity, $C_{u_2}(\{x, z\}) = \{x\}$. Another application of independence yields $C_u(\{x, z\}) = \{x\}$, so xPD_Az.

Similarly, it can be shown that

$$\neg yPD_{N-A}x \to zPD_A y \qquad \text{for all} \quad z \text{ not in } \{x, y\}. \tag{2}$$

Now suppose $N - A \notin \mathscr{F}_f$. Then for some x, $y \in E$, $\neg yPD_{N-A}x$. By (1) and (2),

$$xPD_A z \qquad \text{and} \qquad zPD_A y. \tag{3}$$

But then $\neg zPD_{N-A}x$, so by (1)

$$xPD_A y. \tag{4}$$

(3) also yields $\neg yPD_{N-A}z$, and another application of (1) to this gives

$$zPD_A x. \tag{5}$$

Thus $\neg xPD_{N-A}z$, and (2) on this gives

$$yPD_A x. \tag{6}$$

Finally, from $\neg zPD_{N-A}x$ we use (2) to get

$$yPD_A z. \tag{7}$$

Combining (3)–(7), we see A is decisive between every pair of distinct alternatives in $\{x, y, z\}$. Using the same argument of Blau used in the proof of Theorem 4-3, we see that A is decisive between every pair of alternatives in E, i.e., $A \in \mathscr{F}_f$. $\square$

This series of lemmas allows us to develop a proof of Arrow's second impossibility theorem, supplementing the proofs given in Chapter 4 by Arrow and by Fishburn.

Alternative Proof of Theorem 4-3 (Hansson [158], Kirman and Sondermann [199]) If f satisfies the standard domain constraint, the weak Pareto condition, independence of irrelevant alternatives, and transitive rationality, then all the assumptions of Lemmas 8-4 to 8-8 hold. Hence $\mathscr{F}_f$, the set of weak, global pairwise decisive sets, is an ultrafilter on N. Since N is finite (by the standard domain constraint), Lemma 8-2 tells us $\mathscr{F}_f$ has a singleton base $\{i\}$. Then $\{i\}$ is weakly, globally pairwise decisive. With transitive rationality, $\{i\}$ is a general dictator. $\square$

The payoff from this approach is the insight provided to the case in which N is infinite. As we noted in Chapter 4, if Arrow's conditions are revised only to the extent that the standard domain restriction changes to the domain constraint of Lemma 8-7 (i.e., if infinite N is allowed), then the revised conditions are consistent. An f satisfying such revised conditions is obtained as follows. By Lemma 8-3, there exist free ultrafilters on N; let U be one such. Given u, define the relation $P(u)$ by

$$yP(u)x \qquad \text{iff} \quad \{i \mid xP_{iu}y\} \in U.$$

Then $xR(u)y$ is defined as $\neg yP(u)x$ and C_u is given by the rule that $C_u(v)$ is the set of $R(u)$-best elements of v. Finally, f is defined so as to assign C_u to u. It is an exercise for the reader to confirm that this f satisfies the revised Arrow conditions and that $\mathscr{F}_f = U$ (Hansson [158]).

Kirman and Sondermann have presented some results to show that infinite N cases do not get us as far from dictators as our discussion to this point would suggest. They demonstrate that small decisive sets must still exist. The first trick is to clarify "small" when N is infinite. For this purpose, N is made into an atomless measure space by identifying a set $\mathscr{N}$ of coalitions, i.e., a subset of 2^N and a measure λ on $\mathscr{N}$ such that the following conditions are satisfied:

(1) $\mathscr{N}$ is a σ-algebra, i.e., $\mathscr{N}$ contains $\varnothing$ and N and is closed under complementation and a countable union operation,
(2) λ is a probability measure on $\mathscr{N}$, i.e.,
  (a) λ maps each element of $\mathscr{N}$ into $[0,1]$,
  (b) λ is countably additive, i.e.,

$$\lambda\left(\bigcup_{n=1}^{\infty} E_n\right) = \sum_{n=1}^{\infty} \lambda(E_n),$$

where each $E_n \in \mathcal{N}$ and $n \neq n' \rightarrow E_n \cap E_{n'} = \emptyset$,

    (c) $\lambda(N) = 1$,

(3) $\mathcal{N}$, with λ, is "atomless," i.e.,

    if $\lambda(C) > 0$, there is a $C' \in \mathcal{N}$ with $C' \subseteq C$ and $\lambda(C) > \lambda(C') > 0$.

Since $\mathcal{N}$, with λ, is atomless, no singleton coalition $\{i\}$ has positive measure. This suggests that no individual is decisive. The goal is to show that "arbitrarily" small coalitions (of *positive* measure) can be found that are decisive. We shall say that a collective choice rule f on U, V, where $\mathcal{N}$, with λ, is an atomless measure space, is *measure-dictatorial* if, for each $\varepsilon > 0$, there is a coalition C in $\mathcal{N}$, $C \neq \emptyset$ with $\lambda(C) < \varepsilon$ such that C is weakly, globally pairwise decisive between every pair of distinct alternatives.

Theorem 8-9   There is no collective choice rule f on U, V with $f : u \mapsto C_u$ satisfying

  (i) domain,
    (a) V contains all finite members of $2^E - \{\emptyset\}$,
    (b) $|E| \geq 3$,
    (c) $U = (R_E)^N$,
    (d) f is total on U, V,
  (ii) each C_u has a reflexive, complete, and transitive rationalization $R(u)$,
  (iii) independence of irrelevant alternatives,
  (iv) the weak Pareto condition,
  (v) not measure-dictatorial.

Proof   Since $\mathcal{N}$, with λ, is atomless, we can find for each $\varepsilon > 0$ a finite partition $\pi = (N_1, \ldots, N_m)$ of N into elements of $\mathcal{N}$ such that $\lambda(N_i) < \varepsilon$ for each $i = 1, 2, \ldots, m$. [Exercise: Prove this.] Since, by conditions (i)–(iv), each assumption of Lemmas 8-4 to 8-8 holds, the set of decisive sets for f is an ultrafilter $\mathcal{F}$. The theorem will be proved if we can show that one of the N_i's is in $\mathcal{F}$. But if none of $N_1, \ldots, N_{m-1}$ is in $\mathcal{F}$, each of their complements $N - N_1, \ldots, N - N_{m-1}$ is; then

$$N_m = \bigcap_{i=1}^{m-1} (N - N_i) \in \mathcal{F}. \qquad \square$$

After obtaining this theorem, Kirman and Sondermann topologize N, embed the result in a compact space $\bar{N}$, and prove that if conditions (i)–(iv) of Theorem 8-9 are satisfied, there is an "invisible dictator" $\bar{i}$ in $\bar{N}$, not in N (hence invisible), such that if $\bar{f}$ is the unique extension of f to $(R^E)^{\bar{N}}$, then if $xP_{\bar{i}}y$ on $\bar{u} \in (R^E)^{\bar{N}}$, $\bar{C}_{\bar{u}}(\{x, y\}) = \{x\}$, where $\bar{C}_{\bar{u}} = \bar{f}(\bar{u})$. For details, the interested reader is referred to their paper [158].

Variable Population Size[1]

In this section we no longer assume that a collective choice rule f need work only on profiles of a single fixed size. We demand greater flexibility, replacing

$$U = (R_E)^n \quad \text{for some } n$$

by

$$U = \bigcup_{n=1}^{\infty} (R_E)^n.$$

For such a flexible rule, Smith [321] proposes several interesting new constraints. The one we shall need here is separability. Given $u = (R_1, \ldots, R_r)$ and $u' = (R_1', \ldots, R_s')$, we define $u + u'$ to be the $(r + s)$-element profile $(R_1, \ldots, R_r, R_1', \ldots, R_s')$. With this definition, addition of profiles is associative. Where m is a positive integer, mu will be the mr-element profile $u + u + \cdots + u$ with m summands. A collective choice rule $f: u \mapsto C_u$ satisfies *separability* if whenever $x \in C_u(\{x, y\})$ and $C_{u'}(\{x, y\}) = \{x\}$, we have $C_{u+u'}(\{x, y\}) = \{x\}$.

The following theorem is adapted from Smith's investigations [321].

Theorem 8-10   There does not exist a collective choice rule $f: u \mapsto C_u$ satisfying

   (i)   domain,
      (a) $|E| \geq 3$,
      (b) V contains all one- and two-element members of $2^E - \{\varnothing\}$,
      (c) $U = \bigcup_{n=1}^{\infty} (R_E)^n$,
      (d) f is total on U, V,
  (ii)   triple acyclicity of the base relation,
 (iii)   neutrality,
 (iv)   anonymity,
  (v)   the weak pairwise Pareto condition,
 (vi)   separability,
(vii)   independence of irrelevant alternatives.

Proof   Let $R_1 \in R_E$ satisfy $x P_1 y$ and $R_2 \in R_E$ satisfy $y P_2 x$. By neutrality, anonymity, and independence, $C_u(\{x, y\}) = \{x, y\}$, where $u = (R_1, R_2)$. By the weak Pareto condition, if $u_0 = (R_1)$, then $C_{u_0}(\{x, y\}) = \{x\}$. By separability,

$$C_{u+u_0}(\{x, y\}) = \{x\}.$$

[1] For useful suggestions on this section, I am indebted to the students in the social choice seminar at the University of Minnesota, Spring 1976.

Using anonymity, we obtain

$$u_1 = (R_1, R_1, R_2) \to C_{u_1}(\{x, y\}) = \{x\}. \tag{8}$$

Now suppose $R_3 \in R_E$ satisfies $yI_3 x$. By neutrality, if $u_3 = (R_3)$, then $C_{u_3}(\{x, y\}) = \{x, y\}$. By separability,

$$C_{u_3 + 2u_0}(\{x, y\}) = \{x\}.$$

By anonymity,

$$u_4 = (R_1, R_1, R_3) \to C_{u_4}(\{x, y\}) = \{x\}. \tag{9}$$

Let u be any profile in which a fraction greater than or equal to $\frac{2}{3}$ of all orderings has $xP_{iu}y$. Then with each ordering having $yR_{ju}x$ we can associate two with $xP_{iu}y$, and combining (8) and (9) with applications of anonymity, the weak Pareto condition, and separability we obtain $xP(u)y$. By neutrality, this result works on all pairs $\{x, y\}$. Sets making up a fraction at least as large as $\frac{2}{3}$ of all individuals are weakly, globally pairwise decisive between all pairs of alternatives. The standard voting paradox example (with $n = 3$) then yields a violation of triple acyclicity. $\square$

In comparison with (Hansson's) Theorem 5-7, weakening the regularity condition from transitive rationality to triple acyclicity has been offset only by great strengthenings of some assumptions and adding several very strong new ones. Much further research remains to be done on variable-population problems, but we now turn to a quite different sort of domain revision.

Cardinal Utility

A common response to Arrow's research has been criticism of the independence of irrelevant alternatives criterion, and some claim that consideration of other alternatives would allow the incorporation of information about intensities of preference or cardinal utility. We see, for example, Weldon's attitude [343]: "Arrow's theorem provides ... a *reductio ad absurdum* of the ordinal hypothesis." Where collective choice rules operate on cardinal utilities, a common candidate for avoiding many of the impossibility theorems is something such as

$$\sum_{i=1}^{n} u_i \quad \text{or} \quad \sum_{i=1}^{n} g(u_i)$$

(see, e.g., Kemp and Asimakopulous [197] or Hildreth [165]). Samuelson has suggested that this "solution" to a formal social choice problem is not well founded in classical political philosophy:

> Except for a few utilitarians, drunk on poorly understood post-Newtonian mathematical moonshine, I can find in the ethical writings of recorded cultures scarcely any importance attached to the special welfare functions of additive cardinal utility. [291, p. 36]

We will develop sufficient machinery to present an impossibility theorem on cardinal utilities conjectured by Samuelson [292] and proved by Kalai and Schmeidler [182]. Where r is the set of real numbers, partition r^E into a set Z of nonempty subsets. $X \in Z$ iff $X \neq \varnothing$ and the following conditions are satisfied:

(i) $x, y \in X \rightarrow$ there exist α, $\beta \in r$, $\alpha > 0$, such that $x(a) = \alpha y(a) + \beta$ for all $a \in E$,

(ii) if $x \in r^E$ is in X and there exist α, $\beta \in r$ with $\alpha > 0$, then y, defined by $y(a) = \alpha x(a) + \beta$, is also in X.

An element X of Z is a *cardinal preference relation* over E.

A cardinal collective choice rule is a mapping f from Z^n to Z. Thus transitive rationality is built in here (cardinal rules will be discussed only in this section of this chapter). An element $u \in Z^n$ will be called a *cardinal profile*. f satisfies *cardinal independence of irrelevant alternatives* (CIIA) if for any subset B of cardinality 3,

$$u|_B = u'|_B \qquad \text{implies} \quad f(u)|_B = f(u')|_B.$$

f satisfies the *cardinal Pareto* condition if for every a, $b \in E$ and every $u = (X_1, X_2, \ldots, X_n)$ such that $x_i \in X_i$ implies $x_i(a) > x_i(b)$, we have $x(a) > x(b)$ for every x in $f(u)$.

Now suppose f is a cardinal collective choice rule satisfying the cardinal Pareto condition and CIIA. Given a cardinal preference relation X, define $\pi(X)$ to be the preordering on E determined by X:

$$a\pi(X)b \qquad \text{iff} \quad x(a) \geq x(b) \qquad \text{for all} \quad x \in X.$$

Given $u = (X_1, \ldots, X_n) \in Z^n$, define $\pi(u)$ as $(\pi(X_1), \ldots, \pi(X_n))$. Since E is assumed finite, for any $R \in R_E$, there is an $X \in Z$ such that $\pi(X) = R$. Then from $f : Z^n \rightarrow Z$ we define a collective choice rule

$$\underline{f} : R_E{}^n \rightarrow \mathscr{C} \qquad \text{where} \quad \underline{f}(u) = C_u$$

for $u = (R_1, \ldots, R_n)$ and

$$C_u(v) = \{x \in v \,|\, xR(u)y \text{ for all } y \in v\} \qquad \text{where} \quad R(u) = \pi(f(X_1, \ldots, X_n))$$

for some $X_1, \ldots, X_n$ satisfying $\pi(X_i) = R_i$. $\underline{f}$ has a complete reflexive and transitive rationalization, and $\underline{f}$ is total on $U = R_E{}^n$ and $V = 2^E - \{\varnothing\}$. Since f satisfies the cardinal Pareto condition, it is easily seen that $\underline{f}$ satisfies the weak pairwise Pareto condition. By an argument very similar to Blau's derivation of 2-ary independence from 3-ary independence (see Theorem 3-15), Kalai and Schmeidler use the CIIA condition of f to prove $\underline{f}$ satisfies independence of irrelevant alternatives. Using Arrow's second impossibility theorem (Theorem 4-3), we see that $\underline{f}$ is dictatorial, say by individual j. Then f is dictatorial in the sense that if at $u = (X_1, \ldots, X_n)$, we have $x_j(a) > x_j(b)$

for $x_j \in X_j$, then $x(a) > x(b)$ for $x \in f(u)$. The weaker cardinal independence of irrelevant alternatives has not bypassed Arrow-type problems. What makes the Kalai–Schmeidler study interesting is the use of a continuity assumption on f to show that individual j has even stronger power than already obtained. This allows an impossibility result in which the continuity constraint is traded for a substantially weakened nondictatorship condition. Here we shall prove a part of j's stronger power and then state the full Kalai–Schmeidler result, leaving the reader to study their paper for additional details.

If $|E| = m < \infty$, an element of r^E can be an m-dimensional vector of reals. This set of vectors will be endowed with the usual (Euclidean) topology. Given a cardinal preference relation X, we say $x \in X$ is a zero–one representative of X if

(i)   each least preferred element is assigned the number 0 by x,
(ii)   each most preferred element not also a least preferred element is assigned the number 1 by x.

Convergence in Z is then defined as convergence of the component zero–one representatives. We now use continuity of f to prove that $\pi(f(u))$ gets not only individual j's strict preferences, but also j's indifferences, i.e., that $\pi(f(u)) = \pi(X_j)$.

Given $X = (X_1, \ldots, X_n)$, suppose that for all $x_j \in X_j$, $x_j(a) = x_j(b)$. Using $|E| \geq 4$, pick alternatives c, d and a cardinal preference relation Y_j such that the zero–one representative y_j of Y_j has

$$0 = y_j(c) < y_j(b) = y_j(a) < y_j(d) = 1.$$

Define $Y = (X_1, \ldots, X_{j-1}, Y_j, X_{j+1}, \ldots, X_n)$. Given $E > 0$, choose Y_j^m (for each positive integer m) such that the zero–one representative y_j^m of Y_j^m satisfies

(i) $y_j^m(e) = y_j(e)$ for $e \neq a$,
(ii) $y_j^m(a) = y_j(a) + \varepsilon/m$.

Also choose W_j^m such that the zero–one representative w_j^m of W_j^m satisfies

(i) $w_j^m(e) = y_j(e)$ for $e \neq b$,
(ii) $w_j^m(b) = y_j(b) + \varepsilon/m$.

Define

$$Y^m = (X_1, \ldots, X_{j-1}, Y_j^m, X_{j+1}, \ldots, X_n),$$
$$W^m = (X_1, \ldots, X_{j-1}, W_j^m, X_{j+1}, \ldots, X_n).$$

For each y^m in Y^m, $y^m(a) > y^m(b)$. By continuity, if $y \in Y$, we have $y(a) \geq y(b)$. Similarly, for each w^m in W^m, $w^m(b) > w^m(a)$, so continuity yields $y(b) \geq y(a)$. Hence $y(a) = y(b)$. Since $X|_{\{a,b\}} = Y|_{\{a,b\}}$, $x(a) = x(b)$ for all $x \in X$. This completes our proof that $\pi(f(u)) = \pi(X_j)$. Kalai and Schmeidler, using some ingenious arguments, strengthen this conclusion to $f(X) = X_j$. For this additional result, the reader is referred to their paper. Summarizing, we have:

Theorem 8-11 There is no cardinal collective choice rule f satisfying

   (i)   domain,
      (a) $4 \leqq |E| < \infty$,
      (b) f is total on Z^n and $2^E - \{\varnothing\}$, $n \geqq 3$,
  (ii) cardinal independence of irrelevant alternatives,
 (iii) the cardinal Pareto condition,
 (iv) continuity,
  (v) no cardinal dictator,

there is no j, $1 \leqq j \leqq n$, with $f(X) = X_j$ for each $X = (X_1, \ldots, X_n)$.

For closely related material, see the impossibility results in papers by Fishburn [116], Camacho [74], DeMeyer and Plott [91], and in Chapter 8 of Sen [309].

Extended Preference

Arrow has suggested that his original framework ignores the information that might be available from "extended sympathy." He raises this issue in talking [12, p. 114] about the English tombstone carving:

> Here lies Martin Englebrodde,
> Ha'e mercy on my soul, Lord God,
> As I would do were I Lord God,
> And thou wert Martin Englebrodde.

Interpersonal comparisons of extended sympathy are of the form: state x is better for me than state y is for you; or, in operational form: it is better (in my judgment) to be myself in state x than to be you in state y.

Comparisons of this sort have been formalized by Suppes [329], refined by Sen [309], and used by those authors to get a notion of a grading principle of justice. This grading principle, argues Sen, is the defensible common element in Rawls' maximin criterion [271] and the "contractarian neo-utilitarianism" of Harsanyi [160] and Vickrey [339].

We shall have to adopt important terminology changes for this section. While N is still the set of all individuals and E the set of all social states, an *alternative* now will be an element of the Cartesian product $E \times N$. Individuals are assumed to have preferences over alternatives rather than over social states. $\tilde{R}$ is the set of all complete, reflexive, transitive binary relations on $E \times N$ and $\tilde{R}^n$ is the n-fold Cartesian product of $\tilde{R}$. If $(\tilde{R}_1, \ldots, \tilde{P}_n) \in \tilde{R}^n$, we call $(\tilde{R}_1, \ldots, \tilde{R}_n)$ a *profile*, and $\tilde{R}_i$ is the *extended individual preference ordering* for the ith individual. (In the usual way, we define $\tilde{P}_i$, a strict preference ordering for i, and $\tilde{I}_i$, an indifference relation for i.) $(x, i)\tilde{P}_j(y, k)$ will be interpreted as saying that j would rather be i in state x than be k in state y.

A *general collective choice rule* (on V, U) is a function f on $U \subset \tilde{R}^n$ into $\mathscr{C}(V)$ with $f : u \mapsto C_u$ and $C_u(v) \subseteq v$. The elements of V are the *admissible agenda* and the elements of U are the *admissible profiles*.

The justice criterion that we consider imposing on collective choice rules is, under certain circumstances, an extension of the strong Pareto condition. In our new notation, C_u is said to satisfy the strong Pareto condition if, whenever $u = (\tilde{R}_1, \ldots, \tilde{R}_n)$ and social states x and y are such that $(x, i)\tilde{R}_i(y, i)$ for all i and $(x, i)\tilde{P}_i(y, i)$ for at least one i, then $x \in v \rightarrow y \notin C_u(v)$.

The notion of justice we are here dealing with is founded on preferences that reflect a "veil of ignorance" preventing an individual from knowing what his position would be in a social state. To analyze this, we introduce the set T of all one-to-one correspondences of N onto itself. We define

$$xJ_i y \qquad \text{if there is a } \rho \in T \text{ such that for all } j, (x,j)\tilde{R}_i(y, \rho(j)) \text{ and}$$
$$\text{for at least one } j, (x,j)\tilde{P}_i(y, \rho(j)).$$

We interpret $xJ_i y$ as saying that, according to individual i, x is more just than y. Sen shows [309, p. 153] that J_i is asymmetric and transitive but not total, and defends the concept as follows [309, p. 151]:

> The conflicting claims of the maximin criterion and of utilitarianism are difficult to resolve. Each has some attractive features and some unattractive ones. The grading principle, when suitably constrained, seems to catch the most appealing common elements of the two.
>
> However, since it yields only a strict partial ordering, it is an incomplete criterion. What it does, essentially, is to separate out the relatively noncontroversial part of interpersonal choice . . . .
>
> The extended version of the grading principle is . . . rich. While it does not yield a complete social ordering, it does squeeze as much juice as possible out of the use of "dominance" (or vector inequality) which is the common element in the maximin criterion, utilitarianism, and a number of other collective choice procedures involving interpersonal comparability.

One difficulty in using the J_i partial orderings in determining social choices is that they can conflict with the Pareto condition. Sen has given us [309, p. 155] the following:

Theorem 8-12 When $n \geq 2$, there is a logically possible profile u for which each J_i is incompatible with the Pareto relation $\bar{P}$ defined by $x\bar{P}y$ iff $(x, i)\tilde{R}_i(y, i)$ for all i and $(x, i)\tilde{P}_i(y, i)$ for at least one i.

Proof We will in fact show something stronger, namely that the *weak* Pareto relation $\bar{\bar{P}}$, defined by $x\bar{\bar{P}}y$ iff $(x, i)\tilde{P}_{iu}(y, i)$ for all i, is incompatible with each J_i. Consider the profile u restricted to $\{x, y\} \times N$ as shown in Table 8.1. Clearly $y\bar{\bar{P}}x$ and so $y\bar{P}x$. But it is easily checked that $xJ_i y$ for all $j = 1, \ldots, n$. $\square$

Table 8-1

1	2	3		n
(x,n)	$(x,1)$	$(x,2)$		$(x,n-1)$
$(y,n-1)$	(y,n)	$(y,1)$	$\ldots$	$(y,n-2)$
$(x,n-1)$	(x,n)	$(x,1)$		$(x,n-2)$
$(y,n-2)$	$(y,n-1)$	(y,n)		$(y,n-3)$
$(x,n-2)$	$(x,n-1)$	(x,n)		$(x,n-3)$
$\vdots$	$\vdots$	$\vdots$		$\vdots$
$(y,2)$	$(y,3)$	$(y,4)$		$(y,1)$
$(x,2)$	$(x,3)$	$(x,4)$	$\ldots$	$(x,1)$
$(y,1)$	$(y,2)$	$(y,3)$		(y,n)
$(x,1)$	$(x,2)$	$(x,3)$		(x,n)
(y,n)	$(y,1)$	$(y,2)$		$(y,n-1)$

To circumvent the conflict indicated by this theorem, Sen proposes restrictions on which societies are to be admissible. The first restriction is the *axiom of identity*: u is admissible only if

$$(x,i)\tilde{R}_{iu}(y,i) \qquad \text{iff for all } j, \qquad (x,i)\tilde{R}_{ju}(y,i).$$

Sen interprets this as "each individual j in placing himself in the position of person i takes on the tastes and preferences of i" and claims this restriction "can be justified on ethical grounds as an important part of the exercise of extended sympathy.[2] That employing this axiom *is* a useful circumvention is the content of:

Theorem 8-13 (Sen [309, p. 156]) Under the axiom of identity, for each person i, we have $x\bar{P}y \to xJ_iy$.

Proof Exercise. □

A stronger restriction on profiles is Sen's *axiom of complete identity*: u is admissible only if

$$\tilde{R}_{iu} = \tilde{R}_{ju} \qquad \text{for all} \quad i,j.$$

While many impossibility theorems require the admissibility of all possible profiles, we shall at first require only the admissibility of all those profiles which satisfy the axiom of complete identity. (Of course, this still allows full freedom in the use of restricted preferences, such as $\tilde{R}_i$ restricted to $Ex\{i\}$.)

We use the partial ordering J_i in determining social choices as in the following definition: A general collective choice rule $f: u \mapsto C_u$ is *just* if, for every society u for which xJ_iy for all i, we have $x \in v$ implies $y \notin C_u(v)$. We

---

[2] Thus this approach differs substatially from Rawls's justice as fairness, where the "veil of ignorance" in the original position excludes each agent from the knowledge of others' preferences [271, p. 28]. For Rawls, these agents are mutually disinterested rather than sympathetic [271, p. 153].

shall never choose a social state which *everyone* agrees is less just than some other available social state.

As in Chapter 2, the *weak* Pareto condition may be thought of as the requirement that the set N of all individuals be decisive between all pairs of social states. A set S of individuals is *weakly, globally pairwise decisive for r against s* if, whenever u satisfies $(r, i)\tilde{P}_i(s, i)$ for all $i \in S$, then $r \in v \rightarrow s \notin C_u(v)$. S is said to be *weakly, globally pairwise decisive between r and s* if it is decisive for r against s and for s against r. While the notion of decisiveness has played a key role in nearly all our previous impossibility results, one quickly discovers that in the analysis of grading principles, the idea of decisiveness for any set other than N will have to be modified substantially.

To see this, suppose $n \geq 2$ and that we are looking at a just general collective choice rule for which U contains all societies satisfying the axiom of complete identity. We now consider the consequences of supposing that some nonempty *proper* subset S of N is decisive for r against s and that $\{r, s\} \in V$. Relabeling individuals if necessary, let $1 \in N - S$. Consider a u (which can always be chosen so as to satisfy the axiom of complete identity) for which individuals have extended preference orderings which, restricted to $\{r, s\} \times N$, are

$$(s, 1)$$
$$(r, 2)$$
$$(s, 2)$$
$$\vdots$$
$$(r, n)$$
$$(s, n)$$
$$(r, 1).$$

Then, since $(r, i)\tilde{P}_i(s, i)$ for all $i \in S$, $s \notin C_u(\{r, s\})$. Using the transformation

$$\rho(i) = \begin{cases} i + 1 & \text{for } i = 1, \ldots, n - 1, \\ 1 & \text{for } i = n, \end{cases}$$

we see $sJ_k r$ for all k. Thus the justice condition entails $r \notin C_u(\{r, s\})$. But $C_u(\{r, s\}) = \varnothing$ violates the domain conditions.

The example used reveals a weakness in our condition of decisiveness. For that condition assumes decisiveness is defined in terms of restricted preference orderings (on $Ex\{i\}$ for each $i \in S$), *regardless of information available in the rest of the extended preference ordering*. In particular, if $i \in S$ has $(r, i)\tilde{P}_i(s, i)$, he "counts" in checking decisiveness even if i himself sees s as *more just* than r. In the example, all but one individual prefers r to s, but all find s to be more just than r. Perhaps we could seek a way out by "counting" $(r, i)\tilde{P}_i(s, i)$ toward decisiveness only when s is not more just than r in the eyes of *any* individuals.

That this may also fail is illustrated by the following theorem, which, in essence, is a revision of Sen's impossibility of a Paretian liberal (Theorem 2-3):

Theorem 8-14 (*Impossibility of a just liberal*) There is no just general collective choice rule $f : u \mapsto C_u$ satisfying

(i)   *weak just liberalism*: there exist w, x, y, z, i, and j such that
   (a)   if u is such that $(x, i)\tilde{P}_i(y, i)$ and for no k is yJ_kx, then

$$x \in v \rightarrow y \notin C_u(v),$$

   (b)   if u is such that $(y, i)\tilde{P}_i(x, i)$ and for no k is xJ_ky, then

$$y \in v \rightarrow x \notin C_u(v),$$

   (c)   if u is such that $(w, j)\tilde{P}_j(z, j)$ and for no k is zJ_kw, then

$$w \in v \rightarrow z \notin C_u(v),$$

   (d)   if u is such that $(z, j)\tilde{P}_j(w, j)$ and for no k is wJ_kz, then

$$z \in v \rightarrow w \notin C_u(v),$$

(ii)   *domain restrictions*
   (a) $\{x, y, z, w\} \in V$,
   (b)   U contains all profiles satisfying the axiom of complete identity,
   (c) f is total on V, U.

Proof   For notational simplicity, we take $i = 1$ and $j = 2$.

CASE 1: $\{x, y\} = \{z, w\}$; say $x = z$, $w = y$.   Consider a profile u (and one satisfying the axiom of complete identity can be found), such that the restriction of every $\tilde{R}_i$ to $\{x, y\} \times N$ is

$$(y, 2)$$
$$(x, 2)$$
$$(x, 1)$$
$$(y, 1)$$
$$(x, 3)$$
$$\vdots$$
$$(x, n)$$
$$(y, n).$$

It is easily checked that neither xJ_iy nor yJ_ix holds for any i. Thus the weak just liberalism condition gives us, by individual 1, $y \notin C_u(\{x, y\})$ and, by individual 2, $x \notin C_u(\{x, y\})$. But $C_u(\{x, y\}) = \varnothing$ violates the domain restrictions.

CASE 2: $\{x, y\}$ *and* $\{w, z\}$ *have exactly one element in common, say* $x = w$. Consider a profile u (and one satisfying the axiom of complete identity can be found) such that the restriction of every $\tilde{R}_i$ to $\{x, y, z\} \times N$ is

$$(x, 1)$$
$$(y, 1)$$
$$(z, 1)$$
$$(y, 2)$$
$$(z, 2)$$
$$(x, 2)$$
$$(y, 3)$$
$$(z, 3)$$
$$(x, 3)$$
$$\vdots$$
$$(y, n)$$
$$(z, n)$$
$$(x, n).$$

$(y, i)\tilde{P}_j(z, i)$ for all i, j, so yJ_iz for all i. Therefore justice requires $z \notin C_u(\{x, y, z\})$. Next it is easily checked that yJ_ix and xJ_iz both fail for all i. Thus the weak just liberalism requirement gives us, by individual 1, $y \notin C_u(\{x, y, z\})$ and, by individual 2, $x \notin C_u(\{x, y, z\})$. But $C_u(\{x, y, z\}) = \emptyset$ violates the domain restrictions.

CASE 3: $\{x, y\} \cap \{w, z\} = \emptyset$. Consider a profile u (and one satisfying the axiom of complete identity can be found) such that the restriction of every $\tilde{R}_i$ to $\{x, y, z, s\} \times N$ is

$$(w, 1)$$
$$(x, 1)$$
$$(y, 1)$$
$$(z, 1)$$
$$(y, 2)$$
$$(z, 2)$$
$$(w, 2)$$
$$(x, 2)$$
$$\vdots$$
$$(y, n)$$
$$(z, n)$$
$$(w, n)$$
$$(x, n)$$

Now wJ_ix and yJ_iz for all i, so that justice requires $x \notin C_u(\{x, y, z, w\})$ and $z \notin C_u(\{x, y, z, w\})$. It is easily checked that yJ_ix and wJ_iz both fail for all i. Thus the weak just liberalism requirement gives us, by individual 1, $y \notin C_u(\{x, y, z, w\})$ and, by individual 2, $w \notin C_u(\{x, y, z, w\})$. But $C_u(\{x, y, z, w\}) = \emptyset$ violates the domain restrictions. $\square$

Sen's proof (cf. Theorem 2-2) translates so easily into this one that the result seems unsurprising. Whether it has surprise value or not, Theorem 8-13 does seem to be a rather damaging critique of the Arrow–Sen program of introducing extended sympathy as a resolution of the Arrow problem.

The counterexamples in this proof are all constructed purely by a "layering" process, whereby extended orderings are built up by layering "restricted" orderings, such as

$$(w, 1)$$
$$(x, 1)$$
$$(y, 1)$$
$$(z, 1)$$

on top of one another. The reason Sen's proof translates so easily into a proof of the impossibility of a just liberal is that, with pure layering, we will find xJ_iy only if x is Pareto superior to y.

It might be guessed that this layering process is crucial to our proof techniques. If so, our results will seem weak, for there are many interpretations wherein we would not like to depend on what may be very improbable extended orderings in which, for example, everyone would rather be individual 1, regardless of the social state chosen, than individual 2. If we rule out such extended preferences, can our results be retained?

To illustrate a claim that our theorems are unaffected by ruling out such preferences, suppose we agree, as an extreme, to rule out any case where *any* two successive alternatives have the same second component (i.e., refer to the same individual). Look at the last case in the proof of Theorem 8-3. The extended individual preference ordering in that case was obtained by layering the following individual orderings:

1	2	3	...	n
$(w, 1)$	$(y, 2)$	$(y, 3)$		(y, n)
$(x, 1)$	$(z, 2)$	$(z, 3)$		(z, n)
$(y, 1)$	$(w, 2)$	$(w, 3)$		(w, n)
$(z, 1)$	$(x, 2)$	$(x, 3)$		(x, n)

Instead of layering by individual, we will stack these by rank: first all the top alternatives, then all the second, etc.

This yields

$$(w, 1)$$
$$(y, 2)$$
$$(y, 3)$$
$$\vdots$$
$$(y, n)$$
$$(x, 1)$$
$$(z, 2)$$
$$(z, 3)$$
$$\vdots$$
$$(z, n)$$
$$(y, 1)$$
$$(w, 2)$$
$$(w, 3)$$
$$\vdots$$
$$(w, n)$$
$$(z, 1)$$
$$(x, 2)$$
$$(x, 3)$$
$$\vdots$$
$$(x, n).$$

If every individual has this extended individual preference ordering, we leave our proof nearly intact. We still have wJ_ix and yJ_iz for all i, so that justice requires $x \notin C_u(\{x, y, z, w\})$ and $z \notin C_u(\{x, y, z, w\})$. Also, wJ_iz fails for all i so that, by weak just liberalism, $w \notin C_u(\{x, y, z, w\})$. To apply weak just liberalism to individual 1 on the choice between x and y, we need to have yJ_ix fail. But yJ_ix for all i. For this reason, we alter our example by moving (x, n) from the last position to the second position [ahead of all the (y, i)]:

$$(w, 1)$$
$$(x, n)$$
$$(y, 2)$$
$$\vdots$$
$$(y, n)$$
$$(x, 1)$$
$$(z, 2)$$
$$\vdots$$

$$(z, n)$$
$$(y, 1)$$
$$(w, 2)$$
$$\vdots$$
$$(w, n)$$
$$(z, 1)$$
$$(x, 2)$$
$$\vdots$$
$$(x, n - 1).$$

This will satisfy the weak just liberalism requirements, but now wJ_ix is violated. For this reason, we alter the ordering by moving (w, n) from its low position to the fourth position:

$$(w, 1)$$
$$(x, n)$$
$$(y, 2)$$
$$(w, n)$$
$$(y, 3)$$
$$\vdots$$
$$(y, n)$$
$$(x, 1)$$
$$(z, 2)$$
$$(z, 3)$$
$$\vdots$$
$$(z, n)$$
$$(y, 1)$$
$$(w, 2)$$
$$(w, 3)$$
$$\vdots$$
$$(w, n - 1)$$
$$(z, 1)$$
$$(x, 2)$$
$$(x, 3)$$
$$\vdots$$
$$(x, n - 1).$$

With this extended ordering (which satisfies the extreme second component rule), the proof of the third case carries over intact.

Just as Theorem 8-13 is analogous to Theorem 2-2, we can find extended preference analogs to Theorem 3-2 (which used asymmetric decisiveness) and Theorem 2-4 (on the impossibility of Paretian federalism). Formulation and proof of these analogs is left to the reader.

The analog for federalism would again involve disjoint sets S_1 and S_2 of individuals. Clearly, at least one of these two sets must be composed of less than a strict majority. For some interpretations, perhaps choice among political candidates, we might not want nonmajority sets to be decisive on the occasions when the justice criterion fails to determine the choice. For some such interpretations we might want to impose the following adaptation of the majoritarian condition.

Just Majoritarianism   For every pair of alternatives, x, y, if u is such that not yJ_ix for all $i \in N$ and if $(x, i)\tilde{P}_i(y, i)$ for all i in some set making up a strict majority of N, then $x \in v \rightarrow y \notin C_u(v)$. A simple layering adaptation of the voters paradox yields:

Theorem 8-15   There is no general collective choice rule with $n = 3$ or $n \geq 5$, $|E| \geq 3$, which is just, satisfies just majoritarianism, and satisfies the domain restrictions

(a) V contains all finite subsets of E,
(b) U contains all profiles satisfying the axiom of complete identity,
(c) f is total on U, V.

Proof   Exercise.   □

For some interpretations we may want our decisive-in-the-absence-of-justice-relations sets to be larger than mere majority. But this will not work if there are many alternatives. We will illustrate this by an adaptation of the Fishburn result noted in the discussion following Theorem 2-2.

Theorem 8-16   There is no general collective choice rule with $n \geq 2$, $\#(E) \geq n$, which is just, satisfies the domain restrictions of Theorem 8-15, and satisfies the condition:

For every pair of alternatives x, y, if u is such that not yJ_ix for all $i \in N$ and $(x, i)\tilde{P}_i(y, i)$ for all but one $i \in N$, then $x \in v$ implies $y \notin C_u(v)$.

Proof   Exercise.   □

It is left to the reader to formulate and prove a more general theorem encompassing Theorems 8-14 and 8-15 in analogy with Theorem 2-2.

The class of impossibility theorems so far shown vulnerable to translation into extended preference language are those based on direct decisiveness conditions, stipulating certain subsets of individuals to be decisive between certain pairs of alternatives. But many theorems we have presented in this book are not constructed around these direct decisiveness constraints (other than the weak Pareto condition). These cases, illustrated by Arrow's second impossibility theorem, will now be discussed.

We start by rewriting Arrow's second impossibility theorem in the language of decisiveness: there is no collective choice rule f satisfying

(i) the standard domain constraint (2),

(ii) each $C_u = f(u)$ has a complete, reflexive, and transitive rationalization $R(u)$,

(iii) independence of irrelevant alternatives,

(iv) the weak pairwise Pareto condition: N is weakly, locally pairwise decisive between all pairs of alternatives,

(v) nondictatorship: no singleton set is weakly, locally pairwise decisive between all pairs of alternatives.

Most of the translation of this theorem into extended preference language is straightforward. Instead of (i), the standard domain constraint, we would use:

Extended domain with the axiom of complete identity:

(a) V contains all finite members of $2^E - \{\varnothing\}$,

(b) $|E| \geq 3$,

(c) there is an n, $3 \leq n \leq \infty$, with U equal to the subset of $(\tilde{R})^n$ satisfying the axiom of complete identity,

(d) f is total on U, V.

The transitive rationality condition (ii) is retained without change, while (iv), the weak Pareto condition, is replaced by the constraint that f be just. Independence of irrelevant alternatives, (iii), is dropped in favor of *independence of irrelevant social states*: if u_1 and u_2 are two profiles satisfying

$$u_1|_{v \times N} = u_2|_{v \times N},$$

then $C_{u_1}(v) = C_{u_2}(v)$. What remains is a suitable translation of nondictatorship, and this hinges on a suitable translation of "weakly, locally pairwise decisive." We shall say that a set $S \subseteq N$ is *weakly, locally pairwise E-decisive* (E for "extended") if $C_u(\{x, y\}) = \{x\}$ whenever u satisfies

(i) $(x, i)\tilde{P}_i(y, i)$ for all $i \in S$,

(ii) $(y, i)\tilde{P}_i(x, i)$ for all $i \in N - S$,

(iii) $yJ_k x$ for no $k \in N$.

With all this, we arrive at the *first translation* of Arrow's theorem:

There does not exist any general collective choice rule, $f: u \mapsto C_u$ satisfying

    (i)   independence of irrelevant social states,

    (ii) f is just,

    (iii) no set of just one individual is weakly, locally pairwise E-decisive between every pair of social states,

    (iv) extended domain with the axiom of complete identity,

    (v) each C_u has a complete, reflexive, and transitive rationalization $R(u)$.

This translation does not, however, yield a true theorem, as the following counterexample shows. For each x in E, take any bijective function r_x: $N \rightarrow \{1, \ldots, n\}$ which satisfies

$$(x, i)\tilde{P}(x, j) \rightarrow r_x(i) > r_x(j).$$

(Here $\tilde{R}$ is the extended preference ordering held by all individuals.) Then define i_x to be the inverse of r_x and

$$x(m) \equiv (x, i_x(m)).$$

Define $P(u)$ on E by $xP(u)y$ iff some $m \in \{1, \ldots, n\}$, $t \in \{1, \ldots, m-1\}$ implies $x(t)\tilde{I}y(t)$ while $x(m)\tilde{P}y(m)$. Then $R(u)$ on E is given by $xR(u)y$ iff $\neg\, yP(u)x$. Finally, f is the rule that assigns to each $v \in V$ the set of $R(u)$-best elements of v. (Exercise: Prove this *is* a counterexample.) For a more complete discussion of the class of general social welfare functions serving as counterexamples to the first translation, see Hammond [152] and Strasnick [327].

Unfortunately, the available counterexamples to the first translation all depend heavily on the assumption that the axiom of complete identity is satisfied. While that axiom makes for exciting impossibility results (which are always more disturbing when found on very small domains), it is a poor basis for possibility results since it seems so unlikely that we should find it satisfied by any profiles to be found in applications.

There is, however, a plausible defense for the weaker axiom of identity:

> Placing oneself in the position of another should involve not merely having the latter's objective circumstances but also identifying oneself with the other in terms of his subjective features [309, p. 150].

This leads to the *second translation* of Arrow's theorem:

There does not exist any general collective choice rule $f: u \mapsto C_u$ satisfying

    (i)   independence of irrelevant social states,

    (ii) f is just,

    (iii) no set of just one individual is weakly, locally pairwise E-decisive between every pair of social states,

(iv)   extended domain with the axiom of identity,

(v)   each C_u has a complete, reflexive, and transitive rationalization $R(u)$.

Here the domain constraint has been strengthened by expanding U to be the subset of $(\tilde{R})^n$ satisfying the axiom of identity. Sen has observed that this translation also fails if we determine social choices by a "lexicographic maximin" ordering based on the extended preference relation of, say, individual 1. Seeing why Arrow's proof does not translate will point us to a new notion of local decisiveness, thus to a new no-dictator condition, and so to a third translation which *is* true.

Recall that the proof of Arrow's theorem involves two separate parts. First, it is shown that if a set is locally decisive on some x against some y, then it is locally (and even globally) decisive between all pairs of social states. Then attention is focused on a profile u with the following orderings (restricted to $\{x, y, z\}$):

$$W_1: \quad xyz,$$
$$W - W_1: \quad zxy,$$
$$N - W: \quad yzx.$$

Here W is a smallest decisive set (with at least two members by the no-dictator condition) and W_1 is a one-element subset of W. Since W is decisive, $xP(u)y$. If $zP(u)y$, $W - W_1$ would be locally decisive for z against y and so between all pairs contrary to the choice of W. Therefore, $yR(u)z$, and so $xP(u)y$ by transitivity. But then W_1 is locally decisive for x against z and so between all pairs contrary to the no-dictator condition.

In the translated case, it is also possible to show that, if a set W is weakly, locally pairwise E-decisive for state x against state y, W is weakly, locally pairwise E-decisive between all pairs of social states. The difficulties arise in the second part. No matter how we choose $\tilde{u}$, learning $zP(\tilde{u})y$ would never allow us to deduce that $W - W_1$ is weakly, locally pairwise E-decisive for z against y. This is due to the fact that local E-decisiveness for z against y must be checked against a multiplicity of different cases for the structure of the profile restricted to $\{z, y\} \times N$. In the regular preference case, local decisiveness for z against y is defined in terms of just a single structure of preferences on z and y: everybody in the set has zP_iy, and everybody outside the set has yP_iz. This suggests that we work with a new concept of decisiveness in the case of extended preferences satisfying the axiom of identity.

Accordingly, we seek a new notion of W being decisive for x against y that must satisfy several conditions:

1.   It must be defined in terms of extended preferences satisfying the axiom of identity.

2.   It must involve a *single* structure for the profile restricted to $\{x, y\}$.

3.   It must not conflict with the justice condition the way our earliest naive, translation did.

4.   For the no-dictator condition to be appealing, certain restrictions are placed on the single structure of condition 2:

(a)   Every member of W should have $(x, i)\tilde{P}_i(y, i)$, while every member of $N - W$ should have $(y, i)\tilde{P}_i(x, i)$.

(b)   There should not be anything making the x over y preferences more appealing than the y over x preferences; for example, the structure should not show members of W preferring x to y more intensely (by having them much farther apart in their extended orderings) than members of $N - W$ prefer y to x.

With these conditions, much leeway still remains in the choice of structure to use in the definition. The following choice is made, frankly, because it makes the proof of the third translation work.

A subset W of $N = \{1, \ldots, n\}$ is said to be *narrowly pairwise E-decisive* for x against y if

(i) $W = \{i_1, \ldots, i_n\}$ is a set of *consecutive* integers,[3]

(ii) $xP(\tilde{u})y$ for every profile $\tilde{u}$ in which the extended preference orderings restricted to $\{x, y\} \times N$ are given in Table 8-2.[4]

With this (admittedly nonintuitive) choice of decisiveness condition we state our *third translation* as:

Theorem 8-17   There is no general collective choice rule $f : u \mapsto C_u$ satisfying

(i)   independence of irrelevant social states,

(ii) f is just,

(iii)   no set of just one individual is narrowly pairwise E-decisive between every pair of social states,

(iv)   extended domain with the axiom of identity,

(v)   each C_u has a complete, reflexive, and transitive rationalization $R(u)$.

Proof   This proof mimics Arrow's throughout. We first show that if W is narrowly pairwise E-decisive for some state x against another state y, abbreviated $xD_W y$, then W is narrowly pairwise E-decisive between any two social states. If $W = N$, the conclusion is immediate by the Pareto condition

---

[3] This is purely for notational convenience later. A more elaborate definition could handle decisiveness for more general subsets of individuals.

[4] The structure is written as if $1 < i_1$ and $i_r < n$, but trivial changes can deal with the cases $1 = i_1$ and $i_r = n$.

Table 8-2

If $i \in W$, $\tilde{R}_{i|\{x,y\} \times N}$ is	If $1 \le i < i_1$, $\tilde{R}_{i|\{x,y\} \times N}$ is	If $i_r < i \le n$, $\tilde{R}_{i|\{x,y\} \times N}$ is
(x, i)	(y, i)	(y, i)
(y, i)	(x, i)	(x, i)
$(x, i + 1)$	$(y, i + 1)$	$(y, i + 1)$
$(y, i + 1)$	$(x, i + 1)$	$(x, i + 1)$
⋮	⋮	
(x, i_r)	$(y, i_1 - 1)$	(y, n)
(y, i_r)	$(x, i_1 - 1)$	(x, n)
$(y, i_r + 1)$	(x, i_1)	$(y, 1)$
$(x, i_r + 1)$	(y, i_1)	$(x, 1)$
⋮	⋮	$(y, 2)$
(y, n)	(x, i_r)	$(x, 2)$
(x, n)	(y, i_r)	⋮
$(y, 1)$	$(y, i_r + 1)$	$(y, i_1 - 1)$
$(x, 1)$	$(x, i_r + 1)$	$(x, i_1 - 1)$
$(y, 2)$	⋮	(x, i_1)
$(x, 2)$	(y, n)	(y, i_1)
⋮	(x, n)	⋮
$(y, i_1 - 1)$	$(y, 1)$	(x, i_r)
$(x, i_1 - 1)$	$(x, 1)$	(y, i_r)
(x, i_1)	$(y, 2)$	$(y, i_r + 1)$
(y, i_1)	$(x, 2)$	$(x, i_r + 1)$
⋮	⋮	⋮
$(x, i - 1)$	$(y, i - 1)$	$(y, i - 1)$
$(y, i - 1)$	$(x, i - 1)$	$(x, i - 1)$

(which is subsumed in the requirement that f be just). So we assume $N - W \ne \emptyset$. Let z be any third alternative, and suppose $\tilde{u}$ is any society in which the restrictions of the orderings to $\{x, z\}$ are in the form required for checking decisiveness of W for x against z (Table 8-3). Now look at some society $\tilde{u}_0$ (see Table 8-4), in which the restrictions of the orderings to $\{x, y, z\}$ are what would result if (y, i) is placed above (z, i) for all i in all the orderings in Table 8-3. An examination of these orderings restricted to $\{x, y\}$, together with $xD_W y$ yields $xP(\tilde{u}_0)y$. By the Pareto condition, $yP(\tilde{u}_0)a$. Transitivity then yields $xP(\tilde{u}_0)z$, independence of irrelevant social states yields $xP(\tilde{u})z$, and thus $xD_W z$:

$$xD_W y \to xD_W z. \tag{1}$$

Now if we start with any society $\tilde{u}$ in which the orderings restricted to $\{y, z\}$ are in the form required for checking decisiveness of W for z against y, and then build a $\tilde{u}$ by inserting (x, i) just below (z, i) for all i in all the orderings, we would have $xP(\tilde{u}_1)y$ by $xD_W y$, $zP(\tilde{u}_1)x$ by the Pareto condition,

Table 8-3

| | | | W | | | | | |
1	2	...	i_1	...	i_r	$i_r + 1$	...	n
$(z,1)$	$(z,2)$		(x,i_1)		(x,i_r)	(z,i_r+1)		(z,n)
$(x,1)$	$(x,2)$		(z,i_1)		(z,i_r)	(x,i_r+1)		(x,n)
$(z,2)$	⋮		⋮		(z,i_r+1)	⋮		$(z,1)$
$(x,2)$	(z,i_1-1)		(x,i_r)		(x,i_r+1)	(z,n)		$(x,1)$
⋮	(x,i_1-1)		(z,i_r)		⋮	(x,n)		$(z,2)$
(z,i_1-1)	(x,i_1)	...	(z,i_r+1)	...	(z,n)	$(z,1)$	...	$(x,2)$
(x,i_1-1)	(z,i_1)		(x,i_r+1)		(x,n)	$(x,1)$		⋮
(x,i_1)	⋮		⋮		$(z,1)$	$(z,2)$		(z,i_1-1)
(z,i_1)	(x,i_r)		(z,n)		$(x,1)$	$(x,2)$		(x,i_1-1)
⋮	(z,i_r)		(x,n)		$(z,2)$	⋮		(x,i_1)
(x,i_r)	(z,i_r+1)		$(z,1)$		$(z,2)$	(z,i_1-1)		(z,i_1)
(z,i_r)	(x,i_r+1)		$(x,1)$		⋮	(x,i_1-1)		⋮
(z,i_r+1)	⋮		$(z,2)$		(z,i_1-1)	(x,i_1)		(x,i_r)
(x,i_r+1)	(z,n)		$(x,2)$		(x,i_1-1)	(z,i_1)		(z,i_r)
⋮	(x,n)		⋮		(x,i_1)	⋮		(z,i_r+1)
(z,n)	$(z,1)$		(z,i_1-1)		(z,i_1)	(x,i_r)		(x,i_r+1)
(x,n)	$(z,1)$		(x,i_1-1)		⋮	(z,i_r)		⋮
					(x,i_r-1)			$(z,n-1)$
					(z,i_r-1)			$(x,n-1)$

$zP(\tilde{u}_1)y$ by transitivity, and $zP(\tilde{u})y$ by independence of irrelevant social states:

$$xD_W y \to zD_W y. \tag{2}$$

From (2), interchanging y and z gives

$$xD_W z \to yD_W z. \tag{3}$$

Combining this with (1) gives

$$xD_W y \to yD_W z. \tag{4}$$

From (1), using the permutation

$$\begin{pmatrix} x & y & z \\ y & z & x \end{pmatrix}, \tag{5}$$

we get $yD_W z \to yD_W x$. Combining this with (4), we obtain

$$xD_W y \to yD_W x. \tag{6}$$

From (3), using permutation (5) again, we get $yD_W x \to zD_W x$. Combining this with (6), we have

$$xD_W y \to zD_W x. \tag{7}$$

Table 8-4

			W				
1	2	...	i_1	...	i_r	$i+1$	...	n
$(y,1)$	$(y,2)$		(x,i_1)		(x,i_r)	(y,i_r+1)		(y,n)
$(z,1)$	$(z,2)$		(y,i_1)		(y,i_r)	(z,i_r+1)		(z,n)
$(x,1)$	$(x,2)$		(z,i_1)		(z,i_r)	(x,i_r+1)		(x,n)
$(y,2)$	⋮		⋮		(y,i_r+1)	⋮		$(y,1)$
$(z,2)$	(y,i_1-1)				(z,i_r+1)	(y,n)		$(z,1)$
$(x,2)$	(z,i_1-1)		(x,i_r)		(x,i_r+1)	(z,n)		$(x,1)$
⋮	(x,i_1-1)		(y,i_r)		⋮	(x,n)		$(y,2)$
(y,i_1-1)	(x,i_1)	...	(z,i_r)		(y,n)	$(y,1)$		$(z,2)$
(z,i_1-1)	(y,i_1)		(y,i_r+1)	...	(z,n)	$(z,1)$	...	$(x,2)$
(x,i_1-1)	(z,i_1)		(z,i_r+1)		(x,n)	$(x,1)$		⋮
(x,i_1)	⋮		(x,i_r+1)		$(y,1)$	$(y,2)$		(y,i_1-1)
(y,i_1)	(x,i_r)		(y,n)		$(z,1)$	$(z,2)$		(z,i_1-1)
(z,i_1)	(y,i_r)		(z,n)		$(x,1)$	$(x,2)$		(x,i_1-1)
⋮	(z,i_r)		(x,n)		$(y,2)$	⋮		(x,i_1)
(x,i_r)	(y,i_r+1)		$(y,1)$		$(z,2)$	(y,i_1-1)		(y,i_1)
(y,i_r)	(z,i_r+1)		$(z,1)$		$(x,2)$	(z,i_1-1)		(z,i_1)
(z,i_r)	(x,i_r+1)		$(x,1)$		⋮	(x,i_1-1)		⋮
(y,i_r+1)	⋮		$(y,2)$		(y,i_1-1)	(x,i_1)		(x,i_r)
(z,i_r+1)	(y,n)		$(z,2)$		(z,i_1-1)	(y,i_1)		(y,i_r)
(x,i_r+1)	(z,n)		$(x,2)$		(x,i_1-1)	(z,i_1)		(z,i_r)
⋮	(x,n)		⋮		(x,i_1)	⋮		(y,i_r+1)
(y,n)	$(y,1)$		(y,i_1-1)		(y,i)	(x,i_1)		(z,i_r+1)
(z,n)	$(z,1)$		(z,i_1-1)		(z,i_1)	(y,i_r)		(x,i_r+1)
(x,n)	$(x,1)$		(x,i_1-1)		⋮	(z,i_r)		⋮
					(x,i_r-1)			$(y,n-1)$
					(y,i_r-1)			$(z,n-1)$
					(z,i_r-1)			$(x,n-1)$

Together, (1), (2), (4), (6), and (7) tell us

$$\text{if } xD_W y, \text{ then } rD_W s \qquad \text{for every} \quad \{r,s\} \subseteq \{x,y,z\}. \tag{8}$$

By an adaptation of an argument of Blau [46, p. 310] to our notation, we use this result to prove that if $xD_W y$, then $rD_W s$ for all r, s in E. If $\{r,s\} = \{x,y\}$, (8) guarantees $rD_W s$. Suppose $\{r,s\} \cap \{x,y\}$ consists of just one element, say $r = x$. Then letting $z = s$ in (8), we obtain $rD_W s$. Finally, suppose $\{r,s\} \cap \{x,y\} = \varnothing$. Using (8) once with $z = r$, we have $xD_W y \to rD_W y$. Then using (8) again, with $x = r$ and $z = s$, $rD_W y \to rD_W s$. Therefore $xD_W y \to rD_W s$.

In accordance with this result, we will call a set W decisive if there are states x and y such that $xD_W y$.

Decisive sets exist by the Pareto condition; let W^1 be a smallest decisive set. By the no-dictator condition, W^1 must contain at least two individuals. Without loss of generality, we will assume $W^1 = \{1,2,\ldots,m\}$, where

$2 \leq m \leq n$. We partition W^1 into $W_1 = \{1\}$ and $W_2 = \{2, \ldots, m\}$ and examine a society $\tilde{u}$ with extended preference orderings which, restricted to $\{x, y, z\} \times N$ look like those shown in Table 8-5. Since $xD_{W^1}y$, $xP(\tilde{u})y$. If $zP(\tilde{u})y$, examination of the restrictions to $\{z, y\} \times N$ would show W_2 decisive for z against y (using independence of irrelevant social states), and this would contradict our choice of W^1 as the smallest decisive set. Hence $yR(\tilde{u})z$ and so, by transitivity, $xP(\tilde{u})z$. But then examination of the restrictions to $\{x, z\} \times N$ (and another application of independence of irrelevant social states) proves $xD_{W_1}z$, and so W_1 is decisive contrary to the no-dictator condition. □

Table 8-5

	W^1			$N - W^1$		
W_1	W_2					
1	2	...	m	$m+1$	...	n
$(x,1)$	$(z,2)$		(z,m)	$(y,m+1)$		(y,n)
$(y,1)$	$(x,2)$		(x,m)	$(z,m+1)$		(z,n)
$(z,1)$	$(y,2)$		(y,m)	$(x,m+1)$		(x,n)
$(z,2)$	⋮		$(y,m+1)$	⋮		$(x,1)$
$(x,2)$	(z,m)		$(z,m+1)$	(y,n)		$(y,1)$
$(y,2)$	(x,m)		$(x,m+1)$	(z,n)		$(z,1)$
⋮	(y,m)		⋮	(x,n)		$(z,2)$
(z,m)	$(y,m+1)$		(y,n)	$(x,1)$		$(x,2)$
(x,m)	$(z,m+1)$		(z,n)	$(y,1)$		$(y,2)$
(y,m)	$(x,m+1)$		(x,n)	$(z,1)$		⋮
$(y,m+1)$	⋮		$(x,1)$	$(z,2)$		(z,m)
$(z,m+1)$	(y,n)		$(y,1)$	$(x,2)$		(x,m)
$(x,m+1)$	(z,n)		$(z,1)$	$(y,2)$		(y,m)
⋮	(x,n)		$(z,2)$	⋮		$(y,m+1)$
(y,n)	$(x,1)$		$(x,2)$	(z,m)		$(z,m+1)$
(z,n)	$(y,1)$		$(y,2)$	(x,m)		$(x,m+1)$
(x,n)	$(z,1)$		⋮	(y,m)		⋮
			$(z,m-1)$			$(y,n-1)$
			$(x,m-1)$			$(z,n-1)$
			$(y,m-1)$			$(x,n-1)$

Exercises

1. Confirm the existence of the partition $\pi = (N_1, \ldots, N_m)$ required in the proof of Theorem 8-9.
2. Prove Theorem 8-13.
3. Prove Theorem 8-15.
4. Prove Theorem 8-16.

5. Confirm that the "lexicographic maximin" ordering with the axiom of complete identity gives a counterexample to the first translation of Arrow's theorem.

6. (Sen)   Suppose, with only the axiom of identity, there are two individuals and that social choices are determined by a "lexicographical maximin" ordering based on the extended preference relation of individual 1. Show that individual 2 (not 1!) is narrowly E-decisive.

9 RIGHTS EXERCISING

Most of the impossibility theorems we have discussed have employed one or more of the simplicity conditions: rationality, regularity, or independence conditions. But even if we drop all these, there remain theorems concerning Paretian liberals and just liberals. It is partly freedom from suspect simplicity conditions that make these theorems an important focus of interest. A variety of comments on Sen's theorem have appeared [20, 31, 49, 98, 103, 104, 134, 143, 166, 183, 188, 189, 240, 270, 306, 316, 317, 329b]. The last of these is a survey paper by Sen on the various resolutions of the problem.

The contribution to the discussion of Sen's theorem that I think promises the best *changes in our way of looking at social choice functions* is Gibbard's [143]. The first observation Gibbard makes (and in this respect several of the above-mentioned papers are similar) is that Sen's defense of his condition seems to involve a vector structure on the notion of alternative. Sen's one extended example involves an E of ordered pairs (x_1, x_2), where each x_i takes on one of two values according as individual i does or does not read *Lady Chatterly's Lover*. He also remarks:

> Given other things in the society, if you prefer to have pink walls rather than white, then society should permit you to have this, even if a majority of the community would like to see your walls white. Similarly, whether you should sleep on your back or on your belly is a matter in which the society should permit you absolute freedom, even if a majority of the community is nosey enough to feel that you must sleep on your back.

This suggests that each alternative is a long vector which includes for each individual a component describing sleeping position and another component for each room describing wall color, etc. We formalize all this by restricting our attention in the rest of this chapter to cases satisfying

$$E = M_1 \times M_2 \times \cdots \times M_\mu,$$

where each M_i satisfies $|M_i| \geq 2$. μ is the number of *issues*, i.e., the "number of features in an alternative," and M_i is a set of feature-alternatives. An element x of E is written $x = \langle x_1, x_2, \ldots, x_\mu \rangle$. Alternative x is a *j-variant* of y if x and y differ, if at all, only in their jth component, i.e., $i \neq j$ implies $x_i = y_i$. Now the kind of liberalism suggested by the quotation about wall colors and sleeping positions is captured in Gibbard's:

CONDITION L: For every individual b, there is a j, $1 \leq j \leq \mu$, such that for every pair of j-variants x and y, b is weakly, globally decisive between x and y.

Now Gibbard points out that Condition L generates problems even without the weak Pareto condition:

Theorem 9-1   There is no collective choice rule satisfying

(i)   the standard domain restriction, with $n \geq 2$,
(ii)   Condition L.

Proof   Suppose such an $f : u \mapsto C_u$ exists. For convenience, let Condition L associate feature 1 with individual 1 and feature 2 with individual 2. Let P_1 and W_1 be two elements of M_1, P_2 and W_2 be two elements of M_2, and let $\langle x_3, \ldots, x_\mu \rangle \in M_3 \times M_4 \times \cdots \times M_\mu$. Consider the four alternatives

$$a_{ww} = \langle w_1, w_2, x_3, \ldots, x_\mu \rangle, \qquad a_{wp} = \langle w_1, P_2, x_3, \ldots, x_\mu \rangle,$$
$$a_{pw} = \langle P_1, w_2, x_3, \ldots, x_\mu \rangle, \qquad a_{pp} = \langle P_1, P_2, x_3, \ldots, x_\mu \rangle.$$

Consider a profile u, in which preference orderings restricted to these four alternatives are

$$1: \quad a_{wp} \quad a_{pw} \quad a_{ww} \quad a_{pp},$$
$$N - \{1\}: \quad a_{pp} \quad a_{ww} \quad a_{pw} \quad a_{wp}.$$

When $v = \{a_{ww}, a_{wp}, a_{pw}, a_{pp}\}$, we examine $C_u(v)$:

$a_{ww} \notin C_u(v)$	because	1 is decisive for a_{pw} against a_{ww},
$a_{wp} \notin C_u(v)$	because	2 is decisive for a_{ww} against a_{wp},
$a_{pw} \notin C_u(v)$	because	2 is decisive for a_{pp} against a_{pw},
$a_{pp} \notin C_u(v)$	because	1 is decisive for a_{wp} against a_{pp}.

Thus $C_u(v) = \varnothing$ contrary to the domain restriction. $\square$

To see the way around this theorem, we pick a specific interpretation of the alternatives so that a_{wp} represents 1 having white bedroom walls and 2 having pink bedroom walls. Condition L says 1 and 2 each have a right to choose wall color: if 1 prefers pink walls to white, that preference should be honored by C_u. However, in the proof, we say $a_{ww} \in C_u(v)$ because 1 prefers a_{pw} to a_{ww}—that is *not* the same as saying 1 prefers pink walls to white. Individual 1 prefers pink walls to white just when 2 has white walls; if 2 has pink walls, 1 prefers white to pink. Individual 1 does not have simple, unconditional preferences for pink walls over white; 1 prefers walls that differ in color from 2's. Individual 2, in turn, does not have unconditional preferences for one wall color over another; 2 prefers having walls the same colors as 1's. Gibbard then suggests that a reasonable libertarian claim would disregard "mere" conditional preferences. To formalize all this, we say that individual b *unconditionally prefers* $\bar{x}$ to $\bar{y}$ in u if and only if whenever x and y are j-variants with $x_i = \bar{x}$ and $y_i = \bar{y}$, then $xP_b y$ in u.

CONDITION L': For each b there is j, $1 \le j \le n$, such that if $\bar{x}, \bar{y} \in M_j$, then if b unconditionally prefers $\bar{x}$ to $\bar{y}$ in u and x and y are j-variants with $x_i = \bar{x}$ and $y_i = \bar{y}$, then

$$x \in v \rightarrow y \notin C_u(v).$$

Gibbard illustrates [143, pp. 395–396] that Condition L' *is* consistent with the standard domain restriction. However, Sen's proof can be adapted to show that any such social choice function must violate the weak Pareto condition [143, p. 395]:

Theorem 9-2 (Gibbard) There is no collective choice rule $f: u \mapsto C_u$ satisfying

- (i) the standard domain restriction, $n \ge 2$,
- (ii) the weak Pareto condition,
- (iii) Condition L'.

Proof Without loss of generality $j(1) = 1$, $j(2) = 2$. Define $a_{ww}, a_{wp}, a_{pw}, a_{pp}$ as in the proof of Theorem 9-1, and consider a profile u with the preference orderings (restricted to $\{a_{ww}, a_{wp}, a_{pw}, a_{pp}\}$)

$$1: \quad a_{ww} \quad a_{pw} \quad a_{wp} \quad a_{pp},$$
$$N - \{1\}: \quad a_{pp} \quad a_{pw} \quad a_{wp} \quad a_{ww}.$$

It is easily checked that 1 unconditionally prefers w_1 to p_1 and that 2 unconditionally prefers p_2 to w_2. Let $v = \{a_{ww}, a_{wp}, a_{pw}, a_{pp}\}$. Then

$$a_{ww} \notin C_u(v) \qquad \text{because} \quad \text{2 rejects } a_{ww} \text{ in favor of } a_{wp},$$
$$a_{wp} \notin C_u(v) \qquad \text{because} \quad a_{pw} \text{ is Pareto-superior,}$$

$$a_{pw} \notin C_u(v) \quad \text{because} \quad \text{2 rejects } a_{pw} \text{ in favor of } a_{pp},$$

$$a_{pp} \notin C_u(v) \quad \text{because} \quad \text{1 rejects } a_{pp} \text{ in favor of } a_{wp}.$$

Thus $C_u(v) = \varnothing$ contrary to the domain restriction. ☐

With this inconsistency between Condition L′ and the weak Pareto condition we face two possible resolutions. The first is to retain Condition L′ and reject the Pareto condition. If 1 unconditionally prefers w_1 to p_1 and 2 unconditionally prefers p_2 to w_2, then the appropriate outcome is to let them have their preferences with the result a_{wp}. The argument that a_{pw} is Pareto-superior to a_{wp} would be met by something such as the following:

> That preference stems from busybody interests which ought to be ignored. Each of us should choose the color of his own walls, however little he cares, and suffer the torments of the nosy at the choice the other makes. [143, p. 397]

Gibbard rejects this resolution in favor of retaining the weak Pareto condition and revising Condition L′. (Sen argues [317] against always using the weak Pareto condition, especially in the context of liberalism problems. See a discussion in Chapter 10.) He argues against the first resolution.

> To some libertarians, however, that way of thinking will seem too paternalistic: it keeps 1 and 2 from striking a bargain they would both prefer. They both prefer the outcome with 1's walls pink and 2's white, but on the account [of the first resolution] that outcome is nonoptimal. Many libertarians would hold that 1 and 2 should be free to agree to that outcome. True, the preferences that would make us agree to it stem from nosiness, but a person's motives, such a libertarian could say, are his own business. There is a strong libertarian tradition of free contract, and on that tradition, a person's rights are his to use or bargain away as he sees fit. [143, p. 397, slightly modified]

It is not enough, however, just to stop with a declaration that a_{pw} is the just outcome. We must carefully examine individual decision making and the incentives individual decision makers face. For a_{pw} is vulnerable to both 1, who prefers a_{ww}, and 2, who prefers a_{pp}. Either we will need to invent an elaborate system of enforceable rules keeping 1 and 2 from attempting to achieve these more preferred outcomes, or we will need verification that, with existing incentives, neither 1 nor 2 would decide to change from a_{pw}. Gibbard takes the second route, illustrating his analysis with an example of marriage rights. There are three individuals: Angelina, Edwin, and the judge. The alternatives are described by 2-tuples detailing Angelina's marital possibilities:

w_E = (Angelina marries Edwin, Angelina does not marry the judge),

w_J = (Angelina does not marry Edwin, Angelina marries the judge),

w_0 = (Angelina does not marry Edwin, Angelina does not marry the judge).

The agenda is $v = \{w_E, w_J, w_0\}$, and we examine a society u in which preferences, restricted to these alternatives, are

Angelina:	w_E	w_J	w_0,
Judge:	w_E	w_J	w_0,
Edwin:	w_0	w_E	w_J.

> Angelina wants to marry Edwin but will settle for the judge, who wants whatever she wants. Edwin wants to remain single, but would rather wed Angelina than see her marry the judge. [143, p. 398]

This situation is supplemented with two "libertarian" conditions:

> First, Angelina has a right to marry the willing judge instead of remaining single.... Next, Edwin has the right to remain single rather than wed Angelina....
> [143, p. 398]

Given this, we see

$w_E \notin C_u(v)$ by Edwin's right and his prefernce for w_0 over w_E,

$w_0 \notin C_u(v)$ by Angelina's right and her preference for w_J over w_0,

$w_J \notin C_u(v)$ by the weak Pareto condition (with respect to w_E).

How do we resolve this? The first way mentioned was to drop the weak Pareto condition and so have $C_u(v) = \{w_J\}$. As we have seen, Gibbard does not go this way; he argues:

> Here again, though, a libertarian may want to allow the parties to bargain. Angelina has every right to wed the judge, but she prefers Edwin; Edwin has every right not to wed Angelina, but if he wants her not to wed the judge, then Edwin must wed her himself. Left freely to bargain away their rights, then, Edwin and Angelina would agree to the outcome w_E: wedding each other. Hence, a libertarian may well hold that—deplorable though Edwin's motives be—w_E is a just outcome under the circumstances ....
>
> That means we must deny that Edwin's preferring w_0 to w_E automatically makes w_0 preferable to w_E. He has the right to remain single, but the right is alienable: He can bargain it away to keep Angelina from marrying the judge. For the right is useless to Edwin: Although he prefers w_0 to w_E, and could avoid w_E by exercising his right to w_0 over w_E, Angelina claims her right to w_J over w_0, and Edwin likes w_J no better than w_E. If Edwin exercises his right to avoid w_E, he gets something he likes no better. In such circumstances, even though Edwin has a right to w_0 over w_E and prefers w_0 to w_E, w_E may still be optimal. It may be to Edwin's advantage to waive his right to w_0 over w_E in favor of the Pareto principle. [143, pp. 398–399]

Here then is the second resolution. We have treated the decisiveness component of liberalism as if it *locks in* the outcome: If Edwin prefers w_0 over w_E and w_0 is available, w_E *cannot* be chosen. Gibbard proposes instead that we take the decisiveness condition and break it into two parts: a rights-existence claim and a rights-exercising rule. In the case just mentioned we have been assuming both that Edwin has the right to w_0 over w_E *and* that he will exercise that right if only he prefers w_0 to w_E. Gibbard's quarrel is with the naiveté of the rights-exercising rule. Why would Edwin exercise his right to w_0 over w_E if the consequence in the end is w_j which he likes less than w_E?

Gibbard proposes a revised rights-exercising rule. A *rights system* is a set $\mathbb{R} \subseteq E \times E \times N$; if $\langle x, y, b \rangle \in \mathbb{R}$, we say $\mathbb{R}$ attributes to person b the right to alternative x over alternative y. If b *exercises* $\langle x, y, b \rangle$ at u, then

$$x \in v \rightarrow y \notin C_u(v).$$

The *classical* rights-exercising rule is: b exercises $\langle x, y, b \rangle$ at u if $xP_{bu}y$. Gibbard's revision is an indirect one, saying that b exercises a right unless he waives it.

This obviously requires a criterion for rights-waiving. Informally, b will waive his right to x over y if it gets him into trouble. "Trouble" in this case means ending up with an alternative at least as bad as y. So we let $\sum$ be a finite sequence, $y_1, y_2, \ldots, y_\lambda = x$, of alternatives. If b exercises his right to x over y and then is "forced" to take $y_{\lambda-1}$ over x, $y_{\lambda-2}$ over $y_{\lambda-1}, \ldots, y_1$ over y_2, and if $yR_{bu}y_1$, he has gotten into trouble. How might b be forced to take, say, $y_{\lambda-1}$ over x? In either of two ways:

(A) by the weak Pareto condition, if everyone strictly prefers $y_{\lambda-1}$ to x,

(B) by someone exercising a right to $y_{\lambda-1}$ over x.

Now with (B), we seem to have gotten into a circularity, defining exercising in terms of waiving which now is defined in turn in terms of exercising. Gibbard avoids this circularity by the trick of assuming that the "exercising" in (B) proceeds in accordance with the classical rule. In such a way are we led to Gibbard's rule:

If $\langle x, y, b \rangle \in \mathbb{R}$, b will exercise that right if $xP_{bu}y$ and if b does not waive the right. b waives $\langle x, y, b \rangle$ if there is a finite sequence, $\sum = y_1, y_2, \ldots, y_\lambda$ such that

(a) $y_\lambda = x$,

(b) $yR_{bu}y_1$,

(c) for every $i = 1, 2, \ldots, \lambda - 1$, either

$$(\forall e)y_i P_{eu} y_{i+1}, \qquad \text{or} \qquad (\exists e)[e \neq b \ \& \ \langle y_i, y_{i+1}, e \rangle \in \mathbb{R} \ \& \ y_i P_{eu} y_{i+1}].$$

Gibbard's libertarian requirement then is:

CONDITION L'': For every b there is a j such that for every pair of j-variants x and y, $\langle x, y, b \rangle \in \mathbb{R}$.

The major theorem is:

Theorem 9-3   If $\mu \geq n$, then there *does* exist a social choice function satisfying
satisfying

    (i)   the standard domain restriction,
    (ii) the weak Pareto condition,
    (iii) Condition L″,
    (iv) everyone follows Gibbard's rights-exercising rule.

For a proof see [143, pp. 401–402].

An easy early remark on Gibbard's rule is that it places very heavy demands on the information structure. Not only must each individual know all his rights as well as his own preference ordering, he must know the preference orderings of all other individuals and must know all rights assignments. He must, in addition, be able to carry out evaluations of $\sum$ sequences of arbitrary length. Now one could imagine a central agency to which each individual submits his preference ordering and his rights-exercising strategy, and while this reduces strain on the information transferal system it increases individual's calculation problems on rights exercising (for the strategy will have to describe exercising rules contingent on each of the possible sets of others' preferences). And, of course, there is the obvious problem of providing the agency with incentives to amalgamate preferences and rights-exercising strategies honestly and individuals with incentives to submit true preferences (see the discussion on strategy-proofness in Chapter 6). These are important problems that deserve more attention than they will receive in this chapter, which deals with choosing exercising rules in the presence of a free and perfect information structure.

A second easy observation is that this is an extremely cautious, risk-averse criterion for rights exercising. There may be many $\sum$ sequences starting from x that end up in a y_1 which is vastly preferred to y. But if there is just one ending in a no-better-than-y alternative, the right is to be waived. The moves along the $\sum$ sequence are out of b's control and b is taken to worry about and act upon the worst eventualities. The appropriateness of such caution depends upon the specific interpretation of "alternative" and "individual" and on what rights are assigned. At the level of generality of Gibbard's analysis little can be decided about appropriateness. This chapter will continue the discussion with a flavor of cautious exercising.

Now we proceed to two minor technical issues concerning Gibbard's rule. First, b need not worry about being forced to take $y_{\lambda-1}$ if $y_{\lambda-1}$ is not available, i.e., if $y_{\lambda-1}$ is not in the agenda v. Gibbard is not vary careful about this issue of availability. (While we shall revise this rule to take account of v, it should be pointed out that this alone would have no impact on Gibbard's results.)

The second issue is that in forcing the move from y to x by exercising $\langle x, y, b \rangle$, b does not seem to have gotten into trouble if he is forced in the end to take a y_1 where he is indifferent between y_1 and y. Waiving might be appropriate for a cautious exerciser if $yP_{bu}y_1$ for some $\sum$, but not if only $yR_{bu}y_1$ as in part (b) of the rule. There is evidence in Gibbard's marriage example of his recognition of this problem. Gibbard suggests that this example be solved by Edwin waiving $\langle w_0, w_E, E \rangle$. For there is a $\sum = w_J, w_0$ with $w_E P_{Eu} w_J$ and $\langle w_J, w_0, A \rangle \in \mathbb{R}$. "It may be to Edwin's advantage to waive his right to w_0 over w_E in favor of the Pareto principle." But we can similarly analyze Angelina. For there is a $\sum = w_0$, w_E, w_J with $w_0 R_{Au} w_0$, w_E Pareto-superior to w_J and $\langle w_0, w_E, E \rangle \in \mathbb{R}$. Thus on Gibbard's rule we would have Angelina waive her right to w_J over w_0. This is clearly a terrible result: each waives on the incorrect belief that the other will exercise and each has enough information to know that, if Gibbard's rule is followed by all that their own belief is incorrect. The analysis depends on each individual making a correctable error. Gibbard skirts this by amending the rule slightly so as to require $y_1 \neq y$. But why rule out only those y_1's that are indifferent to y by virtue of identity? The whole collective choice literature has carefully avoided separating identity indifference and just plain indifference. Such separating can also be avoided here by the natural expedient of altering part (b) of the rule to require strict preference.

These two technical issues are incorporated in our *First Revised Rule*:

If $\langle x, y, b \rangle \in \mathbb{R}$, b will exercise that right at (v, u) if $xP_{bu}y$ and if b does not waive that right at (v, u). b waives $\langle x, y, b \rangle$ at (v, u) if there is a finite sequence $\sum = y_1, y_2, \ldots, y_\lambda$ of alternatives in v such that

(a) $y_\lambda = x$,
(b) $yP_{bu}y_1$,
(c) for every $i = 1, 2, \ldots, \lambda - 1$, either

$$(\forall e)[y_i P_{eu} y_{i+1}], \quad \text{or} \quad (\exists e)[e \neq b \ \& \ \langle y_i, y_{i+1}, e \rangle \in \mathbb{R} \ \& \ y_i P_{eu} y_{i+1}].$$

(Again we should point out that these changes alone have no impact on Gibbard's results.)

Sequence Extensions

Gibbard has shown us that the classical rights-exercising rule is unacceptable because it is possible to construct examples in which it seems silly for b to follow that rule. We now begin our task of constructing examples in which it seems silly for b to follow even our First Revised Rule.

Consider the agenda $\{w, x, y, z\}$, over which individuals b and e have the preferences

$$b: \quad xwyz,$$
$$e: \quad ywzx.$$

The rights system is $\mathbb{R} = \{\langle x, y, b\rangle, \langle z, x, e\rangle\}$, and we ask if b should exercise or waive $\langle x, y, b\rangle$. Let $\sum$ be the sequence: z, x. If b considers exercising his right to x over y and expects e (who prefers z to x) to exercise $\langle z, x, e\rangle$, he will run the risk of getting z which he likes less than y. By the First Revised Rule, he should waive $\langle x, y, b\rangle$. But this quite simply ignores the fact that $\sum = z, x$ is part of an extended sequence of alternatives from A, namely, w, z, x. And, although e's expected exercising of $\langle z, x, e\rangle$ yields the undesirable z, the weak Pareto condition would have w eliminate z and b prefers w to y. In effect, the sequence $\sum' = w, z$ repairs the trouble engendered by $\sum = z, x$. This example suggests the following *Second Revised Rule*:

If $\langle x, y, b\rangle \in \mathbb{R}$, b will exercise that right at (v, u) if $xP_{bu}y$ and if b does not waive that right at (v, u). b waives $\langle x, y, b\rangle$ at (v, u) if there is a finite sequence $\sum = y_1, y_2, \ldots, y_\lambda$ of alternatives in v such that

   (a) $y_\lambda = x$,
   (b) $yP_{bu}y_1$,
   (c)   for every $i = 1, 2, \ldots, \lambda - 1$ either

$(\forall e)[y_i P_{eu} y_{i+1}]$,   or $(\exists e)[e \neq b \ \& \ \langle y_i, y_{i+1}, e\rangle \in \mathbb{R} \ \& \ y_i P_{eu} y_{i+1}]$,

   (d)   for every finite sequence, $\sum' = z_1, z_2, \ldots, z_{\lambda'}$, of alternatives in v such that

      (i) $z_{\lambda'} = y_1$,
      (ii) $z_1 P_{bu} y$,
      (iii) for every $i = 1, 2, \ldots, \lambda' - 1$, either

$(\forall e)[z_i P_{eu} z_{i+1}]$,   or $(\exists e)[\langle y_i, y_{i+1}, e\rangle \in \mathbb{R} \ \& \ y_i P_{eu} y_{i+1}]$,

there is a sequence, $\sum'' = w_1, w_2, \ldots, w_{\lambda''}$ of alternatives in v such that

      (iv) $w_{\lambda''} = z_1$,
      (v) $yP_{bu}w_1$,
      (vi)   for every $i = 1, 2, \ldots, \lambda'' - 1$, either

$(\forall e)[w_i P_{eu} w_{i+1}]$,   or $(\exists e)[e \neq b \ \& \ \langle w_i, w_{i+1}, e\rangle \in \mathbb{R} \ \& \ w_i P_{eu} w_{i+1}]$.

In this rule, part (d) says that any extending sequence $\sum'$ that repairs $\sum$ in the eyes of b can enter some other, out-of-control sequence $\sum''$, resulting in an alternative worse than y. Note that b can take part in forcing moves in the repairing sequence; we do not require that the exercise of rights (by the classical rule) be done only by individuals other than b.

   Two remarks are worthwhile regarding this latest revision. First, it causes no significant changes in the theorem that makes up Gibbard's libertarian claim. Second, the revision could be improved if we assume individuals also have information about the choice function. $\sum$ sequences leading to a y_i

worse than y can be "repaired" directly if the choice function always excludes y_1 from $C_u(v)$. The weak Pareto condition and rights-exercising rules are only sufficient, not necessary, conditions for excluding alternatives. Such a change would not affect what follows.

Refinements of the Sequence Concept

In examining a sequence such as $y_1, y_2, \ldots, y_\lambda$, we have supposed that a move from y_{i+1} to y_i can be forced only by either the weak Pareto condition or by a *single* individual exercising a *single* rights triple $\langle y_i, y_{i+1}, e \rangle$. It is useful to expand our concern to sets of individuals and sets of rights triples.

The first expansion can be illustrated by the Angelina–Edwin–Judge example. Gibbard says [143, p. 398]: "Angelina has a right to marry the willing judge instead of remaining single." The introduction of a concept of "willingness" seems quite unnecessary. What we want to say in this case is that the *set* of individuals {Angelina, judge} has a right to being married to each other rather than each remaining single, that this right can be waived by either alone, but that the judge prefers marriage to Angelina over bachelordom and that Angelina correctly believes the judge will not waive their joint right. Thus exercise of the right by {Angelina, judge} in this case depends only on Angelina's waiving decision.

This example is an archetype for all contractual rights. We will henceforth change the notion of a rights system to a subset of

$$E \times E \times (2^N - \{\varnothing\}),$$

where 2^N is the power set of N, the set of all subsets of N. A triple $\langle x, y, T \rangle$ will be exercised [so that $x \in v \to y \notin C_u(v)$] only if every member of T exercises that right. When we are working with a subset consisting of a single individual b, we will, without cause for confusion, continue to write $\langle x, y, b \rangle$ rather than $\langle x, y, \{b\} \rangle$.

The reason for worrying about sets of rights triples at a single forcing step in a sequence is illustrated by Gibbard's other example. Suppose a two-issue space, characterized by the white or pink color of person 1's room and the white or pink color of person 2's room. Each has a "right over own room color," i.e., $\mathbb{R}$ contains

$$\langle (w, w), (p, w), 1 \rangle, \qquad \langle (w, w), (w, p), 2 \rangle,$$
$$\langle (w, p), (p, p), 1 \rangle, \qquad \langle (w, p), (w, w), 2 \rangle,$$
$$\langle (p, w), (w, w), 1 \rangle, \qquad \langle (p, w), (p, p), 2 \rangle,$$
$$\langle (p, p), (w, p), 1 \rangle, \qquad \langle (p, p), (p, w), 2 \rangle.$$

We are currently in state (p, w); person 1 decides to exercise $\langle(w, w), (p, w), 1\rangle$, and person 2 decides to exercise $\langle(p, p), (p, w), 2\rangle$. What happens? The natural answer is (w, p). It seems we should worry about a step from y_{i+1} to y_i being forced as a consequence of the simultaneous joint exercising of several rights over y_{i+1} by several (sets of) individuals. We need a kind of production function where the "inputs" are a current state and a set of rights triples with second component equal to the current state and where the "output" is a new state. We will assume that this function is fixed, independent of v and u, and will represent the function by expressions such as

y_i is the consequence of exercising $\langle y_{i1}, y_{i+1}, S_{i1}\rangle, \ldots,$

$\langle y_{ik(i)}, y_{i+1}, S_{ik(i)}\rangle$ simultaneously.

With those preliminaries, the final revision of Gibbard's rule we shall present is the *Third Revised Rule*:

If $\langle x, y, T\rangle \in \mathbb{R}$ with $b \in T$, b will exercise that right at (v, u) if $xP_{bu}y$ and if b does not waive that right at (v, u). b waives $\langle x, y, T\rangle$ at (v, u) if there is a finite sequence $\sum = y_1, y_2, \ldots, y_\lambda$ of alternatives in v such that

(a) $(\exists S_1, S_2, \ldots, S_k, x_1, x_2, \ldots, x_k)(\langle x_1, y, S_1\rangle \in \mathbb{R}, \langle x_2, y, S_2\rangle \in \mathbb{R}, \ldots,$
$\langle x_k, y, S_k\rangle \in \mathbb{R}\ r \in S_i \to x_i P_{ru}y$ for all i and y_λ is the consequence of exercising $\langle x, y, T\rangle, \langle x_1, y, S_1\rangle, \ldots,$ and $\langle x_k, y, S_k\rangle$ simultaneously),
(b) $yP_{bu}y_1$,
(c) for every $i = 1, 2, \ldots, \lambda - 1$, either

$$(\forall e)[y_i P_{eu} y_{i+1}],$$

or

$$(\exists S_{i1}, S_{i2}, \ldots, S_{ik(i)})\left[b \notin \bigcup_{j=1}^{k(i)} S_{ij}\right.$$

& $(\exists y_{i1}, y_{i2}, \ldots, y_{ik(i)})(\langle y_{i1}, y_{i+1}, S_{i1}\rangle \in \mathbb{R},$
$\langle y_{i2}, y_{i+1}, S_{i2}\rangle \in \mathbb{R}, \ldots,$
$\langle y_{ik(i)}, y_{i+1}, S_{ik(i)}\rangle \in \mathbb{R}$ & $[r \in S_{i1} \to y_{i1} P_{ru} y_{i+1}]$
& $\cdots$ & $[r \in S_{ik(i)}$
$\to y_{ik(i)} P_{ru} y_{i+1}]$ & y_i is the consequence of exercising
$\langle y_{i1}, y_{i+1}, S_{i1}\rangle \cdots$

$\left. \langle y_{ik(i)}, y_{i+1}, S_{ik(i)}\rangle \text{ simultaneously.})\right],$

(d)   for every finite sequence $\sum' = z_1, z_2, \ldots, z_{\lambda'}$ of alternatives in v such that

(i) $z_{\lambda'} = y$,
(ii) $z_1 P_{bu} y$,
(iii) for every $i = 1, 2, \ldots, \lambda' - 1$, either

$$(\forall e)[z_i P_{eu} z_{i+1}],$$

or

$(\exists T_{i1}, T_{i2}, T_{ik'(i)}, z_{i1}, z_{i2}, \ldots, z_{ik'(i)})(\langle z_{i1}, z_{i+1}, T_{i1}\rangle$

$\in \mathbb{R} \cdots \langle z_{ik'(i)}, z_{i+1}, T_{ik'(i)}\rangle \in \mathbb{R} \ \& \ [r \in T_{i1} \rightarrow z_{i1} P_{ru} z_{i+1}]$

$\& \cdots \& \ [r \in T_{ik'(i)} \rightarrow z_{ik'(i)} P_{ru} z_{i+1}] \ \& \ z_i$ is the consequence of exercising

$\langle z_{i1}, z_{i+1}, T_{i1}\rangle \cdots \langle z_{ik'(i)}, z_{i+1}, T_{ik'(i)}\rangle$ simultaneously),

there is a sequence $\sum'' = w_1, w_2, \ldots, w_{\lambda''}$ of alternatives in v such that

(iv) $w_{\lambda''} = z_1$,
(v) $y P_{bu} w_1$,
(vi) for every $i = 1, 2, \ldots, \lambda'' - 1$, either

$$(\forall e)[w_i P_{eu} w_{i+1}],$$

or

$(\exists U_{i1}, U_{i2}, \ldots, U_{ik''(i)}, w_{i1}, w_{i2}, \ldots, w_{ik''(i)})\left(b \notin \bigcup_{j=1}^{k'(i)} U_{ij} \ \& \ \langle w_{i1}, w_{i+1}, U_{i1}\rangle\right.$

$\in \mathbb{R} \cdots \langle w_{ik''(i)}, w_{i+1}, U_{ik''(i)}\rangle \in \mathbb{R} \ \& \ [r \in U_{i1} \rightarrow w_{i1} P_{ru} w_{i+1}]$

$\& \cdots \& \ [r \in U_{ik''(i)} \rightarrow w_{ik''(i)} P_{ru} w_{i+1}] \ \& \ w_i$ is the consequence of exercising

$\langle w_{i1}, w_{i+1}, U_{i1}\rangle \cdots \langle w_{ik''(i)}, w_{i+1}, U_{ik''(i)}\rangle$ simultaneously$\left.\right).$

Using this version of rights exercising, it is still possible to carry out the proof of Gibbard's Pareto-consistent libertarian claim.

Correctable Miscalculations

Up to this point our criticisms of Gibbard's exercising rule have fallen into two classes: Those for which there is a revision allowing Gibbard's analysis to go through, and those such as costless information and caution that we write off as future research lines. Now we take up a problem that seriously affects Gibbard's analysis. The easiest way to get into this is to reexamine the Angelina–Edwin–Judge example. There we saw that there are

situations in which each individual might waive a right because of a miscalculation, correctable with available information, that the other was going
to exercise his right. For that specific example, the problem can be avoided by
a natural revision to Gibbard's rule in which rights are waived only if the
y_1 of a $\sum$ sequence is *strictly* worse than y (not just if it is no better). But does
this adjustment eliminate all cases of correctable miscalculation?

That correctable miscalculation is to be expected arises from the asym-
metry of our rules. Even when everyone is following, say, the Third Revised
Rule, it is part of that exercising rule that everyone is erroneously assuming
that everyone else is following the classical exercising rule. Consider $C_u(\{w,$
$x, y, z\})$, where u has preference orderings for the three individuals as follows:

$$1: \quad yxwz,$$
$$2: \quad zxwy,$$
$$3: \quad xzwy.$$

The rights system will be

$$\mathbb{R} = \{\langle y, z, 1\rangle, \langle z, x, 2\rangle, \langle x, w, 3\rangle\}.$$

Now the Third Revised Rule would have 3 calculate as follows: "Suppose I
exercise $\langle x, w, 3\rangle$. Then 2, who prefers z to x, would exercise $\langle z, x, 2\rangle$, and
then 1, who prefers y to z, would exercise $\langle y, z, 1\rangle$. There is no (repairing)
extension of $\sum = y, z, x$ since no one has rights over y and no alternative in
the agenda is Pareto-superior to y. The $\sum$ sequence would yield for me an
alternative y, strictly worse than w. Thus I should waive $\langle x, w, 3\rangle$." But this is
clearly a miscalculation. Individual 2 would *not* exercise $\langle z, x, 2\rangle$ if he were
also following the Third Revised Rule. The sequence $\sum = y, z$ together with
$\langle y, z, 1\rangle \in \mathbb{R}$ and $yP_{1_u}z$ is 2's rationale for waiving $\langle z, x, 2\rangle$. In assuming 3 to
be following the Third Revised Rule *we are assuming 3 has all the information
about u and $\mathbb{R}$ and so has the information necessary to see that 2 could not
reasonably be expected to behave in the way the Third Revised Rule tells 3 to
expect 2 to behave.* The miscalculation is correctable.

But the mere existence of such an example is not important. The significant question for social choice theory is how serious the phenomenon is for
Gibbard's Pareto-consistent-libertarian possibility theorem (Theorem 9-3)
and its proof.

The effect our introduction of correctable miscalculations has on that
result is to be seen in Theorem 9-4 below. But first we will present more
terminology. We must describe the production function telling us the consequence of simultaneous rights exercising (our function appears natural in
j-variant cases of the sort implied by Gibbard's theorem). We wish to work
with cases such as the white room, pink room example, where the production
function to be used seemed obvious. When both $\langle (w, w), (p, w), 1\rangle$ and $\langle (p, p),$

$(p, w), 2\rangle$ are exercised at (p, w), we expect the consequence to be (w, p). But it is *not* obvious what happens if, say, both $\langle (p, p), (w, w), 1\rangle$ and $\langle (g, g), (w, w), 2\rangle$ are assigned and exercised; are both rooms pink via 1 or both green via 2? Or what other combination? The production function will not be obvious unless the rights system is fairly simple, eliminating the kind of conflict illustrated in the pink–green example. We will focus on such a simple kind of system in a way that ties in very closely with the j-variant idea. A rights system $\mathbb{R}$ will be called *regular* if with each nonempty subset T of N we associate a set $I(T)$ of integers such that if $\langle x, y, T\rangle \in \mathbb{R}$, then x and y differ only in features M_i, where $i \in I(T)$ and furthermore the following rule prevails:

$T_1 \neq T_2 \rightarrow$ [If both $\langle x, y, T\rangle$ and $\langle z, y, T_2\rangle$ are in $\mathbb{R}$,

then $i \in I(T_1) \cap I(T_2)$ implies that the ith components of

x and z are identical].

For regular rights systems we define the *natural* production function: If $\langle x_1, t, T_1\rangle \cdot \langle x_2, y, T_2\rangle, \ldots, \langle x_k, y, T_k\rangle$ are exercised simultaneously, the consequence is z whose ith component is

$$
z_i = \begin{cases} y_i & \text{if } i \notin \bigcup_{j=1}^{k} I(T_j), \\ x_{ji} & \text{if } i \in I(T_j). \end{cases}
$$

Finally, we must settle a problem about agenda. What might we say about b's exercise of $\langle x, y, b\rangle$ at (v, u) if $\langle z, y, e\rangle \in \mathbb{R}$ and the consequence of exercising these rights simultaneously is an alternative *not* in v? At such an abstract level, this question is impossible to answer. Here we resolve this kind of dilemma by working with choice functions and rights systems satisfying the following condition:

A choice function C and rights system $\mathbb{R}$ are *agenda closed* with respect to a production function if every agenda v in domain of C has the property that if $x \in v$ and z is the consequence of the simultaneous exercise of rights over x, then $z \in v$.

Theorem 9-4   There are sets E and N, with $\mu \geq 3$, such that for *every* non-trivial choice function C and rights system $\mathbb{R}$, if

(i) C satisfies the weak Pareto condition,
(ii) C satisfies the libertarian Condition L'' via $\mathbb{R}$,
(iii) $\mathbb{R}$ is regular,
(iv)   the production function is the natural one,
(v) C and $\mathbb{R}$ are agenda closed with respect to the production function,

then there is an agenda v and society u in the domain of C and an individual b such that b makes a correctable miscalculation at (v, u) if everyone follows the Third Revised Rule.

Proof Let $E = \{x_1, x_2, x_3\} \times \{y_1, y_2, y_3\} \times \{z_1, z_2, z_3\}$ and $N = \{1, 2, 3\}$. Without loss of generality, assume that the assignment of features to individuals of the libertarian condition is the identity map; C accords b right to x over y if x and y are b-variants. Thus the rights system $\mathbb{R}$ that C realizes must contain $\langle x, y, b \rangle$ if x and y are b-variants. $\mathbb{R}$ can contain no other triples. For suppose $\mathbb{R}$ contains a triple with third element T. $I(T)$ must be nonempty. Without loss of generality suppose $1 \in I(T)$ and $\langle x, y, S \rangle \in \mathbb{R}$, where x and y differ in at least their first feature. But $\langle z, y, 1 \rangle \in \mathbb{R}$, where z has its first component different from either x or y (here we need three versions for each feature). Thus regularity requires $T = \{1\}$. It is then easily shown that regularity must imply that x and y are 1-variants. So $\mathbb{R}$ contains $\langle x, y, T \rangle$ iff $T - \{b\}$ and x and y are b-variants.

Now consider $v = E$ (which must be in the domain of C by nontriviality and the closure condition) and u given by the presentation shown in Table 9-1 in which higher alternatives are more preferred.

Among the Pareto-optimal alternatives are (x_2, y_2, z_1) and (x_2, y_2, z_2). Should 3 exercise $\langle (x_2, y_2, z_1), (x_2, y_2, z_2), 3 \rangle$? Consider the sequence $\sum = (x_1, y_1, z_1), (x_2, y_1, z_1), (x_2, y_2, z_1)$. If 3 follows the Third Revised Rule, he will note that 2 prefers (x_2, y_1, z_1) over (x_2, y_2, z_1) and 1 prefers (x_1, y_1, z_1) to (x_2, y_1, z_1). The result (x_1, y_1, z_1) is strictly worse in the eyes of 3 than (x_2, y_2, z_2). There is no repairing sequence since no invocation of either the weak Pareto condition or rights exercising (via the classical rule) would lead to a change in the first component away from x_1, and all alternatives with first component x_1 are strictly worse in the eyes of 3 than (x_2, y_1, z_1) except (x_1, y_2, z_1); but 2 would change this to (x_1, y_1, z_1) which is worse than (x_2, y_2, z_2). Thus 3, following the Third Revised Rule, should waive $\langle (x_2, y_2, z_1), (x_1, y_1, z_2), 3 \rangle$.

We now show that the waiving of $\langle (x_2, y_2, z_1), (x_1, y_1, z_2), 3 \rangle$ is a correctable miscalculation. The main point is simply that 2, also following the Third Revised Rule, would not exercise $\langle (x_2, y_1, z_1), (x_2, y_2, z_1), 2 \rangle$. The sequence $\sum = (x_1, y_1, z_1), (x_2, y_1, z_1)$, with 1 exercising his right to (x_1, y_1, z_1) over (x_2, y_1, z_1), yields an alternative (x_1, y_1, z_1) strictly worse in the eyes of 2 than (x_2, y_2, z_1). It is easily seen that there is no repairing sequence. Thus 2 would waive $\langle (x_2, y_1, z_1), (x_2, y_2, z_1), 2 \rangle$.

Finally, a check will show that there is no *other* sequence $\sum$ leading 3 to waive $\langle (x_2, y_2, z_1), (x_2, y_2, z_1), 3 \rangle$ via the Third Revised Rule that does not also involve a correctable miscalculation. □

Table 9-1

1	2	3
(x_1,y_1,z_1)	(x_2,y_1,z_1)	(x_2,y_2,z_1)
(x_1,y_1,z_2)	(x_2,y_2,z_1)	(x_1,y_2,z_1)
(x_1,y_2,z_1)	(x_1,y_1,z_1)	(x_2,y_2,z_2)
(x_1,y_2,z_2)	(x_1,y_2,z_1)	(x_1,y_1,z_1)
(x_1,y_1,z_3)	(x_3,y_1,z_1)	(x_1,y_1,z_2)
(x_1,y_2,z_3)	(x_2,y_1,z_2)	(x_3,y_3,z_1)
(x_1,y_3,z_1)	(x_2,y_1,z_3)	(x_3,y_3,z_2)
(x_1,y_3,z_2)	(x_1,y_1,z_2)	(x_1,y_2,z_2)
(x_1,y_3,z_3)	(x_1,y_1,z_3)	(x_2,y_1,z_1)
(x_2,y_2,z_2)	(x_3,y_1,z_2)	(x_2,y_1,z_2)
(x_2,y_2,z_1)	(x_3,y_1,z_2)	(x_1,y_3,z_1)
(x_2,y_2,z_2)	(x_1,y_2,z_2)	(x_1,y_3,z_2)
(x_2,y_1,z_2)	(x_1,y_2,z_3)	(x_3,y_1,z_1)
(x_2,y_1,z_3)	(x_2,y_2,z_2)	(x_3,y_1,z_2)
(x_2,y_3,z_1)	(x_2,y_2,z_3)	(x_2,y_3,z_1)
(x_2,y_3,z_2)	(x_3,y_2,z_1)	(z_2,y_3,z_2)
(x_2,y_3,z_3)	(x_3,y_2,z_2)	(x_3,y_2,z_1)
(x_2,y_1,z_1)	(x_3,y_2,z_3)	(x_3,y_2,z_2)
(x_3,y_1,z_1)	(x_1,y_3,z_1)	(x_1,y_1,z_3)
(x_3,y_1,z_2)	(x_1,y_3,z_2)	(x_1,y_2,z_3)
(x_3,y_1,z_3)	(x_1,y_3,z_3)	(x_1,y_3,z_3)
(x_3,y_2,z_1)	(x_2,y_3,z_1)	(x_2,y_1,z_3)
(x_3,y_2,z_2)	(x_2,y_3,z_2)	(x_2,y_2,z_3)
(x_3,y_2,z_3)	(x_2,y_3,z_3)	(x_2,y_3,z_3)
(x_3,y_3,z_1)	(x_3,y_3,z_1)	(x_3,y_1,z_3)
(x_3,y_3,z_2)	(x_3,y_3,z_2)	(x_3,y_2,z_3)
(x_3,y_3,z_3)	(x_3,y_3,z_3)	(x_3,y_3,z_3)

One observation on this proof is useful. The elaborate example developed involved, for each individual, only *unconditional* preferences. Thus no return to the conditional–unconditional distinction in the early part of Gibbard's analysis can be invoked to save us from correctable miscalculations.

While I have presented Theorem 9-4 as a criticism of a rights-exercising rule, it might also be seen as a criticism of confining our attention only to regular rights systems. But one must be careful here; regularity of $\mathbb{R}$ is only sufficient and not necessary. The gist of the proof can go through for some nonregular $\mathbb{R}$ if we constrain what rights can be exercised simultaneously.

While economists' models are probably somewhat remiss in their failure to take into account mistakes, miscalculations, and other avoidable errors, I do not think anyone would want to base a libertarian moral philosophy on the assumption that there is a certain kind of error that all people will repeatedly make. The Third Revised Rule is a very weak basis for a moral philosophy.

But it is vitally important to see that this does *not* simply eradicate Gibbard's work and return us to Sen's Paretian liberal problem. Gibbard's paramount contribution is the decomposition of a decisiveness condition (Sen's liberalism) into rights existence and rights exercising. He used this framework to see the "impossibility of a Paretian liberal" as a critique of the classical exercising rule that Sen used. Gibbard's revised rule and our revisions of his revision are all unacceptable, but so is the classical rule. It is Gibbard who has gotten us to ask the right questions.

IO UNSOLVED PROBLEMS

To conclude this book, I will gather together questions and unresolved conjectures on five topics related to earlier material and then address myself briefly to the difficult problems of judging the reasonableness of the conditions employed in the impossibility theorems presented here.

Strategy-Proofness

On this topic several research problems seem important. The first of these has been raised by Pattanaik [253]. Recall that in Chapter 6 we introduced the idea of counterthreats which reduced the amount of expected manipulation. If we increase the possibility of counterthreats, manipulation would be reduced and the requirement of nonmanipulability would be weaker, making an impossibility result harder to obtain. Pattanaik proposes one such change. In the counterthreat mechanism of Chapter 6, a coalition $S \subseteq N - \{i\}$ can meet i's threat to move from u to u' by a counterthreat from u' to u'' only if everyone in S actually prefers $\overline{C_{u''}(v)}$ to $\overline{C_{u'}(v)}$. It is not known if the analog to Theorem 6-4, for the case in which S can move from u' to u'' even if everyone does not prefer the resulting chosen elements, is true.

A second area of research would combine the work on counterthreats with work on abandoning single-valuedness. There are no known impossibility theorems that work with a notion of strategy-proofness by counterthreats defined for circumstances in which $C_u(v)$ need not be a singleton.

The third area involves further study of possibilities of good social choice procedures under certain assumptions about narrowing $C_u(v)$ to single alternatives. Gibbard's work on using chance mechanisms with known probabilities [144, 145] has been mentioned, but much remains to be done with other mechanisms and even with Gibbard's mechanisms, in which he has had to assume away the possibility of individual indifference.

Arrow's Theorem and the Justice Criterion

In Chapter 8, we presented three possible translations of Arrow's theorem into the language of extended preference and grading principles of justice. The third, which uses a rather awkward decisiveness condition, was proven true. In Exercise 6 of Chapter 8 we looked at a case of a social choice function based on lexicographical maximin with respect to the extended preference relation of individual 1. By the third translation, someone must be narrowly E-decisive—but it is *not* individual 1! We need a true translation of Arrow's theorem to the grading principles case which builds upon a nondictatorship condition that would be violated for that example by individual 1, i.e., that would rule out having the social choice procedure depend only on information embodied in the preference relation of a single individual.

Variable Population Size

Also in Chapter 8, we discussed a theorem, adapted from Smith [321], on collective choice rules that have to be flexible enough to deal with populations of all sizes. Too little work has been done in this area and the great strength of the conditions used in Theorem 8-10—particularly in comparison with Theorem 5-7—suggest room for considerable improvement.

Impossibility Results without a Pareto Condition

Theorem 4-13, by Wilson, dropped the Pareto condition from Arrow's theorem and used some rather mild new conditions (weak nonimposition, nonnull, and no inverse dictator). Wilson's theorem was an adaptation of Arrow's and so required full transitive rationality as the regularity constraint. It would be very interesting to see how far the other theorems presented here (especially those in Chapter 4 with weaker regularity constraints) could be dealt with in a similar manner. The difficulty of Wilson's techniques seems to have delayed progress here, but I expect the theorems that result will be worth the effort.

Social Choice from Individual Choice

Throughout this book, we have assumed that *individuals'* choices are founded on reflexive, complete, and transitive preferences. Even setting aside the weakness of the empirical support for transitivity, the theorems we have examined here themselves suggest the need for concern over our assumptions about individual choice procedures. For May [218] has pointed out that Arrow's formalism can be reinterpreted so that "society" is a single individual and "individual ordering" is the ranking of the single individual by one of many criteria:

> In this hypothetical case each of us, when faced with the need to make a decision, will be a deliberative assembly where isolated individuals with divergent interests confront each other. (Barbut [27, p. 163])

Arrow's theorem then points out the impossibility of aggregating ranking by different criteria into a single overall transitive preference relation for the individual. The assumption of reflexive, complete, and transitive preferences Barbut calls a "psychology without nuance." Of course, if we demand of a collective rule that it not only aggregate such regular individual choice procedures but even some very "irregular" ones, impossibility results will be easier to obtain. This approach may allow us to prove some theorems that work with broader domains while dropping some conditions, such as positive responsiveness, that might not always seem desirable. Note that Wilson [353] and Brown [67] have expressed theorems in which individual preferences were allowed to be semiorders, but, in fact, their proofs nowhere required a profile of semiorders that was not a profile of transitive relations and their theorems work with the standard domain constraint (cf. Exercise 4 of Chapter 4). Nothing is really known about what results can be obtained when f is forced to work with profiles that are composed of, say, acyclic relations or choice functions satisfying Property β.

Evaluation of Conditions

Any one of the impossibility theorems we have presented will seem disturbing only if all the conditions required seem to be "reasonable" constraints on a social choice procedure—not that we might be concerned only with conditions that seem completely reasonable to us. To paraphrase Archibald [4, p. 321], there are many reasons, besides our own value judgements, for finding a criterion interesting: it may be important to other people; it may raise interesting technical questions; it may appeal in many ways to our curiosity without having our moral approbation. But clearly theorems with apparently desirable constraints will be more difficult to deal with than those with undesirable but technically interesting constraints. I do not propose to describe here a sieve that cleanly separates desirable or reasonable conditions from those not desirable. I could not do it even if I proposed to. What I do want is to present some observations on such separation procedures that might aid some very confused discussions in the literature.

First, we make the obvious point (especially obvious after our remarks, in the previous section, on May's interpretation) that there are a variety of possible interpretations of such "primitive" terms of our formalism as "alternative" and "individual." Conditions desirable under one interpretation may be undesirable under another. Nothing has contributed more to the fruitless nature of most discussions of constraints such as independence of irrelevant alternatives than the effort either to discuss them in an interpretation-free context or naively to transfer a judgment of unreasonableness for one interpretation over to another.

Second, related to the first, we should not judge constraints in isolation from whatever other constraints we are planning to impose. For example, Blau [46] points out that nonimposition may make no sense for aggregation procedures working over a restricted domain. If, for every u, we must have $xP_{iu}y$ for all i, why insist that for some u, $C_u(\{x, y\}) = \{y\}$? Similarly, Little [205] argued that a nondictatorship condition need not be compelling if $|E| = 2$. Little is certainly correct when he says: "It is foolish to accept or reject a set of ethical axioms one at a time [205, p. 143]."

Next I would like to make some observations on two broad classes of constraints, simplicity conditions, and decisiveness conditions, for these have been at the heart of all our theorems. Let us discuss decisiveness conditions first. As noted in Chapter 9, it is enlightening to decompose decisiveness conditions into rights allocations and rights-exercising rules. As we discovered at some length, we do not really have any very good rights-exercising rules with which to work, and from that point of view, all decisiveness conditions are suspect. But this is not the only basis for criticizing decisiveness requirements. For other perspectives, we focus attention on the Pareto conditions.

Clearly, the Pareto conditions make sense only if N has the "correct" interpretation. Even when everyone in N strictly prefers x to y, that is not very compelling unless N includes everyone affected by the choice between x and y. And "everyone" may include individuals from whom (perhaps because they have not been born) it is difficult to obtain preference information. When you have the right N and independence of irrelevant alternatives prevails, so that in choosing between x and y only preferences between x and y need be consulted, unanimity on those preferences seems determining. But if independence is not assumed, why could unanimity not be overruled by information somewhere else in the system? In any case there is significant dissent even when N is correct and independence holds. Sen believes (cf., e.g., Sen [317]) that the main moral from the Paretian liberal problem is that we have to look behind preferences. In the cases Sen examines, everyone may prefer x to y, but some do so for "clearly wrong" reasons. Sen suggests that in having a set decisive for x against y, it should prevail not just when they all prefer x to y and do not waive their right, but only when their preferences reflect good motivations. In any case, we must allow the possibility that N would waive its rights on occasion.

Turning to simplicity conditions, I will focus on regularity conditions such as Property α:

$$S \subseteq T \rightarrow [C(T) \cap S \subseteq C(S)].$$

Three observations may be made. First, they are terribly strong conditions and, even in their weakest forms, make impossible choice procedures satisfying other conditions that, under some interpretations, all seem reasonable. Second, they are not well defended. Only since Plott broke out the independence of path part of transitive rationality for defense has there been serious analysis of when and why regularity conditions should be invoked. Third, these conditions may encounter problems with the rights-exercising games discussed in Chapter 9. Given an agenda $\{x, y, z\}$, y might be chosen because someone waives his right to x over y for fear of then getting stuck with z. But on $\{x, y\}$ the right might be exercised to get x chosen. This yields a clear violation of Property α.

Regularity and independence conditions make sense only where we can find good arguments for them as, for example, in terms of resource conservation. Varian [336] has attempted to work with some automata-theoretic notions of computational complexity and this is very interesting work, but even this is not well founded in terms of resource uses.

Clearly the remarks of this section do not go too far in dispelling what Sen calls [318] the "Arrowian gloom," as exemplified by Riker [279]:

> After this theorem, one feels the same sort of retrospective pity for the arithmeticians of proportional representation as for the geometers who tried to square the circle until it was discovered that π was a transcendental number.

But not all of us feel the gloom. Some feel that impossibility theorems have tremendously clarified the boundary of what is possible in the way of "good" social choice. We who work in the field have such a distorted view that we begin to believe everyone should rejoice when a deep new impossibility theorem is discovered.

MATHEMATICAL APPENDIX

As was observed in the Introduction, this appendix will not serve as a useful way to learn concepts not previously encountered. They are provided here to recall material once learned but now only vaguely remembered and to provide some agreement on terminology and notation. For more complete discussions, the reader is directed to Fishburn's *Mathematics of Decision Theory*.

A. Logic

I. Given propositions p and q, we can form new propositions as follows:

(a) $\neg p$ or not p: the *denial* of p, which is true just when p is false.

(b) $p \& q$: read "p and q"; the *conjunction* of p and q, which is true just when both p and q are true.

(c) $p \vee q$: read "p or q"; the *disjunction* of p and q, which is true just when either p or q, or both, are true.

(d) $p \rightarrow q$: read "if p, then q" or "p implies q"; *implication*. This proposition is false just when p is true and q is false. Alternative readings of this expression are: "p is a sufficient condition for q" and "q is a necessary condition for p."

(e) $p \Leftrightarrow q$: read "p if and only if q," sometimes abbreviated as "p iff q"; *equivalence*. This proposition is true just when either p and q are both true or both are false. An alternative reading of this expression is: "p is a necessary and sufficient condition for q." $p \Leftrightarrow q$ is usually proven by separate proofs of $p \to q$ and $q \to p$ because of the validity of the equivalence

$$(p \Leftrightarrow q) \Leftrightarrow [(p \to q) \& (q \to p)].$$

II. Given a 1-ary predicate Fx asserting that x has property F, we form two important propositions:

(a) $(\exists x)(Fx)$: read "there is an x such that F of x"; This is true just when there exists at least one element a in the universe of discourse, for which the proposition Fa is true.

(b) $(\forall x)(Fx)$: read "for all x, Fx"; this is true just when Fa is true for each and every a in the universe of discourse.

III. The end of a proof is marked by a square $\square$, which is Halmos's modern version of "Q.E.D."

B. Sets

I. Sets are presented within braces either as an explicit list,

$$\{1, 2, 3\}$$

or as a description of its elements,

$$\{x : Fx\}$$

(read: "the set of x such that Fx). The Greek epsilon $\in$ is used to indicate membership or elementhood:

$$1 \in \{1, 2, 3\}.$$

Denial of membership,

$$\neg(4 \in \{1, 2, 3\})$$

is usually rewritten as

$$4 \notin \{1, 2, 3\}.$$

II. Sets are *equal* just when they have exactly the same members:

$$\{1, 2, 3\} = \{3, 2, 1\}$$
$$= \{3, 1, 3, 2, 2, 2\}$$
$$= \{x \mid x \text{ is an integer and } 0 < x < 4\}.$$

III. Set A is a *subset* of a set B if all the elements of A are elements of B, i.e., if the proposition

$$(\forall x)(x \in A \to x \in B)$$

is true. The relation is written $A \subseteq B$. An equivalent expression for this relation is: B is a *superset* of A. Set equality, $A = B$, prevails when both $A \subseteq B$ and $B \subseteq A$ are true. If $A \subseteq B$ but $A \neq B$, we write $A \subsetneqq B$ and say that A is a *proper* subset of B. Among the subsets of a set A, one is of particular importance, namely the set $\varnothing$, containing *no* elements. $\varnothing$ is called the *null* set or *empty* set and is a subset of all other sets. The set of *all* subsets of $\{1, 2, 3\}$ is then

$$\{\varnothing, \{1\}, \{2\}, \{3\}, \{1, 2\}, \{1, 3\}, \{2, 3\}, \{1, 2, 3\}\}.$$

In general, given a set S, the set of all subsets of S is called the *power set* of S and is written 2^S.

IV.   Given sets A and B, the set of all elements they have in common is called their *intersection* and is written $A \cap B$:

$$A \cap B = \{x \,|\, x \in A \,\&\, x \in B\}.$$

If $A \cap B = \varnothing$, we say A and B are *disjoint*. Note that $A \subseteq B$ is equivalent to $A \cap B = A$.

V.   Given A and B, the set of elements in A or B, or both, is called their *union* and is written $A \cup B$:

$$A \cup B = \{x \,|\, (x \in A) \vee (x \in B)\}.$$

Note that $A \subseteq B$ is equivalent to $A \cup B = B$.

VI.   Given A and B, the set of elements in A but not in B is called their *difference* or the *relative complement* of B in A and is written $A - B$:

$$A - B = \{x \,|\, x \in A \,\&\, x \notin B\}.$$

If A is fixed, we speak of just the *complement* of B and write this as

$$\tilde{B}.$$

Note that $A \subseteq B$ is equivalent to $A - B = \varnothing$.

VII.   The *cardinality* of a set S, written $|S|$, is the number of elements in S:

$$|\{1, 2, 3\}| = |\{4, 5, 6\}| = 3.$$

$S = \varnothing$ is equivalent to $|S| = 0$. To say S has only finitely many elements, we write

$$|S| < \infty.$$

If $|S| = 1$, we say S is a *singleton* set.

C.   Relations and Functions

I.   Our set notation disregards the order in which elements are written, so that $\{1, 2\} = \{2, 1\}$. We switch from braces to parentheses to indicate that order *is* taken into account:

$$(1,2) \neq (2,1).$$

In general, *ordered pairs* satisfy the condition

$$(x, y) = (u, v) \qquad \text{iff} \quad x = u \quad \text{and} \quad y = v.$$

II. The *Cartesian product* of sets A and B, $A \times B$, is a set of ordered pairs defined by

$$A \times B = \{(x, y) | x \in A \ \& \ y \in B\}.$$

Thus

$$\{1, 2, 3\} \times \{x, y\} = \{(1, x), (2, x), (3, x), (1, y), (2, y), (3, y)\}.$$

Note that this is not the same as

$$\{x, y\} \times \{1, 2, 3\} = \{(x, 1), (x, 2), (x, 3), (y, 1), (y, 2), (y, 3)\}.$$

$A \times B = B \times A$ only if either $A = B$ or $A = \emptyset$ or $B = \emptyset$.

III. *Ordered n-tuples* such as $(x_1, x_2, \ldots, x_n)$ are characterized by satisfaction of the condition

$$(x_1, x_2, \ldots, x_n) = (y_1, y_2, \ldots, y_n) \qquad \text{iff} \quad x_1 = y_1, x_2 = y_2, \ldots \quad \text{and} \quad x_n = y_n.$$

The *Cartesian product* of sets $A_1, A_2, \ldots, A_n$ is

$$\prod_{i=1}^{n} A_i = A_1 \times A_2 \times \cdots \times A_n$$

$$= \{(x_1, x_2, \ldots, x_n) : x_1 \in A_1 \ \& \ x_2 \in A_2 \ \& \ \cdots \ \& \ x_n \in A_n\}.$$

Given a set A, the n-fold Cartesian product of A is

$$\prod_{i=1}^{n} A = \underbrace{A \times \cdots \times A}_{n \text{ factors}}$$

and is written A^n.

IV. A (binary) *relation* on A to B is a subset of $A \times B$. A binary relation on A is a relation on A to A, i.e., a subset of A^2. Thus, if A is the set of positive integers, the relation of strict inequality is given by

$$< \ = \{(1, 2), (1, 3), (2, 3), (1, 4), (2, 4), (3, 4), (1, 5), \ldots\}.$$

Often, instead of the notation $(x, y) \in R$, we write xRy, e.g., we write $2 < 3$ rather than $(2, 3) \in <$. We use the xRy notation in developing the following definitions of binary relations:

R on A is

(1) *reflexive* if xRx for all x in A,

(2) *connected* if xRy or yRx for all x, y in A such that $x \neq y$,

(3) *transitive* if $(xRy \;\&\; yRz) \rightarrow xRz$ for all x, y, z in A,

(4) *quasitransitive* if the relation P defined by

$$xPy \qquad \text{iff} \quad xRy \quad \text{and} \quad \neg yRx$$

is transitive,

(5) *acyclic* if $x_1 p x_2, x_2 p x_3, \ldots, x_{n-1} p x_n$ imply $\neg x_n p x_1$.

Given a binary relation R on A and a subset B of A, an element $x \in B$ is *R-maximal* in B if

$$\neg(\exists y)(y \in B \;\&\; yPx).$$

x is *R-best* in B if

$$(\forall y)(y \in B \rightarrow xRy).$$

An R-best element is R-maximal, but an R-maximal element need not be R-best. If R is complete, x is R-maximal iff it is R-best.

A *partial function* f from A to B is a relation from A to B satisfying

$$(x, y) \in f \;\&\; (x, z) \in f \rightarrow y = z,$$

i.e., it is "single-valued." The members x of A such that there is a y in B with $(x, y) \in f$ constitute a set called the *domain* of f. The members y of B such that there is some x in A with $(x, y) \in f$ comprise a set called the *range* of f. If $(x, y) \in f$, we also write $y = f(x)$. A set is *countable* if it is the range of some function on the positive integers.

If, for every $x \in A$, there is a y in B such that $(x, y) \in f$, i.e., if the domain of f is all of A, then f is called *total*. The word "function" alone will be used for total functions, and we will write $f : A \rightarrow B$ to indicate that f is a total function from A to B.

A function $f : A \rightarrow B$ is *injective* if $f(a) = f(b)$ implies $a = b$; it is *surjective* if the range of f is B; it is *bijective* if it is both injective and surjective.

A bijective function from a set A to itself is called a *permutation* of A. For small sets A, we will represent a permutation by two rows inside one set of parentheses, elements in the lower row being the images of the corresponding elements in the first row. As an example,

$$\begin{pmatrix} 1 & 2 & 3 & 4 \\ 3 & 2 & 4 & 1 \end{pmatrix}$$

describes a permutation f from $\{1, 2, 3, 4\}$ to itself satisfying

$$f(1) = 3, \qquad f(2) = 2, \qquad f(3) = 4, \qquad f(4) = 1.$$

Given a binary relation (possibly a function) R on A, if B is a subset of A, the *restriction* of R to B, written $R|_B$, is defined as $R \cap (B \times B)$. If $u = (R_1,$

$R_2, \ldots, R_n)$ is an n-tuple of binary relations on A and $B \subseteq A$, then by the restriction of u to B, written $u|_B$, we mean

$$(R_1|_B, R_2|_B, \ldots, R_n|_B).$$

D. Integers

From number theory we borrow one special function from the set of reals to the set of integers. The *greatest integer function* is defined by

$$[x] = i,$$

where i is the largest integer not exceeding x:

$$[\pi] = [3] = 3, \qquad [-\pi] = -4.$$

E. Zorn's Lemma

We shall make use of one result from set theory that is much deeper than those obtained in Section B. This result is Zorn's lemma, an equivalent of the axiom of choice. Let X be a nonempty set. $Q \neq \varnothing$ is a *nonempty ascending chain* of subsets of X if $Q \subset 2^X$, and for every pair of elements A, B of Q, either $A \subseteq B$ or $B \subseteq A$. Zorn's lemma is the proposition that X contains a $\subseteq$-maximal element if it is true that for every nonempty ascending chain Q of subsets of X, the set

$$\bigcup_{Y \in Q} Y$$

is also an element of X.

F. Notation Note

Profiles (cf. Chapter 1) or restrictions of profiles to proper subsets of E will be displayed by writing individual preference orderings horizontally with less preferred alternatives appearing to the right of less preferred alternatives:

$$i: \quad xyz$$

means xP_iy and yP_iz (and xP_iz).

Indifference will be indicated by parentheses:

$$i: \quad x(yz)$$

means xP_iy and yI_iz (and xP_iz). Brackets will be used to allow some relations to go unspecified. If only strict preferences are allowed,

$$i: \quad x[yz]$$

means xP_iy and xP_iz and *either* yP_iz or zP_ix. If individuals are allowed indifference, $[yz]$ could mean yI_iz. The main convention in using the bracket notation is that, in going from one profile to a related one, the bracketed relation remains unchanged. If at u_1 we have

$$i: \quad [xy],$$

we are allowing any relation between x and y. If u_2 is constructed by inserting z and we write

$$i: \quad [xy]z,$$

then it is understood that the unspecified relation between x and y is the *same* for i at both u_1 and u_2.

SELECTED BIBLIOGRAPHY
AND REFERENCES

Without pretending to completeness, this bibliography includes a number of books and papers which, while not referenced in the text, are closely related to social choice impossibility results.

1. Ahmad, Kabir, An Adaptive Approach to Social Choice, unpublished manuscript, Princeton Univ. 1975.
2. Allingham, Michael, *General Equilibrium.* New York: Halsted, 1975.
3. Arbib, Michael A., Man-Machine Symbiosis and the Evolution of Human Freedom, *The American Scholar* **43**, No. 1 (Winter 1973–1974), 38–54.
4. Archibald, G. C., Welfare Economics, Ethics and Essentialism, *Economica* [N.S.] **26**, No. 104 (November 1959), 316–327.
5. Arkhipoff, Oleg, Le probleme de l'Agregation dans la measure de la qualities de la vie: reformulation et generalisation du theoreme d'Arrow, *Annales de l'Institut National de la Statistique et des Studes Economiques*, No. 18 (January/April 1975).
6. Arkhipoff, Oleg, Problems in Welfare Measurement, unpublished.
7. Arrow. Kenneth J., A Difficulty in the Concept of Social Welfare, *Journal of Political Economy* **58**, No. 4 (August 1950),.
8. Arrow, Kenneth J., *Social Choice and Individual Values.* New York: Wiley, 1951.
9. Arrow, Kenneth J., Le principe de rationalité dans les décisions collectives, *Economie Appliquée*, **5**, No. 4 (October–December 1952).
10. Arrow, Kenneth J., Utilities, Attitudes, Choices: A Review Note, *Econometrica* **26**, No. 1 (January 1958), 1–23.
11. Arrow, Kenneth J., Rational Choice Functions and Orderings, *Economica* [N.S.] **26**, No. 102 (May 1959), 121–127.
12. Arrow, Kenneth J., *Social Choice and Individual Values*, 2nd ed. New York: Wiley, 1963.
13. Arrow, Kenneth J., Public And Private Values, in *Human Values and Economic Policy* (Sidney Hook, ed.), pp. 3–21. New York: New York Univ. Press, 1967.

14. Arrow, Kenneth J., The Place of Moral Obligation in Preference Systems, in *Human Values and Economic Policy* (Sidney Hook, ed.), pp. 117–119. New York: New York Univ. Press, 1967.

15. Arrow, Kenneth J., Values and Collective Decision Making, in *Philosophy, Politics and Society, Vol. 3* (Peter Laslett and W. G. Runciman, eds.), pp. 215–232. Oxford: Blackwell, 1967.

16. Arrow, Kenneth J., Tullock and an Existence Theorem of Politics, *Public Choice* **4** (Spring, 1969), 105–111.

17. Arrow, Kenneth J., Formal Theories of Social Welfare, in *Dictionary of the History of Ideas* (Philip P. Wiener, ed.), pp. 277–284. New York: Scribner's, 1973.

18. Arrow, Kenneth J., Extended Sympathy and the Possibility of Social Choice, *American Economic Review* **67**, No. 1 (February 1977), 219–225.

 * Arrow, Kenneth J. See also Barbut, Marc.

 * Asimakopulous, A. See also Kemp, Murray C.

19. d'Aspremont, Claude and Louis Gevers, Equity and Informational Basis of Collective Choice, *Review of Economic Studies* **44**, No. 137 (June 1977), 199–209.

20. Bailey, Martin J., Liberalism and Pareto-Optimality, unpublished manuscript, Univ. of Maryland, 1975.

21. Bailey, Martin J., Welfare Economies and Social Orderings, unpublished manuscript, Univ. of Maryland, 1976.

22. Banach, Stefan and Alfred Tarski, Sur la decomposition des ensembles de points en parties respectivement congruents, *Fundamenta Mathematicae* **6** (1924).

23. Banerji, D., Choice and Order: or First Things First, *Economica* [N.S.] **31**, No. 122 (May 1964), 158–167.

24. Barbera, Salvador, The Manipulability of Social Choice Mechanisms That Do Not Leave Too Much to Chance, *Econometrica*, forthcoming.

25. Barbera, Salvador, Manipulation of Social Decision Functions, *J. Economic Theory* **15**, No. 2 (August 1977), 266–278.

26. Barbera, Salvador, Nice Decision Schemes, unpublished manuscript, Univ. Autónoma de Madrid, 1976.

27. Barbut, Marc, Quelques aspects mathématiques de la décision rationnelle, *Les Temps Modernes* **15**, No. 164 (October 1959), 725–745. Translated by Corrine Hoexter as "Does the Majority Ever Rule?" *Portfolio and Art News Annual*, No. 4 (1961), 79–83, 161–168 with an introduction by Kenneth J. Arrow.

28. Bartoszynski, Robert, Power Structure in Dichotomous Voting, *Econometrica* **40**, No. 6 (November 1972), 1003–1019.

29. Batra, Raveendra N., and Prasanta K. Pattanaik, Transitivity of Social Decisions under Some More General Group Decision Rules Than Majority Voting, *Review of Economic Studies* **38**, No. 3 (July 1971), 295–306.

30. Batra, Raveendra N., and Prasanta K. Pattanaik, Transitive Multistage Majority Decisions with Quasi-Transitive Individual Preferences, *Econometrica* **40**, No. 6 (November 1972), 1121–1135.

31. Batra, Raveendra N., and Prasanta K. Pattanaik, On Some Suggestions for Having Non-Binary Social Choice Functions, *Theory and Decision* **3**, No. 1 (October 1972), 1–11.

32. Baumol, William, Review (of *Social Choice and Individual Values*), *Econometrica* **20**, No. 1 (January 1952).

33. Bergson, Abram, *Essays in Normative Economics*. Cambridge, Massachusetts: Harvard Univ. Press, 1966.

34. Bergstrom, Theaedore C., Maximal Elements of Acyclic Relations on Compact Sets, *Journal of Economic Theory* **10**, No. 3 (June 1975), 403–404.

35. Bernholz, Peter, Logrolling, Arrow Paradox and Decision Rules—a Generalization, *Kyklos* **27**, No. 1 (1974), 49–61.

36. Bernholz, Peter, Is a Parentian Liberal Really Impossible? *Public Choice* **20** (Winter 1974), 99–108.

37. Binmore, K. Social Choice and Parties, *Rev. Economic Studies* **43**, No. 135 (October 1976), 459–464.

38. Binmore, K., Arrow's Theorem with Conditions, mimeographed, London School of Economics, 1974.

39. Binmore, K., An Example in Group Preference, *Journal of Economic Theory* **10**, No. 3 (June 1975), 377–385.

40. Black, Duncan, *The Theory of Committees and Elections*. London and New York: Cambridge Univ. Press, 1958.

41. Black, Duncan, On Arrow's Impossibility Theorem, *Journal of Law and Economics* **12**, No. 2 (October 1969), 227–248.

42. Blackorby, Charles, Degrees of Cardinality and Aggregate Partial Orderings, *Econometrica* **43**, No. 5–6 (September–November 1975), 845–852.

43. Blackorby, Charles, and C. Donaldson, Utility vs. Equity: Some Plausible Quasi-orderings, Discussion Paper No. 75–105, Dept. of Economics, Univ. of British Columbia, 1975.

44. Blair, Douglas H., Path-Independent Social Choice Functions: A Further Result, *Econometrica* **43**, No. 1 (January 1975), 173–174.

45. Blair, Douglas H., Georges Bordes, Jerry S. Kelly, and Kotaro Suzumura, Impossibility Theorems without Collective Rationality, *Journal of Economic Theory* **13**, No. 3 (December 1976), 361–379.

46. Blau, Julian H., The Existence of Social Welfare Functions, *Econometrica* **25**, No. 2 (April 1957), 302–313.

47. Blau, Julian H., Arrow's Theorem with Weak Independence, *Economica* [N.S.] **38**, No. 152 (November 1971), 413–420.

48. Blau, Julian H., A Direct Proof of Arrow's Theorem, *Econometrica* **40**, No. 1 (January 1972), 61–67.

49. Blau, Julian H., Liberal Values and Independence, *Review of Economic Studies* **42**, No. 131 (July 1975), 395–403.

50. Blau, Julian H., Neutrality, Monotonicity and the Right of Veto: Comment, *Econometrica* **44**, No. 3 (May 1976), 603.

51. Blau, Julian H., and Rajat Deb, Social Decision Functions and Veto, *Econometrica* **45**, No. 4 (May 1977), 871–879.

52. Blau, Julian H., and Donald J. Brown, The Structure of Social Decision Functions, unpublished manuscript, 1977.

53. Blin, Jean-Marie, Preference Aggregation and Statistical Estimation, *Theory and Decision* **4**, No. 1 (September 1973), 65–84.

54. Blin, Jean-Marie, *Patterns and Configurations in Economic Science*. Dordrecht, Reidel, 1973.

56. Blin, Jean-Marie and Mark A. Satterthwaite, Individual Decisions and Group Decisions: The Fundamental Differences, unpublished manuscript, Northwestern Univ. (November 1975).

57. Blin, Jean-Marie, Strategyproofness and Single-peakedness, unpublished manuscript, Northwestern Univ. (December 1975).

58. Blin, Jean-Marie, On Preferences, Beliefs and Manipulation within Voting Situations, *Econometrica* **45**, No. 4 (May 1977), 881–888.

59. Bloomfield, S., An Axiomatic Formulation of Constitutional Games, Tech. Rep. 71–18, Stanford Univ., 1971.

60. Bordes, Georges, Consistency, Rationality, and Collective Choice, *Rev. Economic Studies* **43**, No. 135 (October 1976), 447–457.
  * Bordes, Georges. See Blair, Douglas.
61. Boulding, Kenneth, Some Contributions of Economics to the General Theory of Value, *Philosophy of Science* **23**, No. 1 (January 1956), 1–14.
62. Bowman, V. J., and Claude S. Colantoni, Majority Rule under Transitivity Constraints, *Management Science* **19** (May 1973), 1029–1041.
63. Brissaud, Marcel, Agregation des préférences individuelles, *Comptes Rendus* (Sér. A) **278**, No. 9 (25 February 1974), 637–639.
64. Brown, Donald J., An Approximate Solution to Arrow's Problem, *Journal of Economic Theory* **9**, No. 4 (December 1974), 375–383.
65. Brown, Donald J., Acyclicity and Choice, unpublished manuscript (1973).
66. Brown, Donald J., Why Acyclicity unpublished manuscript (1973).
67. Brown, Donald J., Collective Rationality, Cowles Foundation Discussion Paper No. 393, Yale Univ. (April 3, 1975).
68. Brown, Donald J., Aggregation of Preferences, *Quarterly Journal of Economics* **89**, No. 3 (August 1975), 456–469.
69. Brown, Donald J., Acyclic Aggregation over a Finite Set of Alternatives, unpublished manuscript, Yale Univ. (1975).
  * Brown, Donald J., See also Blau, Julian H.
70. Buchanan, James M., Social Choice, Democracy and Free Markets, *Journal of Political Economy* **62**, No. 2 (April 1954), 114–123.
71. Buchanan, James M., Individual Choice in Voting and the Market, *Journal of Political Economy* **62**, No. 4 (August 1954), 334–343.
72. Buchanan, James M., and Gordon Tullock, *The Calculus of Consent*. Ann Arbor: Univ. of Michigan Press, 1962.
73. Comacho, Antonio and Jon C. Sonstelie, Cardinal Welfare, Individualistic Ethics and Interpersonal Comparisons of Utilities: a Note, *Journal of Political Economy* **82** No. 3 (May/June 1974), 60–61.
74. Camacho, Antonio, Cardinal Utility and the Problem of Social Choice, unpublished manuscript, Northwestern Univ. (18 July 1972).
75. Campbell, Colin D., and Gordon Tullock, A Measure of the Importance of Cyclical Majorities *Economic Journal* **75**, No. 304 (December 1965), 853–857.
76. Campbell, Colin D., and Gordon Tullock, The Paradox of Voting—a Possible Method of Calculation, *American Political Science Review* **60**, No. 3 (September 1966), 684–685.
77. Campbell, Donald E., A Collective Choice Rule Satisfying Arrow's Five Conditions in Practice, in *Theory and Applications of a Collective Choice Rule*, Institute for Quantitative Analysis of Social and Economic Policy, Working Paper No. 7206 (Univ. of Toronto), 1972.
78. Campbell, Donald E., Social Choice and Intensity of Preference, *Journal of Political Economy* **81**, No. 1 (January/February 1973), 211–218.
79. Campbell, Donald E., Democratic Preference Functions, *Journal of Economic Theory* **12**, No. 2 (April 1976), 259–272.
80. Campbell, Donald E., Freedom of Choice and Social Choice, mimeographed (1975).
81. Chernoff, Herman, Rational Selection of Decision Functions, *Econometrica* **22**, No. 4 (October 1954), 422–443.
  * Cimbala, Steven J., See Friedland, Edward I.
  * Colantoni, Claude S. See Bowman, V. J.
82. Coleman, James S., The Possibility of a Social Welfare Function, *American Economic Review* **56**, No. 5 (December 1966), 1105–1122.

83. Contini, Bruno, A Note on Arrow's Postulates for a Social Welfare Function, *Journal of Political Economy* **74**, No. 3 (June 1966), 278–280.
84. Craven, J., Majority Voting and Social Choice, *Review of Economic Studies* **38** (2), No. 114 (April 1971), 265–267.
85. Czayka, L., and H. Krauch, A Graph-Theoretical Approach to the Aggregation of Individual Preference Orderings, *Theory and Decision* **3**, No. 1 (October 1972), 12–17.
86. Davidson, Donald, John C. C. McKinsey, and Patrick Suppes, Outline of a Formal Theory of Value, I, *Philosophy of Science* **22**, No. 2 (April 1955), 140–160.
87. Davis, John Marcell, The Transitivity of Preferences, *Behavioral Science* **3**, No. 1 (January 1958), 26–33.
88. Davis, Richard G., Comment on Arrow and the "New Welfare" Economics, *Economic Journal* **68**, No. 272 (December 1958), 834–835.
89. Day, Richard H., Rational Choice and Economic Behavior, *Theory and Decision* **1**, No. 3 (March 1971), 229–251.
* Deb, Rajat. See Blau, Julian H.
90. DeMeyer, Frank, and Charles Plott, The Probability of a Cyclical Majority, *Econometrica* **38**, No. 2 (March 1970), 345–354.
91. DeMayer, Frank, and Charles Plott, A Welfare Function Using "Relative Intensity of Preference," *Quarterly Journal of Economics* **85**, No. 1 (February 1971), 179–186.
92. Diamond, Peter A., Cardinal Welfare, Individualistic Ethics, and Interpersonal Comparisons of Utility: Comment, *Journal of Political Economy* **75**, No. 5 (October 1967), 765–766.
* Donaldson, C. See Blackorby, Charles.
93. Dummett, Michael and Robin Farquharson, Stability in Voting, *Econometrica* **29**, No. 1 (January 1961), 33–43.
94. Encarnación, José, Jr., On Independence Postulates Concerning Choice, *International Economic Review* **10**, No. 2 (June 1969), 134–140.
95. Fagen, Richard R., Some Contributions of Mathematical Reasoning to the Study of Politics, *American Political Science Review* **60**, No. 4 (December 1961), 888–900.
96. Farquharson, Robin, Sur une generalisation de la notion d'equilibrium, *Comptes Rendus* **240** (3 January 1955), 46–48.
97. Farquharson, Robin, *Theory of Voting*. New Haven, Connecticut: Yale Univ. Press, 1969.
* Farquharson, Robin. See Dummett, Michael.
98. Farrell, Michael J., Liberalism in the Theory of Social Choice, *Rev. Economic Studies* **43**, No. 133 (February 1976), 3–10.
99. Feldman, Allan M., and D. Weiman, Class Structure and Envy, mimeographed, Brown Univ., 1975.
    Feldman, Allan M., "A Very Unsubtle Version of Arrow's Impossibility Theorem," *Economic Inquiry* **12**, No. 4 (December 1974), 534–546.
100. Ferejohn, John A., and David Grether, On a Class of Rational Social Decision Procedures, *Journal of Economic Theory* **8**, No. 4 (August 1974), 471–482.
101. Ferejohn, John A., and David Grether, Weak Path Independence, *Journal of Economic Theory* **14**, No. 1 (February 1977), 19–31.
102. Fine, Ben J., A Note on "Interpersonal Aggregation and Partial Comparability," *Econometrica* **43**, No. 1 (January 1975), 173–174.
103. Fine, Ben J., Individual Liberalism in a Paretian Society, *Journal of Political Economy* **83**, No. 6 (December 1975), 1277–1281.
104. Fine, Ben J., Interdependent Preferences and Liberalism in a Paretian Society, Birkbeck Coll., Univ. of London, Discussion Paper No. 15 (1974).
105. Fine, Ben, and Kit Fine, Social Choice and Individual Ranking, *Review of Economic Studies* **41**, No. 127 (July 1974), 303–322; **41**, No. 128 (October 1974), 459–475.

106. Fine, Kit, Some Necessary and Sufficient Conditions for Representative Decision on Two Alternatives, *Econometrica* **40**, No. 6 (November 1972), 1083–1090.

107. Fine, Kit, Conditions for the Existence of Cycles under Majority and Non-Minority Rules, *Econometrica* **41**, No. 5 (September 1973), 889–899.

   * Fine, Kit, See Fine, Ben.

108. Fishburn, Peter C., Preferences, Summation and Social Welfare Functions, *Management Science* **16**, No. 3 (November 1969), 179–186.

109. Fishburn, Peter C., The Irrationality of Transitivity in Social Choice, *Behavioral Science* **15**, No. 2 (March 1970), 119–123.

110. Fishburn, Peter C., Comments on Hansson's "Group Preferences," *Econometrica* **38**, No. 6 (November 1970), 933–935.

111. Fishburn, Peter C., Arrow's Impossibility Theorem: Concise Proof and Infinite Voters, *Journal of Economic Theory* **2**, No. 1 (March 1970), 103–106.

112. Fishburn, Peter C., Intransitive Individual Indifference and Transitive Majorities, *Econometrica* **38**, No. 3 (May 1970), 482–489.

113. Fishburn, Peter C., Suborders on Commodity Spaces, *Journal of Economic Theory* **2**, No. 4 (December 1970), 321–328.

114. Fishburn, Peter C., Should Social Choice Be Based on Binary Comparisons? *Journal of Mathematical Sociology* **1**, No. 1 (January 1971), 133–142.

115. Fishburn, Peter C., Lotteries and Social Choices, *Journal of Economic Theory* **5**, No. 2 (October 1972), 189–207.

116. Fishburn, Peter C., Even Chance Lotteries in Social Choice Theory, *Theory and Decision* **3**, No. 1 (October 1972), 18–40.

117. Fishburn, Peter C., *Mathematics of Decision Theory*. Mouton, The Hague, 1972.

118. Fishburn, Peter C., *The Theory of Social Choice*. Princeton, New Jersey: Princeton Univ. Press, 1973.

119. Fishburn, Peter C., Transitive Binary Social Choices and Intraprofile Conditions, *Econometrica* **41**, No. 4 (July 1973), 603–615.

120. Fishburn, Peter C., Summation Social Choice Functions, *Econometrica* **41**, No. 6 (November 1973), 1183–1196.

121. Fishburn, Peter C., Social Choice Functions, *SIAM Review* **16**, No. 1 (January 1974), 63–90.

122. Fishburn, Peter C., On Collective Rationality and a Generalized Impossibility Theorem, *Review of Economic Studies* **41**, No. 128 (October 1974), 445–459.

123. Fishburn, Peter C., Impossibility Theorems without the Social Completeness Axiom, *Econometrica* **42**, No. 4 (July 1974), 695–704.

124. Fishburn, Peter C., Choice Functions on Finite Sets, *International Economic Review* **15**, No. 3 (October 1974), 729–749.

125. Fishburn, Peter C., Dictators on Blocks: Generalizations of Social Choice Impossibility Theorems, *Journal of Combinatorial Theory B* **20** (1976).

126. Fishburn, Peter C., Semiorders and Choice Functions, *Econometrica* **43**, No. 5–6 (September–November 1975), 975–977.

127. Fitzroy, Felix R., Review of A. K. Sen's *Collective Choice and Social Welfare*, *Kyklos* **24**, No. 4 (1971), 815–818.

128. Fleming, J. Marcus, A Cardinal Concept of Welfare, *Quarterly Journal of Economics* **66**, No. 3 (August 1952), 366–384.

129. Fleming, J. Marcus, Cardinal Welfare and Individualistic Ethics: Comment *Journal of Political Economy* **65**, No. 4 (August 1957), 355–357.

130. Frey Bruno S., Review (in German) of P. K. Pattanaik's *Voting and Collective Choice*, *Kyklos* **25**, No. 4 (1972), 895–896.

131. Friedland, Edward I., and Stephen J. Cimbala, Process and Paradox: The Significance of Arrow's Theorem, *Theory and Decision* **4**, No. 1 (September 1973), 51–64.

*   Fu, K. S. See Piccoli, Mary Louise.
132. Gärdenfors, Peter, Positionalist Voting Functions, *Theory and Decision* **4**, No. 1 (September 1973), 1–24.
133. Gärdenfors, Peter, Manipulation of Social Choice Functions, *Journal of Economic Theory* **13**, No. 2 (October 1976), 217–228.
134. Gardner, Roy, The Logic of the Liberal Paradox, unpublished manuscript, Cornell Univ., 1974.
135. Gardner, Roy, Some Implications of the Gibbard–Satterthwaite Theorem, unpublished manuscript, Cornell Univ., 1974.
136. Gardner, Roy, Two Theories of Misrevealed Preference for Representable Elections, unpublished manuscript, Cornell Univ., 1974.
137. Garman, Mark and Morton Kamien, The Paradox of Voting: Probability Calculations, *Behavioral Science* **13**, No. 4 (July 1968), 306–316.
138. Gauthier, D., Acyclicity, Neutrality and Collective Choice, mimeographed, Dept. of Philosophy, Univ. of Toronto, 1974.
139. Georgescu-Roegen, Nicholas, The Relation between Binary and Multiple Choices: Some Comments and Further Results, *Econometrica* **37**, No. 4 (October 1969), 728–730.
140. Gerber, D., Metrizing Social Preference, *Theory and Decision* **3**, No. 1 (October 1972), 41–48.
*   Gevers, Louis. See d'Aspremont, Claude.
141. Gibbard, Allan, Social Choice and the Arrow Conditions, unpublished manuscript (1969).
142. Gibbard, Allan, Manipulation of Voting Schemes: A General Result, *Econometrica* **41**, No. 4 (July 1973), 587–601.
143. Gibbard, Allan, A Pareto Consistent Libertarian Claim, *Journal of Economic Theory* **7**, No. 4 (April 1974), 388–410.
144. Gibbard, Allan, Manipulation of Schemes that Mix Voting with Chance, *Econometrica* **45**, No. 3 (April 1977), 665–681.
145. Gibbard, Allan, Straightforwardness of Game Forms with Lotteries on Alternatives, unpublished manuscript, Univ. of Pittsburgh (February 1976).
146. Gibbard, Allan, Social Decision, Strategic Behavior and Best Outcomes: An Impossibility Result, unpublished manuscript, Northwestern Univ.(June 1976).
147. Gleser, Leon Jay. The Paradox of Voting, *Public Choice* **7**, (Fall 1969), 47–63.
148. Goodman, Leo A., and Harry Markowitz, Social Welfare Functions Based on Individual Rankings, *American Journal of Sociology* **58**, No. 3 (November 1952), 257–262.
149. Graaf, Jan deV., *Theoretical Welfare Economics*. London and New York: Cambridge Univ. Press, 1957.
*   Grether, David. See Ferejohn, John A.
150. Guha, Ashok S. Neutrality, Monotonicity and the Right of Veto, *Econometrica* **40**, No. 5 (September 1972), 821–826.
151. Guilbaud, G. Th., Les Théories de l'Interet General et la Problème Logique de l'Agrégation, *Economie Appliquée* **5**, No. 4 (October–December 1952), 501–584. English Transl.: Theories of the General Interest and the Logical Problem of Aggregation, in *Readings in Mathematical Social Sciences* (Paul F. Lazarsfeld and Neil W. Henry, eds.), pp. 262–307. Chicago: Science Research Associates, 1966.
152. Hammond, Peter J., Equity, Arrow's Conditions and Rawls' Difference Principle, *Econometrica* **44**, No. 4 (July 1976), 793–804.
153. Hansson, Bengt, Choice Structures and Preferences Relations, *Synthese* **18**, No. 4 (October 1968), 443–458.
154. Hansson, Bengt, Fundamental Axioms for Preference Relations, *Synthese* **18**, No. 4 (October 1968), 423–442.

155. Hansson, Bengt, Group Preferences, *Econometrica* **37**, No. 1 (January 1969), 50–54.
156. Hansson, Bengt, Voting and Group Decision Functions, *Synthese* **20**, No. 4 (December 1969), 526–537.
157. Hansson, Bengt, Transitivity and Topological Structure of the Preference Space, in *Proceedings of the First Scandinavian Logic Symposium* (Uppsala, 1970).
158. Hansson, Bengt, The Existence of Group Preferences, *Public Choice* **28** (Winter, 1976), 89–98.
159. Hansson, Bengt, The Independence Condition in the Theory of Social Choice, *Theory and Decision* **4**, No. 1 (September 1973), 25–49.
160. Harsanyi, John C., Cardinal Welfare, Individualistic Ethics, and Interpersonal Comparisons of Utility, *Journal of Political Economy* **63**, No. 4 (August 1955), 309–321.
161. Harsanyi, John C., Ethics in Terms of Hypothetical Imperatives, *Mind* **69**, No. 267 (July 1958), 305–316.
162. Harsanyi, John C., Non-linear Social Welfare Functions, or, Do Welfare Economists Have a Special Exemption from Bayesian Rationality, mimeographed, Univ. of California, Berkeley (1975).
163. Hayden, Richard, A Note on Intransitivity and Rationality in Majority Decision, *Economica* [N.S.] **42**, No. 165 (February 1975), 92–96.
164. Herzberger, Hans G., Ordinal Preference and Rational Choice, *Econometrica* **41**, No. 2 (March 1973), 187–237.
165. Hildreth, Clifford, Alternative Conditions for Social Orderings, *Econometrica* **21**, No. 1 (January 1953), 81–94.
166. Hillinger, Claude and Victoria C. Lapham, The Impossibility of a Paretian Liberal: Comment by Two Who Are Unreconstructed, *Journal of Political Economy* **79**, No. 6 (November/December 1971), 1403–1405.
167. Houthakker, Hendrik S., On the Logic of Preference and Choice, in *Contributions to Logic and Methodology* (A.T. Tyminieniecka, ed.), pp. 193–207. Amsterdam: North-Holland Publ., 1965).
168. Hurwicz, Leonid, The Design of Resource Allocation Mechanisms, *American Economic Review* **62**, No. 2 (May 1973), 1–30.
169. Inada, Ken-Ichi, Elementary Proofs of Some Theorems about the Social Welfare Function, *Annals of the Institute of Statistical Mathematics* **6**, No. 1 (1954), 115–122.
170. Inada, Ken-Ichi, Alternative Incompatible Conditions for a Social Welfare Function, *Econometrica* **23**, No. 4 (October 1955), 396–399.
171. Inada, Ken-Ichi, On the Economic Welfare Function, *Econometrica* **32**, No. 3 (July 1964), 316–338.
172. Inada, Ken-Ichi, A Note on the Simple Majority Decision Rule, *Econometrica* **32**, No. 4 (October 1964), 525–531.
173. Inada, Ken-Ichi, On the Simple Majority Decision Rule, *Econometrica* **37**, No. 3 (July 1969), 490–506.
174. Inada, Ken-Ichi, Majority Rule and Rationality, *Journal of Economic Theory* **2**, No. 1 (March 1970), 27–40.
175. Inada, Ken-Ichi, Social Welfare Functions and Social Indifference Surfaces, *Econometrica* **39**, No. 3 (May 1971), 599–623.
176. Jamison, Dean T., and Lawrence J. Lau, Semiorders and the Theory of Choice, *Econometrica* **41**, No. 5 (September 1973), 901–912.
177. Jamison, Dean T., and Lawrence J. Lau, Semiorders and the Theory of Choice: A Correction, *Econometrica* **43**, No. 5–6 (September–November 1975), 975–977.
178. Johansen, Leif, An Examination of the Relevance of Kenneth Arrow's General Possibility Theorem to Economic Planning, *Economics of Planning* **9**, Nos. 1–2 (1969), 5–41.
179. Kalai, Ehud and Eitan Muller, Characterization of Domains Admitting Nondictatorial

Social Welfare Functions and Nonmanipulable Voting Procedures, unpublished manuscript, Northwestern Univ. (10 August 1976).

180. Kalai, Ehud, Elisha A. Pazner, and David Schmeidler, Collective Choice Correspondences as Admissible Outcomes of Social Bargaining Processes, *Econometrica* **44**, No. 2 (March 1976), 233–240.

181. Kalai, Ehud, Eitan Muller, and Mark A. Satterthwaite, Social Welfare Functions When Preferences Are Convex and Continuous: Impossibility Results, unpublished manuscript, Northwestern Univ. (1976).

182. Kalai, Ehud and David Schmeidler, Aggregation Procedure for Cardinal Preferences: A Formulation and Proof of Samuelson's Impossibility Conjecture, *Econometrica* **45**, No. 6 (September 1977), 431–38.

 * Kamien, Morton. See Garman, Mark.

183. Karni, Edi, Individual Liberty, The Pareto Principle and the Possibility of a Social Choice Function, Working Paper no. 32, The Foerder Institute for Economic Research, Tel-Aviv Univ. (September 1974).

184. Karni, Edi and David Schmeidler, Independence of Non-Feasible Alternatives, and Independence of Non-Optimal Alternatives, *Journal of Economic Theory* **12**, No. 3 (June 1976), 488–493.

185. Kats, Amoz, On the Social Welfare Function and the Parameters of Income Distribution, *Journal of Economic Theory* **5**, No. 3 (December 1972), 377–382.

186. Kats, Amoz, Non-Binary Relations, Choice Sets and Maximal Sets, unpublished manuscript, VPI (1975).

187. Keeney, R. L., and C. W. Kirkwood, Group Decision Making Using Cardinal Social Welfare Functions, Center Technical Report No. 83, Massachusetts Institute of Technology (October 1973).

188. Kelly, Jerry S., The Continuous Representation of a Social Preference Ordering, *Econometrica* **39**, No. 3 (May 1971), 593–597.

189. Kelly, Jerry S., Voting Anomalies, the Number of Voters and the Number of Alternatives, *Econometrica* **42**, No. 2 (March 1974), 239–251.

190. Kelly, Jerry S., Necessity Conditions in Voting Theory, *Journal of Economic Theory* **8**, No. 2 (June 1974), 149–160.

191. Kelly, Jerry S., The Impossibility of a Just Liberal, *Economica* **43**, No. 169 (February 1976), 67–75.

192. Kelly, Jerry S., Rights-Exercising and a Pareto Consistent Libertarian Claim, *Journal of Economic Theory* **13**, No. 1 (August 1976), 138–153.

193. Kelly, Jerry S., Strategy-proofness and Social Choice Functions without Single-Valuedness, *Econometrica* **45**, No. 2 (March 1977), 439–446.

194. Kelly, Jerry S., Algebraic Results on Collective Choice Rules, *Journal of Mathematical Economics* **3**, No. 3 (December 1976), 285–293.

 * Kelly, Jerry S. See Blair, Douglas.

195. Kemeny, John G., Mathematics without Numbers, *Daedalus* **88**, No. 4 (Fall 1959), 577–591.

196. Kemp, Murray C., Arrow's General Possibility Theorem, *Review of Economic Studies* **21** (3), No. 56 (1953–1954), 240–243.

197. Kemp, Murray C., and A. Asimakopulos, A Note on Social Welfare Functions and Cardinal Utility, *Canadian Journal of Economics and Political Science* **18**, No. 2 (May 1952), 195–200.

198. Kemp, Murray C., and Yew-Kwang Ng, On the Existence of Social Welfare Functions, Social Orderings and Social Decision Functions, *Economica* **43**, No. 169 (February 1976), 59–66.

 * Kirkwood, C. W. See Keeney, R. L.

199. Kirman, Alan P., and Dierter Sondermann, Arrow's Theorem, Many Agents and Invisible Dictators, *Journal of Economic Theory* **5**, No. 2 (October 1972), 267–277.

200. Klahr, David, A Computer Simulation of the Paradox of Voting, *American Political Science Review* **60**, No. 2 (June 1966), 384–390.

201. Kolm, Serge-Christophe, Optimum Production of Social Justice, in *Public Economics* (Julius Margolis and H. Guitton, eds.), pp. 145–200. New York: Macmillan, 1969.

202. Kramer, Gerald H., An Impossibility Result Concerning the Theory of Decision Making, in *Mathematical Applications in Political Science* (Joseph L. Bernd, ed.), Vol. III, pp. 39–51. Univ. Press of Virginia, Charlottesville, 1967.

203. Kramer, Gerald H., Sophisticated Voting over Multidimensional Choice Spaces, *Journal of Mathematical Sociology* **2** (1972), 165–180.

  * Krauch, H. See Czayka, L.

204. Kuga, Kiyoshi, and Hiroaki Nagatani, Voter Antagonism and the Paradox of Voting, *Econometrica* **42**, No. 6 (November 1974), 1045–1067.

  * Lapham, Victoria C. See Hillinger, Claude.

  * Lau, Lawrence J. See Jamison, Dean T.

205. Little, Ian M.D., Social Choice and Individual Values, *Journal of Political Economy* **60**, No. 5 (October 1952), 422–432.

206. Little, Lan M. D., L'avantage Collectif, *Economie Appliquée* **5**, (October–December, 1952), 455–468.

207. Lorimer, Peter, A Note on Orderings, *Econometrica* **35**, No. 3–4 (July–October, 1967), 537–539.

208. MacKay, Alfred F., A Simplified Proof of an Impossibility Theorem, *Philosophy of Science* **40**, No. 2 (June 1973), 175–177.

209. Majumdar, Tapas, A Note on Arrow's Postulates for a Social Welfare Function: Comment, *Journal of Political Economy* **77**, No. 4, Part I (July/August 1969), 528–531.

210. Majumdar, Tapas, Amartya Sen's Algebra of Collective Choice, *Sankya* **35**, Ser. B, Part 4 (December 1973), 533–542.

  * Markowitz, Harry. See Goodman, Leo A.

  * Marschak, Jacob. See Radner, Roy.

211. Mas-Colell, Andreu and Hugo F. Sonnenschein, General Possibility Theorems for Group Decisions, *Review of Economic Studies* **39**, No. 2 (April 1972), 185–192.

212. Maskin, Eric, A Theorem on Utilitarianism unpublished manuscript, Harvard Univ. and the Univ. of Cambridge (October 1975).

213. Maskin, Eric, Arrow Social Welfare Functions on Restricted Domains: The Two Person Case, unpublished manuscript, Harvard Univ. and the Univ. of Cambridge (October 1975).

214. Maskin, Eric, Arrow Social Welfare Functions and Cheat-Proof Game Forms on Restricted Domains: the Two-Person Case, unpublished manuscript, Harvard Univ. and the Univ. of Cambridge (October 1975).

215. Maskin, Eric, Decision-Making under Ignorance with Implications for Social Choice, unpublished manuscript, Harvard Univ. and the Univ. of Cambridge (November 1975).

216. May, Kenneth O., A Set of Independent, Necessary and Sufficient Conditions for Simple Majority Decision, *Econometrica* **20**, No. 4 (October 1952), 680–684.

217. May, Kenneth O., Note on Complete Independence of the Conditions for Simple Majority Decision, *Econometrica* **21**, No. 1 (January 1952), 172–173.

218. May, Kenneth O., Intransitivity, Utility and the Aggregation of Preference Patterns, *Econometrica* **22**, No. 1 (January 1954), 1–13.

219. May, Robert M., Some Mathematical Remarks on the Paradox of Voting, *Behavioral Science* **16**, No. 2 (March 1971), 143–151.

220. Mayston, David J., *The Idea of Social Choice*. New York: St. Martin's, 1975.
221. Mayston, David J., Alternatives to Irrelevant Alternatives, Univ. of Essex, Dept. of Economics Discussion Paper No. 61 (March 1975).
 * McKinsey, John C. C. See Davidson, Donald.
222. McManus, Maurice, Social Welfare Maximization When Tastes Change, unpublished manuscript (1975).
223. Miller, Nicholas R., Logrolling and the Arrow Paradox: A Note, *Public Choice* **21** (Spring 1975), 107–110.
224. Mirkin, B.G., Arrow's Approach to the Problem of Reconciling Opinions (Russian), *Mathematics and Sociology* (Russian), pp. 254–262. Akad. Nauk. SSSR Sibersk. Otdel Inst. Ekonom. i Organizacii Promysl. Proizvod., Novosibirsk, 1972.
225. Mishan, Ezra J., An Investigation into Some Alleged Contradictions in Welfare Economics, *Economic Journal* **67**, No. 267 (September 1957), 445–454.
226. Mishan, Ezra J., Arrow and the "New Welfare Economics": a Restatement, *Economic Journal* **68**, No. 271 (September 1958), 595–597.
227. Mishan, Ezra J., Review of J. Rothenberg's *The Measurement of Social Welfare*, *Economica* [N.S.] **30**, No. 119 (August 1963), 314–319.
228. Moon, John W., A Problem on Rankings by Committees, *Econometrica* **44**, No. 2 (March 1976), 241–246.
229. Muller, Eitan and Mark A. Satterthwaite, An Impossibility Theorem for Voting with a Different Interpretation, *Journal of Economic Theory* **14**, No. 2 (April 1977), 412–418.
 * Muller, Eitan. See Kalai, Ehud.
230. Murakami, Yasusuke, Some Logical Properties of Arrowian Social Welfare Functions, *Journal of Economic Behavior* **1**, No. 1 (April 1961), 77–84.
231. Murakami, Yasusuke, A Note on the General Possibility Theorems of the Social Welfare Function, *Econometrica* **29**, No. 2 (April 1961), 244–246.
232. Murakami, Yasusuke, *Logic and Social Choice*. New York: Dover, 1968.
 * Nagatani, Hiroaki. See Kuga, Kiyoshi.
233. Nash, John F., The Bargaining Problem, *Econometrica* **18**, No. 2 (April 1950), 155–162.
234. Negishi, Takashi, On Social Welfare Function, *Quarterly Journal of Economics* **77**, No. 1 (February 1963), 156–158.
235. Ng, Yew-Kwang, The Possibility of a Paretian Liberal: Impossibility Theorems and Cardinal Utility, *Journal of Political Economy* **79**, No. 6 (November/December 1971), 1397–1402.
 * Ng, Yew-Kwang, See Kemp, Murray C.
236. Nicholson, Michael B., Conditions for the "Voting Paradox" in Committee Decisions, *Metroeconomica* **7**, Nos. 1–2 (July–August, 1965), 29–44.
237. Niemi, Richard G., and William H. Riker, The Choice of Voting Systems, *Scientific American* **234**, No. 6 (June 1976), 21–27.
238. Niemi, Richard G., and Herbert Weisberg, A Mathematical Solution for the Probability of the Paradox of Voting, *Behavioral Sciences* **13**, No. 4 (July 1968), 317–323.
239. Nozick, Robert, *Anarchy, State, and Utopia*. New York: Basic, 1974.
240. Osborne, D. K., On Liberalism and the Pareto Principle, *Journal of Political Economy* **83**, No. 6 (December 1975), 1283–1287.
240a. Osborne, D. K., Irrelevant Alternatives and Social Welfare, *Econometrica* **44**, No. 5 (September 1976), 1001–1015.
241. Park, R. E., Comment (on Coleman), *American Economic Review* **57**, No. 5 (December 1967), 1300–1304.
242. Parks, Robert P., Choice Paths and Rational Choice, unpublished manuscript, (Washington Univ. (March 4, 1974).

243. Parks, Robert P., The Possibility of Social Choice, unpublished manuscript, (Washington Univ. (October 1974).

244. Parks, Robert P., An Impossibility Theorem for Fixed Preferences: a Dictatorial Bergson-Samuelson Welfare Function, *Rev. of Economic Studies* **43**, No. 3 (October 1976), 447–450.

245. Parks, Robert P., Further Results on Path Independence, Quasi-transitivity and Social Choice, *Public Choice* **26** (Summer 1976), 75–87.

246. Pattanaik, P. K., Risk, Impersonality and the Social Welfare Function, *Journal of Political Economy* **76**, No. 6 (November/December 1968), 1152–1169.

247. Pattanaik, Prasanta K., *Voting and Collective Choice*. London and New York: Cambridge Univ. Press, 1971.

248. Pattanaik, Prasanta K., On the Stability of Sincere Voting Situations, *Journal of Economic Theory* **6**, No. 6 (December 1973), 558–574.

249. Pattanaik, Prasanta K., and Manimay Sengupta, Conditions for Transitive and Quasi-transitive Majority Decisions," *Economica* [N.S.] **41**, No. 164 (November 1974), 414–423.

250. Pattanaik, Prasanta K., Stability of Sincere Voting under Some Classes of Non-Binary Group Decision Procedures, *Journal of Economic Theory* **8**, No. 2 (June 1974), 206–224.

251. Pattanaik, Prasanta K., Strategic Voting without Collusion under Binary and Democratic Group Decision Rules, *Review of Economic Studies* **42**, No. 129 (January 1975), 93–103.

252. Pattanaik, Prasanta K., Threats, Counter-Threats, and Strategic Voting, unpublished manuscript (1975).

253. Pattanaik, Prasanta K., Counter-Threats and Strategic Manipulation under Voting Schemes, *Rev. Economic Studies* **43**, No. 133 (February 1976), 11–18.

 *   Pattanaik, Prasanta. See Batra, Raveendra; Sen, Amartya K.

254. Pazner, Elisha A., and Eugene Wesley, Infinite Voters and the Possibility of a Cheatproof Social Choice Function, unpublished manuscript (1974).

255. Pazner, Elisha A., and Eugene Wesley, A Limit Theorem on the Cheatproofness of the Plurality Rule, unpublished manuscript (1974).

256. Pazner, Elisha A., and Eugene Wesley, Stability of Social Choices in Infinitely Large Societies, unpublished manuscript, Northwestern Univ. and Tel-Aviv Univ. (1975).

257. Pazner, Elisha A., and Eugene Wesley, Stability of Social Choices in Infinitely Large Societies, *J. Economic Theory* **14**, No. 2 (April 1977), 252–262.

258. Pazner, Elisha A., and Eugene Wesley, Stability of Social Choices in Infinitely Large in Large Societies, Discussion Paper No. 155, Center for Mathematical Studies in Economics and Management Science, Northwestern Univ. (June 1975).

 *   Pazner, Elisha. See Kalai, Ehud.

259. Peacock, Alan T., and Charles K. Rowley, Pareto Optimality and the Political Economy of Liberalism, *Journal of Political Economy* **80**, No. 3, Part 1 (May–June 1972), 476–490.

260. Peleg, Bezalel, A Note on the Manipulation of Large Voting Schemes, unpublished manuscript, The Hebrew Univ. (August 1976).

261. Piccoli, Mary Louise, Andrew B. Whinston, and K. S. Fu, Choice Functions and Social Preference Orderings Modelled by Heuristic Grammatical Inference, *Progress in Cybernetics and Systems Research* (Robert Trappl and F. deP. Hanika, eds.), pp. 15–23. New York: Wiley, 1975.

262. Piccoli, Mary Louise and Andrew B. Whinston, Social Choice and Formal Language Theory, *Journal of Cybernetics* **3**, No. 2 (1973), 40–50.

263. Plott, Charles R., Recent Results in the Theory of Voting, in *Frontiers in Quantitative Economics* (Michael Intriligator, ed.). Amsterdam: North-Holland Publ., 1971.

264. Plott, Charles R., Ethics, Social Choice Theory and the Theory of Economic Policy, *Journal of Mathematical Sociology* **2**, No. 2 (July 1972), 181–208.

265. Plott, Charles R., Individual Choice of a Decision Process, in *Probability Models of Collective Decision Making* (Richard Niemi and Herbert Weisberg, eds.), pp. 83–87. Columbus, Ohio: Merill, 1972.

266. Plott, Charles R., Path Independence, Rationality and Social Choice, *Econometrica* **41**, No. 6 (November 1973), 1075–1091.

267. Plott, Charles R., Rationality and Relevance in Social Choice Theory, unpublished manuscript, California Inst. of Technology, 1971.

268. Plott, Charles R., Axiomatic Social Choice Theory: An Overview and Interpretation, *American Journal of Political Science* **20**, No. 3 (August 1976), 511–596.

* Plott, Charles R. See also DeMeyer, Frank.

269. Radner, Roy and Jacob Marschak, Notes on Some Proposed Decision Criteria, in *Decision Processes* (Robert M. Thrall, Clyde H. Coombs, and R. L. Davis, eds.), pp. 61–68. New York: Wiley, 1954.

270. Ramachandra, V. S., Liberalism, Non-Binary Choice and Pareto Principle, *Theory and Decision* **3**, No. 1 (October 1972), 49–54.

271. Rawls, John, *A Theory of Justice*. Cambridge, Massachusetts: Harvard Univ. Press, 1971.

272. Ray, Paramesh, Independence of Irrelevant Alternatives, *Econometrica* **41**, No. 5 (September 1973), 987–991.

273. Rescher, Nicholas, *The Logic of Decision and Action*. Pittsburgh: Univ. of Pittsburgh Press, 1967.

274. Rescher, Nicholas, *Introduction to Value Theory*. Englewood Cliffs, New Jersey: Prentice-Hall, 1969.

275. Rescher, Nicholas, Some Observations on Consensus Methodology, *Theory and Decision* **3**, No. 2 (December 1972), 175–179.

276. Richardson, Gregory, Information and the Manipulation of Social Choice Mechanisms, unpublished manuscript, Cornell Univ. (1974).

277. Richter, Marcel K., Revealed Preference Theory, *Econometrica* **34**, No. 3 (July 1966), 635–645.

278. Richter, Marcel K., Rational Choice, in *Preferences, Utility and Demand* (John S. Chipman, Leonid Hurwicz, Marcel K. Richter, and Huge F. Sonnenschein, eds.), pp. 29–58. New York: Harcourt, 1971.

279. Riker, William H., Voting and the Summation of Preferences, *American Political Science Review* **60**, No. 4 (December 1961), 900–911.

280. Riker, William H., Arrow's Theorem and Some Examples of the Paradox of Voting, in *Mathematical Applications in Political Science* (John M. Claunch, ed.), pp. 41–60. Dallas, Texas: Southern Methodist Univ. Press, 1965.

* Riker, William H. See also Niemi, Richard G.

281. Ringbom, Marten, Rescher's Determination of a Social Preference Ranking, *Theory and Decision* **3**, No. 2 (December 1972), 170–174.

282. Roberts, Fred S., What If Utility Functions Do Not Exist, *Theory and Decision* **3**, No. 2 (December 1972), 126–139.

283. Roberts, Marc J., Alternative Social Choice Criteria: A Normative Approach, unpublished manuscript, Harvard Univ. (1971).

284. Rosenthal, Robert W., Voting Majority Sizes, *Econometrica* **43**, No. 2 (March 1975), 293–299.

285. Rothenberg, Jerome, Conditions for a Social Welfare Function, *Journal of Political Economy* **61**, No. 5 (October 1953), 389–405.

286. Rothenberg, Jerome, *The Measurement of Social Welfare*. Englewood Cliffs, New Jersey: Prentice-Hall, 1961.

*   Rowley, Charles K. See Peacock, Alan T.
287.   Runciman, Walter G., and Amartya K. Sen, Games, Justice and the General Will, *Mind* **74**, No. 296 (October 1965), 554–562.
288.   Salles, Maurice, A General Possibility Theorem for Group Decision Rules with Pareto-Transitivity, *Journal of Economic Theory* **11**, No. 1 (August 1975).
289.   Salles, Maurice, A Note on Inada's "Majority Rule and Rationality," *Journal of Economic Theory* **8**, No. 4 (August 1974), 539–540.
290.   Samuelson, Paul A., *Foundations of Economic Analysis*. Cambridge, Massachusetts: Harvard Univ. Press, 1947.
291.   Samuelson, Paul A., Comment on Welfare Economics, in *A Survey of Contemporary Economics* (B. F. Haley ed.), Vol. II, pp. 36–38. Homewood, Illinois: Irwin, 1952.
292.   Samuelson, Paul A., Arrow's Mathematical Politics, in *Human Values and Economic Policy* (Sidney Hook, ed.), pp. 41–51. New York: New York Univ. Press, 1967.
293.   Samuelson, Paul A., Maximum Principles in Analytical Economics, *American Economic Review* **62**, No. 3 (June 1972), 249–262.
294.   Saposnik, Rubin, Power, the Economic Environment and Social Choice, *Econometrica* **42**, No. 3 (May 1974), 461–470.
295.   Saposnik, Rubin, On the Transitivity of the Social Preference Relation under Simple Majority Rule, *Journal of Economic Theory* **10**, No. 1 (February 1975), 1–7.
296.   Saposnik, Rubin, Social Choice with Continuous Expression of Individual Preferences, *Econometrica* **43**, No. 4 (July 1975), 683–690.
*   Sargent, Thomas J. See Williamson, Oliver E.
297.   Satterthwaite, Mark A., *The Existence of a Strategy Proof Voting Procedure: a Topic in Social Choice Theory*. Ph.D. Dissertation, Univ. of Wisconsin, 1973.
298.   Satterthwaite, Mark A., Strategy-proofness and Arrow's Conditions: Existence and Correspondence Theorems for Voting Procedures and Social Welfare Functions, *Journal of Economic Theory* **10**, No. 2 (April 1975), 187–217.
*   Satterthwaite, Mark A. See also Blin, Jean-Marie; Kalai, Ehud; Muller, Eitan.
299.   Schick, Frederick, Arrow's Proof and the Logic of Preference, *Philosophy of Science* **36**, No. 2 (June 1969), 127–144.
300.   Schmeidler, David and Hugo F. Sonnenschein, Two Proofs of the Gibbard–Satterthwaite Theorem on the Possibility of a Strategy-proof Social Choice Function, in *Proceedings of a Conference on Decision Theory and Social Ethics* (W. Essler and H. Gottinger, eds.). Dordrecht: Reidel. forthcoming.
301.   Schmeidler, David, A Condition for the Completeness of Partial Preference Relations, *Econometrica* **39**, No. 2 (March 1971), 403–404.
*   Schmeidler, David See also Kalai, Ehud; Karni, Edi.
302.   Schwartz, Thomas, On the Possibility of Rational Policy Evaluation, *Theory and Decision* **1**, No. 1 (October 1970), 89–106.
303.   Schwartz, Thomas, Rationality and the Myth of the Maximum, *Noûs* **6**, No. 2 (May 1972), 97–117.
304.   Schwartz, Thomas, Notes on the Abstract Theory of Collective Choice, mimeographed, Carnegie-Mellon Univ. (1974).
305.   Schwartz, Thomas, Serial Collective Choice, unpublished manuscript, Carnegie-Mellon Univ. (1975).
306.   Seidl, C., On Liberal Values, mimeographed, Univ. of Vienna (1975).
307.   Sen, Amartya K., Quasi-transitivity, Rational Choice and Collective Decisions, *Review of Economic Studies* **36** (3), No. 107 (July 1969), 381–393.
308.   Sen, Amartya K., and Prasanta K. Pattanaik, Necessary and Sufficient Conditions for Rational Choice under Majority Decision, *Journal of Economic Theory* **1**, No. 2 (August 1969), 178–202.

309. Sen, Amartya K., *Collective Choice and Social Welfare*. San Francisco: Holden-Day, 1970.

310. Sen, Amartya K., The Impossibility of a Paretian Liberal, *Journal of Political Economy* **78**, No. 1 (January/February 1970), 152–157.

311. Sen, Amartya K., Interpersonal Comparison and Partial Comparability, *Econometrica* **38**, No. 3 (May 1970), 393–409.

312. Sen, Amartya K., Choice Functions and Revealed Preference, *Review of Economic Studies* **38** (3), No. 115 (July 1971), 307–317.

313. Sen, Amartya K., Interpersonal Comparison and Partial Comparability: A Correction, *Econometrica* **40**, No. 5 (September 1972), 959.

314. Sen, Amartya K., Behavior and the Concept of Preference, *Economica* [N.S.], Vol. 40, No. 159 (August 1973), 241–259.

315. Sen, Amartya K., Choice, Orderings and Morality, in *Practical Reason* (Stephen Körner, ed.). Oxford: Blackwell, 1972, 1974.

316. Sen, Amartya K., Is a Paretian Liberal Really Impossible: A Reply, *Public Choice* **21** (Spring 1975), 111–113.

317. Sen, Amartya K., Liberty, Unanimity and Rights, *Economica* **43**, No. 171 (August 1976), 217–245.

318. Sen, Amartya K., Social Choice Theory: A Re-Examination, *Econometrica* **45**, No. 1 January 1977), 53–89.

 * Sen, Amartya K. See also Runciman, Walter G.

319. Simpson, Paul B., On Defining Area of Voter Choice: Professor Tullock on Stable Voting, *Quarterly Journal of Economics* **83**, No. 3 (August 1969), 478–490.

320. Simpson, Paul B., Independence of Irrelevant Alternatives and Majority Type Voting, unpublished manuscript, Univ. of Oregon (1975).

321. Smith, John H., Aggregation of Preferences with Variable Electorate, *Econometrica* **41**, No. 6 (November 1973), 1027–1041.

322. Smith, Tony, On the Existence of Most-Preferred Alternatives, *International Economic Review* **15**, No. 1 (February 1974), 184–194.

 * Sondermann, Dieter. See Kirman, Alan P.

323. Sonnenschein, Hugo, Relationship between Transitive Preferences and the Structure of Choice Space, *Econometrica* **33**, No. 3 (July 1965), 624–634.

324. Sonnenschein, Hugo, Reply to "A Note on Orderings," *Econometrica* **35**, No. 3–4 (July–October 1967), 540–541.

 * Sonnenschein, Hugo F. See also Mas-Colell, Andreu; Schmeidler, David.

 * Sonstelie, Jon C. See Comacho, Antonio.

325. Stearns, Richard, The Voting Problem, *American Mathematical Monthly* **66**, No. 9 (November 1959), 761–763.

326. Stevens, Dana N., A Very Unsubtle Version of Arrow's Impossibility Theorem: A Subtle Comment, *Economic Inquiry* **14**, No. 2 (June 1976), 297–299.

327. Strasnick, Steven, Social Choice and the Derivation of Rawls' Difference Principle, *The Journal of Philosophy* **73**, No. 4 (26 February 1976), 85–99.

328. Suppes, Patrick, *Axiomatic Set Theory*. Princeton, New Jersey: Van Nostrand-Reinhold, 1960.

329. Suppes, Patrick, Some Formal Models of Grading Principles, *Synthese* **16**, No. 3/4 (December 1966), 284–306.

 * Suppes, Patrick See also Davidson, Donald.

329a. Suzumura, Kotaro, Remarks on the Theory of Collective Choice, *Economica* **43**, No. 172 (November 1976), 381–390.

329b. Suzumura, Kotaro, On the Consistency of Libertarian Claims, unpublished manuscript (1976).

* Suzumura, Kotaro. See Blair, Douglas H.

* Tarski, Alfred. See Banach, Stefan.

330. Taylor, Michael, Proof of a Theorem on Majority Rule, *Behavioral Science* **14**, No. 3 (May 1969), 228–231.

331. Taylor, Michael, The Problem of Salience in the Theory of Collective Decision-Making, *Behavioral Science* **15**, No. 5 (September 1970), 415–430.

332. Taylor, Michael, The Theory of Collective Choice, mimeographed, Univ. of Essex (1971).

333. Taylor, Michael, Review Article: Mathematical Political Theory, *British Journal of Political Science* **1**, Part 3 (July 1971), 339–382.

* Thorsen, Stuart J. See Wendell, Richard E.

334. Tullock, Gordon, The Irrationality of Intransitivity, *Oxford Economic Papers* [N.S.] **16**, No. 3 (November 1964), 401–406.

335. Tullock, Gordon, The General Irrelevance of the General Possibility Theorem, *Quarterly Journal of Economics* **81**, No. 2 (May 1967), 256–270.

* Tullock, Gordon. See also Buchanan, James M; Campbell, Colin D.

336. Varian, Hal, Complexity of Social Decisions, unpublished manuscript.

337. Vickrey, William S., Goals of Economic Life: An Exchange between Economics and Philosophy, in *Goals of Economic Life* (A. D. Ward, ed.), pp. 148–177. New York: Harper, Row, 1952.

338. Vickrey, William, Utility, Strategy and Social Decision Rules, *Quarterly Journal of Economics* **74**, No. 4 (November 1960), 507–535.

339. Vickrey, William S., Risk, Utility and Social Policy, *Social Research* **28**, No. 2 (Summer 1961), 205–217.

340. Waldner, Ilmar, The Empirical Meaningfulness of Interpersonal Utility Comparisons, *Journal of Philosophy* **69**, No. 4 (February 1972), 87–103.

341. Waldner, Ilmar, The Possibility of Rational Policy Evaluation, *Theory and Decision* **4**, No. 1 (September 1973), 85–90.

342. Walsh, Vivian C., On the Significance of Choice Sets With Incompatibilities, *Philosophy of Science* **34**, No. 3 (September 1967), 243–250.

* Weiman, D. See Feldman, Alan.

* Weisberg, Herbert. See Niemi, Richard G.

343. Weldon, J. C., On the Problem of Social Welfare Functions, *Canadian Journal of Economics and Political Science* **18**, No. 4 (November 1952), 452–463.

344. Wendell, Richard E., and Stuart J. Thorson, Some Generalizations of Social Decisions under Majority Rule, *Econometrica* **42**, No. 5 (September 1974), 893–912.

* Wesley, Eugene. See Pazner, Elisha. A.

* Whinston, Andrew B. See Piccoli, Mary Louise.

345. Williamson, Oliver E., and Thomas J. Sargent, Social Choice: a Probabilistic Approach, *Economic Journal* **77**, No. 308 (December 1967), 797–813.

346. Wilson, Robert, The Theory of Syndicates, *Econometrica* **36**, No. 1 (January 1968), 119–132.

347. Wilson, Robert, The Finer Structure of Revealed Preference, *Journal of Economic Theory* **2**, No. 4 (December 1970), 348–353.

348. Wilson, Robert, Stable Coalition Proposals in Majority-Rule Voting, *Journal of Economic Theory* **3**, No. 3 (September 1971), 254–271.

349. Wilson, Robert, A Revision of Arrow's General Possibility Theorem, Stanford Business School Paper No. 181 (1971).

350. Wilson, Robert, A Game-Theoretic Analysis of Social Choice, in *Social Choice* (Bernhardt Lieberman, ed.), pp. 393–407. New York: Gordon and Breach, 1971.

351. Wilson, Robert, The Game-Theoretic Structure of Arrow's General Possibility Theorem, *Journal of Economic Theory* **5**, No. 1 (August 1972), 14–20.

352. Wilson, Robert, Social Choice Theory without the Pareto Principle, *Journal of Economic Theory* **5**, No. 3 (December 1972), 478–486.

353. Wilson, Robert, On the Theory of Aggregation, *Journal of Economic Theory* **10**, No. 1 (February 1975), 89–99.

354. Young, Hobart P., An Axiomatization of Borda's Rule, *Journal of Economic Theory* **9**, No. 1 (September 1974), 43–52.

355. Young, Hobart P., A Note on Preference Aggregation, *Econometrica* **42**, No. 6 (November 1974), 1129–1131.

356. Zeckhauser, Richard, Voting Systems, Honest Preferences, and Pareto Optimality, *American Political Science Review* **67** No. 3 (September 1973), 934–946.

AUTHOR INDEX

Numbers in parentheses are reference numbers and indicate that an author's work is referred to although his name is not cited in text. Numbers in italics refer to pages on which the complete references are listed.

SUBJECT INDEX